Walking Israel

ALSO BY MARTIN FLETCHER

Breaking News

Walking Israel

MARTIN FLETCHER

Thomas Dunne Books
St. Martin's Griffin
New York

THOMAS DUNNE BOOKS.
An imprint of St. Martin's Press.

WALKING ISRAEL. Copyright © 2010 by Martin Fletcher. All rights reserved. Printed in the United States of America. For information, address St. Martin's Press, 175 Fifth Avenue, New York, N.Y. 10010.

www.thomasdunnebooks.com
www.stmartins.com

Maps by Daniel Fletcher

Grateful acknowledgment is given for permission to reprint the following: "Yad Mordechai" from *Open Closed Open: Poems by Yehuda Amichai*, translated from the Hebrew by Chana Bloch and Chana Kronfeld. Copyright © 2000 by Chana Bloch and Chana Kronfeld. Reprinted by permission of Houghton Mifflin Harcourt. All rights reserved.

The Library of Congress has cataloged the hardcover edition as follows:

Fletcher, Martin, 1947–
    Walking Israel : a personal search for the soul of a nation / Martin Fletcher. — 1st ed.
        p. cm.
    Includes bibliographical references and index.
    ISBN 978-0-312-53481-3
    1. Israel—Description and travel.   2. Fletcher, Martin, 1947—Travel—Israel.
I. Title.
    DS107.5.F54 2010
    956.9405'4—dc22

2010029256

ISBN 978-0-312-53482-0 (trade paperback)

First St. Martin's Griffin Edition: September 2011

10   9   8   7 6   5   4   3   2   1

For Hagar and the boys,

who are now men

Contents

Introduction: What a Country   1

1. In the Beginning   11

2. The Bride of Galilee: Lebanon Border to Achziv   23

3. Revenge of the Jews: Achziv to Kibbutz Lohamei Hagheta'ot   55

4. Four Faces of the Truth: Lohamei Hagheta'ot to Acre   91

5. The Cream Arabs of Haifa: Acre to Haifa   115

6. Remaking Utopia: Haifa to Beit Oren   143

7. The Call to Arms: Beit Oren to Herzliya   173

8. The Off-White City: Herzliya to Tel Aviv   209

9. We're All in This Together: Tel Aviv to Ashkelon   245

10. Journey's End: Ashkelon to Gaza   273

Notes   291

Index   295

Walking Israel

INTRODUCTION

What a Country

One November afternoon in 1992, just before sunset, two friends and I took out a sixteen-foot Hobie Cat off the Israeli coast at Herzliya for one last rip out to sea. The wind was blasting at twenty-five knots, right on the edge of safety, but we knew the waters well and relished it. How dumb could we be? A half hour in we were racing on one hull, sail taut, leaning hard into the wind, powering through the waves, when a freak gust tore into the sail, shooting us like corks into the sea and leaving the boat upside down. At first it was routine—capsizing a catamaran is half the fun. But for two hours we struggled to right our vessel. We grew tired, and as dusk fell we got scared. We were alone, it was late, and we were in serious trouble. For some reason, the mast and hulls began to fill with water and the catamaran sank. Buoyed by the trampoline, it became a deadweight just below the surface.

Soon the only light came from the stars and a half-moon. Giving up on the boat, we dove underneath and cut off the mast and sail, hoping at least to raise the trampoline above the water so we could sit on it and warm up. As we watched the sail, our only means of control, float away, we began drifting faster out to sea. Making matters worse, the hulls were now full of water and so heavy we still couldn't force the trampoline right way up.

We resolved to hang on to the submerged boat until rescue came. But it didn't.

The air was cool and the water frigid. In our three-millimeter rubber suits and life jackets, my friend Ziv Levanon and I could probably have survived by waiting to be rescued in the morning. However, our third sailor, Eitan, a tough and lean eighteen-year-old, wore only his swimming trunks. After half an hour in the water, his teeth were chattering, and he was beginning to fade. We knew hypothermia could kill him in hours, and that his only chance was to keep moving by swimming to shore.

Ziv, the owner of our sailing club, grew up on a kibbutz by the sea and was confident he could make it, but I was a poor swimmer. After three hours drifting, the coast was now about two miles away, and there was a gentle current pulling us south and west, away from land. The waves were low, but strong. We knew we had to act, and quick. So with Eitan listless between us, Ziv and I slipped into the sea and struck out for Israel's coast, kicking hard, pushing the submerged trampoline, which had become our life raft.

It was tough. Riding high in the peak of the waves, I could make out a tiny smudge of dark matter that was dry land, but in the waves' troughs all I saw was a wall of water. My legs were weak and heavy, and I shivered with cold. Sometimes I swallowed seawater, then hacked it out, gulping in clean air while treading in place. No way would I let go of the trampoline. I didn't despair, or at least not too much. Nothing weightier crossed my mind than the British music hall ditty "I Do Like to Be Beside the Seaside," emphasis on the "Do" and the "Sea." That and the thought of how good a warming tot of rum would feel.

We made slow progress. To keep my spirits up, I glanced periodically to shore, spotting the familiar sandy beach and the low cliffs of the coast around Tel Aviv, which now appeared as shadows in the night. As the hours passed and the coast approached, the beaches where I had spent so many pleasurable hours took on new meaning, embodying not just the good life

I had come to enjoy as a foreign correspondent based in Israel, but life itself, and also, I imagined, human civilization through the ages. The tiny orange dots of light coming from seaside homes and hotels recalled the bonfires that had once lit the way for sailors as they approached the Holy Land. How many men had struggled to swim ashore over the generations? I knew there were thousands of shipwrecks along the coast. This led to other, more personal thoughts. With every exhausted stroke, I swore I'd pray every day, nay, twice a day. If you only save me, O God, I'll be a new man and help everybody. Please, save me! I'll be nice to my wife. I'll even be fair to Jewish settlers!

Ziv, Eitan, and I stuck together in the dark sea and followed moonlit channels of light to land. It took us eight hours, but we made it, and at four thirty in the morning we were hauling ourselves onto the sandy beach by our fingernails, like three Robinson Crusoes.

Desperate men couldn't have landed at a more fitting place: Tel Baruch, north of Tel Aviv, Israel's most notorious hooker hangout. The ladies, dressed in skintight white pants and the tiniest of bulging tank tops, or screaming red microskirts and what appeared to be lace bras, were resting at a bonfire between tricks, while the legs of their johns lolled out the backs of pickups. Israel's first prime minister, David Ben-Gurion, reputedly said Israel would not be a real country until it had prostitutes, and here they were. On seeing us, the women first appeared alarmed, their mouths gaping as Ziv and I, in our dripping rubber suits, hugging the almost naked Eitan, emerged through the mist, our teeth chattering and our bodies numb with cold. They must have thought the SM gays had arrived. Then one of the prostitutes, a stocky rinsed blonde, who in retrospect was probably a man, wrapped blankets around us and filled us with steaming mint tea. With towels they rubbed our heads, and I remember wondering where else the towels had been, but being too tired to care. They were happy we had landed among them, like more thieves in the night.

After establishing that we were unharmed by our ordeal, the hookers' driver, a gaunt, tattooed man who informed us that he was on weekend furlough from jail, kindly drove us home in his beat-up old Peugeot. He wouldn't take any money, but all the way he tried to sell us on the charms of his "girls." His parting advice was a delightful non sequitur: "Stay out of jail— crime doesn't pay."

My house was dark, and at first I silently thanked God that Hagar, my wife, was unaware of my misadventure. But our bed was empty. I phoned the sailing club and sure enough, there she was, keeping a terrified vigil with friends who also feared we had drowned. The coast guard was searching for us in vain. "Uh, hello," I said. Hagar burst into tears.

I checked on the kids, who were sleeping peacefully, dimmed the bathroom light, put on a CD, ran a hot oily bath, and slid gratefully in, feeling my skin tingle and heat pulse through my body. As I waited for Hagar, chuckling at yet another brush with death, I savored the reaction of one of our hooker hosts, a buxom lady who hugged me to keep me warm. "What a country," she had said. "They came from the sea. They could have been terrorists and killed us. Or police and arrested us. And what do we do? We give 'em a cup of tea! But they are cute in rubber," she said, patting my stomach. And then she repeated, "What a country!"

Walking Israel is a rather different sort of book about the people and society of modern Israel. I don't emphasize, as have most authors, the blood feud between Jews and Arabs and their numbing peace plans, nor do I provide an account of the City of Peace, Jerusalem, or follow in the footsteps of Jesus. Rather, I relate my own personal journey of discovery along an often ignored but fascinating landscape that was such a beacon of hope for me that desperate night: Israel's historic coast.

During the summer of 2008, I spent two weeks trekking along the entire coast, visiting seaside communities from the Lebanon border to the tip of the Gaza Strip. My idea was simple: Get away from the narrow focus of my daily grind as a news reporter, enjoy a leisurely stroll along beautiful terrain, stop off in interesting places and talk to interesting people, then follow up on issues that fascinated me. Looking with fresh and open eyes at Israel, its past and present, I wanted to write a book that would take readers beyond the familiar yet constricted stories of guns and bombs and closer to the true nature of this unique country. I wanted to write a book that would have a very simple, often overlooked, message: This quirky, surprising, complex, difficult, and disturbing country is actually a great place.

Israelis are hard to impress. When I told my wife's brother, Yaariv, of my plan to walk from Rosh Hanikra on the Lebanon border all the way south to Yad Mordechai and the border with Gaza, in a couple of weeks, he scoffed: "In the army, we walked eighty miles in twenty-seven hours, with a twenty-pound backpack." My friend Fossi jeered: "So what? On my first day in the navy commandos they gave us lousy new shoes, backpacks with twenty kilos of sand, then made us go into the water, doubling the load. We had to run and run, sixty miles in fourteen hours, and on the way we had to free a truck stuck in the sand."

Okay, so I'm not eighteen and I wasn't climbing Mount Everest. It wasn't as ambitious or dangerous a trip as my three-week trek across the Hindu Kush mountains reporting on the Afghan mujahideen's battle against the Soviets, or my week chasing the French Foreign Legion in Zaire. Israel's entire coastline is only 110 miles, not quite the length of Long Island, New York, or from Washington, D.C., to Charlottesville, Virginia. You can drive the whole way on one gallon of fuel, if you believe Chrysler's claim for its hybrid jeep. But when you consider the extraordinary span of history crammed into this tiny coastline, it has to be the most fascinating, action-packed hundred miles in the world.

This tiny sliver of land shaped like a curved dagger has always been the site of raw passions, where empires collided and great religions were born. Here Canaanites and Philistines fought, the Romans ruled, Christianity and Islam clashed, and the armies of Alexander the Great and Napoleon and the Ottomans stormed to shore. Yet today the coast is interesting not so much as a place of war, but as a place of peace. Seventy percent of Israel's people, Jews and Arabs, live within ten miles of the beach, along the coastal plain, in relative harmony. Take a walk through Israel's coastal communities and you find a much more dynamic, diverse, and energizing place than you see in the headlines—a society with the second-largest per-capita buyers of books in the world; where each small town has a major orchestra; where, as I found, prostitutes trade on the cliff and serve mint tea to those in need; and where a resigned humor trumps all.

When a stooped former soldier told me he had been a prisoner of war in Syria for a year, I clucked in sympathy. "Hah," he said, as he pulled up his sleeve and displayed the number tattooed on his forearm, "it was like a sanatorium after Auschwitz." Jewish and Arab men share the same henpecked joke: A woman buys her husband two neckties for his birthday. He proudly wears one and she cries: "What, you don't like the other one?"

For all the attention focused on this tiny land, and all the effort spent on fixing its problems, Israel has to be the most analyzed yet least understood country in the world. I am always struck by the worried question of first-time visitors: "Is it safe to come?" Yet after a week here they exclaim, "Wow, Israel's such a great place. I had no idea!"

An Israeli intellectual, the "new historian" Benny Morris, summed up the dichotomy as follows: "Zionism has always had two faces: a constructive, moral, compromising and considerate aspect; and a destructive, selfish, militant, chauvinistic-racist one. Both are sincere and real. . . . The simultaneous existence of these two facets was one of the most significant keys to the success of Zionism."[1]

The media doesn't talk much about the pleasing side of Israel, nor, in news terms, does it need to. Rather, it sticks to a familiar and unhappy story, that of a brutal military dictatorship whose relationship with the Palestinians is defined by force. This familiar Israel, unlike the compassionate one I encountered during my sailing misadventure, is a place of violent passions, religious fervor, and tribal intensity, which the Palestinians match slogan for slogan and prayer for prayer. The clashing dreams of Jews and Arabs lead periodically to bullets and bombs, stones and grenades, funerals and parades—grim fodder for news media. Everything else pales; if it isn't "news," reporters pay little attention, and as a result many wonderful, surprising, and profound aspects of the country go unreported. I've often reflected over the years that the large majority of Israelis living along the coast could be in a completely different country for all the world hears about them.

As a reporter covering Israel and the region for European and American television since 1973, I myself have hardly been blameless. Most of my work has dealt with people and events located away from the coast, east of a line that zigzags from north to south, through Jenin, Nablus, Ramallah, Jerusalem, Bethlehem, and Hebron. This line includes the Jewish settlements and every main point of friction. I hadn't realized how typecast my own coverage of Israel was until I phoned the news desk in New York one day and the desk editor immediately interrupted in alarm, "Martin, has there been a bomb?" as if there could be no other reason for me to call. What made it even more galling was that I had to respond, "Yes, in Jerusalem, ten dead so far."

In writing *Walking Israel*, I've tried to remedy this important and unfortunate media distortion that presents Israel as such an unappealing place. The book's chapters consist of personal stories from my trip as well as insights I gleaned from a year of follow-up interviews and historical research, broadened by my three decades of reporting experience in the region. I've organized the book both geographically and topically; each chapter deals with an individual community in coastal Israel, the chapters proceeding from north to south. Each chapter also discusses a specific issue I encountered while visiting that community. By dealing with coastal Israel one place and issue at a time, I've tried to build up a comprehensive picture of the country that the world rarely sees, one that is closer to reality than the portrait of a place of permanent conflict, peopled by the grim and the gruff, in their God-given land. The Israel you'll find in this book isn't only a place of violence and "us against them," but a truer mix of surprise, complexity, humanity, and humor. It is the country first-time visitors are often so pleased to discover, the country I myself encountered the night my boat capsized.

I've written *Walking Israel* not just because I believe that journalists should strive to report the whole story, but because I'm convinced that Israel and its people have long gotten a raw deal in the world's eyes. Don't get me wrong: Israel is hardly a Garden of Eden. Building a country on land inhabited by another people was never going to be anything less than excruciating. But relentless insistence on Israel's faults, rather than fair recognition of its virtues, has increasingly legitimized a question that applies to no other country on the planet: Does Israel have the right to exist? This book offers an unequivocal answer: Yes. Despite the injustice and violence we all hear about, I hope the reader will agree that the good outweighs the bad, and indeed that the good can overcome the bad, to create a country that all Israelis, Jews and Arabs, can be proud of. That may seem naïve, a distant goal, but then, so was the coast to my friends and me that cold November night.

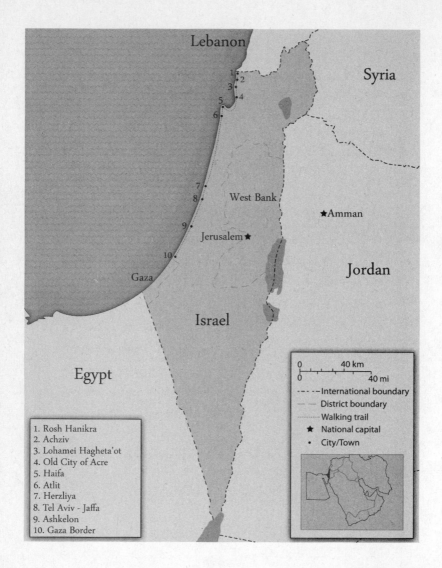

Lebanon

Syria

1
2
3
4
5
6

West Bank

★Amman

7
8
9
Jerusalem ★

10

Gaza

Jordan

Israel

Egypt

1. Rosh Hanikra
2. Achziv
3. Lohamei Hagheta'ot
4. Old City of Acre
5. Haifa
6. Atlit
7. Herzliya
8. Tel Aviv - Jaffa
9. Ashkelon
10. Gaza Border

0   40 km
0   40 mi
- - - International boundary
- - District boundary
.... Walking trail
★   National capital
•   City/Town

1

In the Beginning

It is said of Abraham that in his wanderings over many lands, he came to Mesopotamia where he saw the inhabitants spending their time in eating and drinking and in all forms of frivolity. Therefore he said: "May I never have a share in any of these lands." When he came to Erez Israel and arrived at the ladders of Tyre, he saw the inhabitants of the land ploughing and tilling the soil at the appointed time and sowing and reaping in due course. Therefore he said: "This is the land that I would ask of the Lord as my portion." And the Lord said to him: "Unto thy seed have I given this land!"

—ZEV VILNAY, *Legends of Palestine,* 1932

June 21, 2008. I, too, stood at the Ladder of Tyre, and I looked down upon the Promised Land. And it was wondrous, although most of the inhabitants plowing and tilling the land today were from Thailand. Below me lay Israel, locked in conflict all its life. And I thought, If Abraham knew what a mess he was starting, he may well have turned right around and legged it back to Mesopotamia.

Abraham did continue into the promised land, whether by way of the coast, as the legend tells, or by following the more likely hilly trail out of Mesopotamia and across the Jordan River. In Canaan, it is written, the Lord then promised Abraham that at the age of a hundred he would have a son, and "you . . . will greatly increase your numbers."[1] His descendants did indeed multiply but the land that is Israel today is far smaller than Abraham's biblical portion—three hundred miles long and barely seventy miles at its widest—smaller than El Salvador.

On his grumpy travels through the Holy Land in 1867, Mark Twain claimed to have been taken aback by its humble proportions: "The state of Missouri could be split into three Palestines." He'd expected "a country as large as the United States . . . I suppose it was because I could not conceive of a small country having so much history."[2] But as well as an unrivaled biblical legacy and history, ancient and modern, Israel includes in that small space an astonishing geographical diversity.

Israel's borders range from the lowest point on earth, the Dead Sea, whose water level is sinking at the alarming rate of three feet a year, to the Red Sea's sparkling azure waters in the south. Northward, the border tracks the Jordan River along a crack in the earth's crust called the Jordan rift valley to the mountains and waters of Galilee, ending at the wooded foothills of Mount Lebanon. There the frontier wends westward along mountain ridges, cutting fifty miles through cypress forests and olive groves until the Ladder of Tyre, where it plunges down to the Mediterranean, or, as it was known in Abraham's time, the Great Sea. From here, it follows sandy beaches straight south to Gaza. Inland, half the country is desert.

Israel also packs a rare amount of cultural diversity into its tight borders. Jews account for some 80 percent of Israel's population, yet the Jewish population is far from homogeneous. Although a handful of Jews trace their lineage back to the Roman destruction of the Second Temple in 70 CE, most landed in the late nineteenth and twentieth centuries, answering the Zionist call to reclaim the land God promised to Abraham, or fleeing persecution in Europe and Arabia.

They're a noisy bunch, gregarious and excitable, spontaneous and combustible, a vivid mix of the orient and occident—hummus meets *Kartoffelsalat*. They're also a bundle of contradictions: selfish and generous, bigoted and tolerant, arrogant and—well—maybe not so humble. Their national character is that there is no national character. They are too varied. The only accurate generalization is that they are, in my opinion, the worst drivers in the world.

The clearest cultural divide among Israel's Jews is religious. Black-garbed Orthodox Jews obey every ancient kosher law and as many of the 613 *mitzvot*, or commandments, as are feasible. The laws of Moses determine every aspect of their lives today, from diet and sex to education and prayer rituals. Their lives are anchored in their history, and they wear their odd black clothes and fur hats specifically to set themselves apart from secular Jews. The latter set their own rules, and their dress and customs would seem equally at home in New York, London, or Rome. Yet they, too, cling to their Jewish traditions and roots. The loudest and longest argument among Jews is reserved for their most basic dispute: Who actually is a Jew? And who decides?

Mark Twain found the Holy Land's landscape unimpressive, calling it "rocky and bare, repulsive and dreary," but he repeatedly emphasized the link between the people and their past. He was right. Here, history is not merely something you read about; it's ever-present.

When I called a government spokesman to ask how many people had been murdered in the past calendar year, his defensive reply was: "Which calendar is that? The Jewish calendar, right? Not the Muslim calendar or Gregorian?"

For many, the Bible is as familiar as the daily newspaper. A friend of mine loves to tell the story of his first Israeli taxi ride. He was nearing his destination, a part of town with a street named after the biblical Judean king Hizkiyahu, and another street named after Matisyahu, the leader of the Hasmonean revolt. The driver called in to inquire about his next assignment. The dispatcher told him to pick up an old lady at her apartment in King Hizkiyahu Street. But the driver couldn't hear over the crackling taxi radio and asked, "Did you say King Matisyahu Street?"

The dispatcher snapped: "Hizkiyahu, Hizkiyahu! Matisyahu was never king!"

Another enduring distinction among Israel's Jews is that between Ashkenazim, Jews of mostly European origin, and Sephardim, Jews from mostly Muslim countries. For decades, the difference was stark and easy to spot: Ashkenazim have light skin and money and get their way; Sephardim are dark-skinned, poor, and don't.

I saw tensions between Ashkenazim and Sephardim play out in the sunset years of such prejudice at a wedding in the Tel Aviv Hilton. A matchmaker had brought a poor Sephardi girl and a wealthy Ashkenazi boy together in a traditional *shidduch*, and now they were getting married. The Sephardim brought their own band with Mizrahi, Middle Eastern music, while the Ashkenazim insisted on their own Klezmer ensemble, whose music harked back to the Polish shtetl. The Sephardim gave in and their band went home, but the bride's party was left muttering and frustrated.

The dispute turned violent after the marriage ceremony. The bride's uncle had brought his seven-year-old niece to dance on the floor reserved for Orthodox men, who celebrate separately from the women. Her presence so outraged one bearded man in a black coat that he kicked the little girl's bottom. This infuriated the girl's uncle, who tried to punch the Orthodox man. The groom shouted, while the bride locked herself in the bathroom. Finally she stormed out of the hotel with her furious and humiliated family hot on her heels. I don't know what became of the married couple, but I would guess they didn't enjoy much bliss that night in the bridal suite.

Sephardic Jews complained of their lowly status for decades. Today, thanks to education, intermarriage, and common sense, the issue is moot: Sephardic Jews populate the government and the ranks of senior army officers and business leaders in almost equal numbers. More important, marriage celebrations run about fifty-fifty in Klezmer and Mizrahi music.

Differences run just as deep, though are more muted, among Israel's Arabs. They divide into four groups—Muslims, Christians, Bedouin, and Druze—each of which breaks down further along clan and regional lines. Each local Arab community has its own values, morals, and loyalties. The communities unite only in a marriage of convenience in their struggle for equality with the Jews, and usually, in a more discreet manner, in support of the political goals of their Palestinian cousins.

Much has been written about the Arabs' inevitable victory over the Jews, not in the battle of the bullet or the ballot, but of the womb. Arab birthrates worry many in Israel's government, and individual reproductive feats on the Arab side are startling. A Palestinian friend sat in our kitchen with another friend of his, and my wife asked him how many children he now had, as he always seemed to have a bag of diapers in his car. "Seventeen," Abed answered.

"What?" my wife said. "Do you know what a condom is?" Then she asked Abed's friend how many children he had.

He smiled proudly. "Twenty-two." Each had three wives.

Although the birthrate remains sky-high among Palestinians in the West Bank and Gaza, it has plummeted among Arabs who live inside Israel and who are exposed to secular values. Orthodox Jews, meanwhile, average around eight children per family, while ten or more is common. Apart from fulfilling their religious duties, many Orthodox Jews speak openly of outbreeding the Arabs. Demographers differ in their analysis of the statistics: Some predict Arabs will soon claim a majority in the Holy Land; others say that this will never happen. But there's another side to the baby boom: By 2050, some analysts anticipate, half of all Jews in Israel will be Orthodox, leading to a subversion of the state's secular nature.

If the Arabs wield their large families as a weapon, the Jews rely on immigration. Recent immigration from the former Soviet Union has profoundly influenced Israeli culture and created new tensions between Jews and Arabs, as I experienced firsthand during the late 1990s, when I hired two Arabs and four Russians to renovate my home.

The two Arabs, Abed and Suleiman, were fairly typical Arab construction workers, poorly educated but nice enough fellows hailing from the Israeli town of Taibe. The Russians had to have been the most educated and accomplished group of construction workers on the planet. Pyotr, the chess master, mixed and poured the concrete. Sasha, the architect, built the walls. Shimon, the actor and writer, laid the tiles. His friend Leonid, the movie stuntman, did the heavy lifting.

Actually, a crew like this was hardly unique in Israel during the 1990s. Many of the million Soviet immigrants who arrived in Israel lacked jobs, and few were fortunate enough to find immediate employment in their professions. Doctors worked as kindergarten teachers and scientists as night watchmen. So many professional musicians stepped off the planes clutching violins, flutes, and guitars that when one man appeared without an instrument, people joked—oh, he must be the piano player.

Initially, the work at my house proceeded without incident. Then one day the Arabs argued with two of the Russians about who would use the wheelbarrow. Leonid, the stuntman, was a kung fu expert, but Abed wasn't to be messed with, either; his muscles rippled from carrying bricks all his life. Their argument became louder until one pushed the other. Suddenly they were rolling on the ground, wrestling and punching each other in the face.

Suleiman, tall and powerful, grabbed Shimon from behind, holding him fast so he couldn't intervene. As these two shouted and struggled on the sidelines, Abed and Leonid kept grunting and swinging at each other, drawing blood. At one point, Abed had Leonid in a headlock. In a sudden kung fu move, Leonid hurled him over, landed on top of him, and smashed him in the eye.

"Please stop," I shouted feebly. "I'll buy another wheelbarrow."

Eventually my wife jumped in the middle and pulled them apart by the hair. They cleaned up and, as is often the case after mindless violence in Israel, shared a plate of hummus and a good laugh. Later, pondering their juvenile escapade, I realized it wasn't about the wheelbarrow but rather about who languished at the bottom of Israeli society, the newly arrived Russian immigrants or the local Arabs. I didn't buy another wheelbarrow, and as time passed it became clear who the losers really were. The Russians eventually found work closer to their professions, while the two Arabs remained construction workers.

Immigrants' education and drive have strengthened Israel from the beginning. Whereas other countries struggle to incorporate immigrants of different ethnicities, Israel has largely succeeded: It has created jobs, built homes, and educated newcomers at a rate unmatched in modern times. Even the million-strong Soviet immigration of the nineties pales when compared to Israel's achievement after the 1948 War of Independence. In the forties and fifties, the Jewish population doubled in size within four years and tripled within ten. Not to be outdone, Israel's Arab population grew eightfold in sixty years. Today there are 7.4 million Israelis, of whom 20 percent are Arabs.

Of course, Israel's rapid growth was far from painless. Israeli bureaucrats, mostly Ashkenazi immigrants from Germany and Poland, routinely assigned poor Sephardic Jews from North African countries to distant development towns while finding comfortable accommodations in Tel Aviv and Jerusalem for the more familiar European Jews. In 1991, Israel's secret "Operation Solomon" spirited fifteen thousand largely illiterate Ethiopian Jews out of their country in thirty-six hours aboard thirty-six jets and crash-landed them into the twentieth century. It was a triumph for Israel's ingathering of the Jews but hard for the Ethiopians. Brought from their mountain villages, ignorant of modern plumbing, dependant on handouts, facing racial prejudice, their social hierarchies overturned, the Ethiopians became confused and lost. Before long, they were committing suicide at an unprecedented rate.

Over time, the Ethiopians' absorption has improved, with the young growing up fluent in Hebrew and slowly filtering into all areas of life. Yet despite the overall success of absorption, difficulties for individual immigrants persist. Even newcomers from developed countries such as Britain and the United States complain about how hard it is to make it in Israel, where ties formed in school and the army last a lifetime and *protekzia*, personal contacts, win the day.

Still, Israelis, old and new, stand united by an overarching sense of shared struggle and pride. Little more than sixty years old, pressured by immigrant needs, Israeli Arab demands for true equality, Orthodox Jewish demands for the dominance of their laws, and the still-unresolved conflict with the Palestinians, Israel has shown extraordinary resilience. In a number of areas, it has even scored some remarkable successes.

For its size, Israel stands in a league of its own in science, agriculture, weapons industries, and high tech. In 2008, more Israeli companies were listed on NASDAQ than companies from Europe, China, India, Korea, and Japan combined.[3] Half the exhibitors at international high-tech fairs in New York often hail from Israel. And the rush for patents from Israeli medical research facilities such as the Weizmann Institute dwarfs those of countries ten times Israel's size. Within a year of the global economic collapse of 2008, Israel's stock exchange regained all its losses and then some. Israel's currency, the shekel, grew so strongly that for months the Bank of Israel bought a hundred million dollars a day to stop its rise. Real estate prices soared in Tel Aviv even as they tanked around the world.

Israel's prodigious economic, scientific, and financial success, so out of proportion for its size, stems from its identification not with its immediate Arab neighbors but with its friends across the Mediterranean. From the German immigrants in the thirties who wore jackets and ties in the summer heat to today's moneyed classes who vacation in Europe and America, Israelis face not the blazing sun that rises over Jordan's mountain plateau but the cooling sun that sinks across the waters. Their ambitions lie with NATO, the OECD, the EU, and Eurovision—with the distant west—not with the east on its doorstep.

These contradictions add up to a human tapestry as colorful and intricate as any on earth. My ambition, in setting out on my coastal walk, was to study this fascinating yet confusing place. In preparing to engage with Israel's complexity, I took particular pleasure in simplicity. I stuffed a backpack with two of each item of clothing. I checked that I had the basics: spectacles, credit card, and sun lotion. I charged my cell phone and promised to call home every night. I took a vacation from NBC. And then I set off on my journey of discovery, the adventure I had long imagined.

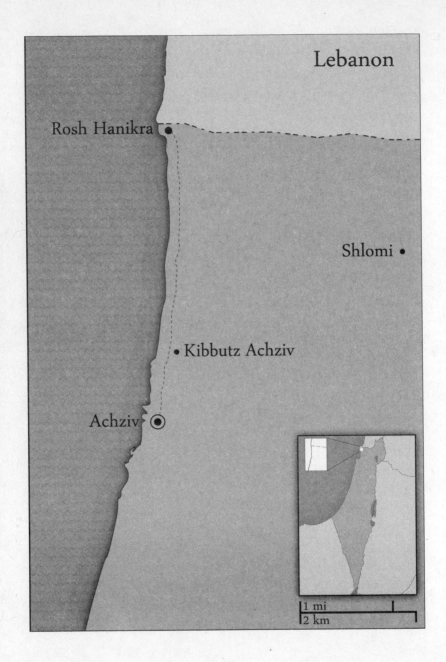

2

The Bride of Galilee

LEBANON BORDER TO ACHZIV

With Rosh Hanikra to my back, Lebanon's hills slope down to the coastal plain that stretches all the way to the Nile and beyond. From the border post high on the cliff, I can see clear across western Galilee to the distant Mount Carmel, which drops to the sparkling waters of Haifa Bay. The plain is filled with green fields and forests dotted with the red roofs of farming communities, while the white walls of Acre jut into the choppy sea. Eight tiny islands, rock outcrops, lie off the coast. They once comprised part of the landmass, just as the rocky outcrops along the edge of the water were once covered in forest and vineyards. Birds hoot and waves crash into the chalk cliffs. The sea air is crisp and tart. A film of spray floats on the wind, which brings the deep sweet scent of purple thyme. Beneath the ground, the pounding surf has chiseled labyrinthine grottoes that fill with seawater and empty as the tide sucks out. And there is a reminder down there, too, of more peaceful times: the remains of the railroad that linked Haifa with Lebanon and Syria. Today the tracks are broken and overgrown.

Under the 1949 armistice agreement drawn up by the United Nations, a small concrete pillar, Post Number One, marked Israel's border with Lebanon. Today it perches precariously on the steep cliff at Rosh Hanikra, known in antiquity as the Ladder of Tyre. Overrun by shrub and purple flowers, the humble slab stands as a reminder of better times, when Jews would ignore the border to drink mint tea and whiskey in the homes of Lebanese friends. Israel's high-tech border post looms above it, a porcupine of razor wire, antennae, radar posts, electronic monitoring systems, watchtowers, and metal gates that befits a country nominally at war with its northern neighbor for the last sixty years.

It was seven o'clock in the morning. The sea was flinty, roiling gray, and white gulls honked and squawked as they wheeled over spray from the waves that pounded the rocks. I was standing on the coastal road, leaning against the border post's locked blue gate, jotting down the first notes of the first day of my hike down the coast (". . . the gate has a Star of David motif. . ."). A stern, white-haired man with a bushy white mustache interrupted me. *"Ma ahta oseh?"* he demanded in Hebrew—what are you doing?

Harsh queries from strangers are common in Israel, and their exact tone of voice determines the response. He sounded a bit too gruff for me, so I answered in kind in English, "And why do you want to know?" I immediately regretted my rudeness to an elderly man and explained: "I'm making a few notes for a story I may write." After a suspicious stare, he stalked away, glaring at me over his shoulder.

What I was really doing was thinking about the first three miles of my journey. I planned to follow the beach from Rosh Hanikra down to Achziv, a spit of land with low hills clearly visible by a small lagoon. There, at the northernmost houses on Israel's coast, I would take a closer look at a group mostly ignored by journalists but critical to Israel's future, the country's Arab citizens.

The coastal route had always been one of the main gateways into the Holy Land from the north, but in 1948 it was the emergency exit for thousands of Arabs fleeing, or forced to flee, to Lebanon. These terrified refugees and their descendants still inspire the Palestinian conflict with Israel. Yet today almost one in five Israelis is Arab, descended from the families who stayed. There is always the question: Are they the enemy within, an Arab fifth column that could rise up and attack the Jews? Or are they the vanguard of peace between Arabs and Jews? Caught up in the violence between Palestinians and Israelis, like most reporters I had generally ignored these Israeli Arabs and their delicate balancing act. In Achziv, which the Arabs call Al-Zib, I hoped to learn more about what had been termed "the quietest minority in the world."

Twenty yards away, across the road, the worried older man appealed to a female border guard sitting on a white plastic chair in the shade. Indicating me with his chin, trying not to draw my attention, he whispered, "That man makes me feel bad. Maybe you should call somebody—he's writing!"

True; now I was struggling to record his exchange with the soldier. She seemed unimpressed and sank back in her chair. "*Nu?*" she responded. So?

"Call your officer—quickly," he said, a little louder.

The soldier, about eighteen years old with a round, innocent face and

light brown hair pulled back into a knot, stood up and summoned a colleague. Oh no, I thought. Would I get arrested before I'd even started my
trek? For writing? I continued jotting down notes, describing the scene as it
unfolded. I couldn't make out what the two soldiers said, but then the first
girl shrugged and called out to the man, "Why shouldn't he write?"

I grinned to myself.

"*Hoo lo achad mi shelaanu,*" the man answered, as if this explained everything.

I couldn't help but chuckle and look up. "*Hoo lo achad mi shelaanu*"—he
isn't one of us—has a clear subtext in Israel. It means he isn't Jewish,
he isn't Israeli, he can't be trusted, so he isn't on our side, and therefore he
must be against us. "One of us" is the ultimate seal of belonging in the Holy
Land, where Us has a biblical sense of the chosen people. You either belong, or you don't. An Arab, a Goy, cannot be "one of us"; it's a reason Israeli
Arabs are viewed with suspicion, regardless of their social status. In fact,
Israeli security officials have developed a lexicon of euphemistic, "politically
correct" questions to determine if travelers are "one of us." At the entrance
to Ben-Gurion Airport, armed guards ask departing passengers where
they come from. They don't care about the answer. They just want to know
if the speaker has an Arab accent. If so, the follow-up is usually "Step aside,
please." Inside the terminal, the query to foreigners: "Did you speak any Hebrew before you came to Israel" means: Did you study for a bar mitzvah?
"Do you have any family in Israel?" means: Are you Jewish?

All this flashed through my mind. Yet after so many years spent reporting in Israel, I understood the old man's fears. He was trying to save the
country; what more can an old Jew do? Fortunately for me, the soldier he
addressed apparently didn't share his concerns. She shrugged again and
answered, "It's a free country."

Perfect! I added exclamation marks to my notes and tilted my head to
see his reaction. Our eyes met as he turned and stalked away.

NO CHURLS, THIEVES, CADS, OR MISERS!

Seeing freedom of the press victorious, I left the coast road and stumbled down a steep, narrow, rocky path to the pebble beach, my backpack already digging into my shoulders. In addition to the essentials listed above I carried a laptop, a cell phone, a digital camera and a digital recorder (with separate chargers for each), sandals, a bedroll and a sleeping bag, two bottles of water, dried fruits and nuts, my trusty Swiss army knife, notebooks, pens, and two books, one on the Crusades and one on Napoleon's Holy Land misadventures. My pack weighed a ton. I wore hiking boots with thick socks, khaki shorts with lots of pockets, a reddish T-shirt, and a silly floppy hat with a flap to cover my neck. At 7:30 a.m. on this, the longest day of the year, it was already eighty degrees and humid. By noon it would reach a hundred. I was already sweating, but the good news was that two weeks later, when I hoped to reach Gaza, I should have lost an inch or two from my stubborn paunch.

It was only about an hour's walk to Achziv, legendary in antiquity as a base of a Canaanite cult of temple prostitutes dedicated to the fertility goddess Ashtoreth, and in modern times as a hippie paradise called Achzivland. During the 1960s and '70s, topless Israeli girls and foreign backpackers competed for the attentions of the happy landlord, Eli Avivi, who claims to have slept with thousands of girls and to have taken naked photos of most of them. I was looking forward to meeting him.

Achziv was also home, fittingly enough, to Club Med. For six consecutive years in the early sixties, the Achziv holiday village was voted Club Med's most popular resort, even though it had little to offer beyond volleyball and the beach. The view from the straw bungalows, set among eucalyptus groves yards from the sea, was spectacular, and the first brochure praised the "fun, cosmopolitan atmosphere," while promoting its "Arabian village ambience." No mention was made of why it seemed so authentic, or of the Arabs whose home it had once been. The fun ended in 1995, when a Katyusha rocket fired from Lebanon killed a French cook near the pool. The violent history of the place had caught up with it.

Around the time of the patriarch Abraham, Achziv was a walled city. Later it became a Canaanite city, mentioned in the Bible as part of the territory of the tribe of Asher. The Bible also relates that King Solomon gave the city of Achziv to the king of Tyre, in return for cedar, cypress, and gold to help build the Temple in Jerusalem. And this was just the beginning. Phoenician tombstones were found here, as were Roman milestones. A stone tablet with Greek writing was found next to synagogue remains from earlier millennia, when the town had been regarded as the religious boundary of ancient Israel. Christian Crusaders built a fortress here, which in turn was destroyed by Saladin, to prevent any future heathen foothold. Then came Muslim farmers and fishermen who for centuries used the ancient carved stones to build foundations for their homes.

By the mid-twentieth century, two thousand Muslims were living here in the village they called Al-Zib. Their fig and pomegranate orchards and lush pastures covered five square miles, much of it on low hills and fields overlooking the Mediterranean. It was a place so beautiful that the British police chief called it the prettiest village in Palestine, and the Arabs called it the Bride of Galilee. But peaceful, it wasn't. In 1946, fourteen fighters of the Palmach, the Jewish militia, died while trying to blow up a nearby bridge. Revenge came two years later, during Israel's War of Independence, when Jews razed the Bride of Galilee, sparing only the mosque and the home of the mukhtar, the village head. All those remains of ancient city walls, tombstones, columns, carvings, inscribed tablets, and modern Arab gravestones were left strewn around, a historical treasure trove waiting to be collected and cataloged by archaeologists. Instead, Avivi, a former sailor turned beach bum, turned up in 1952. He used some of the precious artifacts to construct wood and stone houses that he rented out, and he preserved the rest in his museum of found objects, which today is housed in the high vaulted rooms of the mukhtar's former home.

I dawdled during my modest hike along the water's edge to Achziv, sitting on rocks, eating dried fruit and drinking bottled water, admiring the view, and generally congratulating myself on finally fulfilling a dream. For so long I had wanted to take time out from my insane schedule as a foreign correspondent to think more deeply about this place that I called home.

A man approached, a charming geologist and family friend whom I had arranged to meet named Yigal Sela. After greeting each other, we cast about near the beach, admiring fossilized tree roots in the limestone sediment and ancient grape presses carved into the rock. Yigal said this was evidence that the coast was once well to the west, and that hundreds of yards of land were now drowned in the sea. He pointed out where sea turtles had once nested and told me the Latin names for flowers I had previously known only as yellow or blue. He had helped found the kibbutz at Rosh Hanikra and had joined Israel's nature reserve authority in 1954. One of his main concerns, as the young Israel struggled to survive, was to protect the indigenous sea turtles. In those early years, he often ran into a bum on the beach, and gave the homeless man food and drink. That man, he told me, was Avivi, whom I was now even more eager to meet.

I thanked the gentle geologist and strolled up from the beach toward the main road, then followed a road sign marked ELI AVIVI. The path guided me along a private access road lined with trees and wild bougainvillea. Passing through a tall metal gate, I entered a large compound composed of bizarre structures, some with pointy wooden roofs like Swiss chalets, others flat and squat like bunkers, with windows of all shapes and sizes. The bases of these buildings were of rock and ancient stones, and their frames were mismatched old wood and glass, as if a beachcomber had built his fantasy home—which, as it turns out, is exactly what happened. Avivi had stunning views over the ancient natural fishing harbor and terraces that led down to the Mediterranean. To the left as I entered, several people sat inside a semicircular wall built of limestone blocks taken from the Arab homes. In the center of this courtyard salon, an old man sat. He had a deeply tanned pate, long gray hair beginning at his ears, and a gray beard. It was Avivi himself, lording it at table with saucers of nuts, a bowl of fruit, and little mugs of tea, all in the shade of a spreading carob tree. He seemed nothing short of an aging robber baron holding court.

As I asked him about his colorful life, Avivi volunteered that he wasn't nearly the man he once was. Aged seventy-four, he munched happily on the Arab sweetcakes his wife, Rina, served, but his voice was feeble and slow, and his list of hospital visits, in which he seemed to take some pride, was impressive. "I've been in hospital a hundred times in ten years," he whispered. "I've had a prostate operation, and I need another one. I had four heart attacks, I've had four bypasses, I have diabetes . . ."

As he elaborated, an attractive young girl in a swimsuit walked by and called out, "Regards from my mother."

Avivi shot back: "How old are you?"

She smiled sheepishly. "Twenty-four."

"Too old for me," he said in a raspy voice, and followed up with, "Just kidding, just kidding, come sit with us." He burst into a fit of coughing, spluttering and spitting, and she continued to the beach.

Avivi, of Persian origin, followed the Israeli maxim of creating facts on the ground. He discovered this stretch of beach as a navy commando, liked what he saw, and after sailing around the world as a merchant seaman, returned, living on cigarettes and food handouts, including those from Yigal Sela. He moved into a half-destroyed house that had belonged to the Sa'adi family of Arab refugees, improved it, took over some land, built another house, took over more land, put a fence around it all, and began charging admission on the theory that, as he put it, "People came to look, so why shouldn't they pay?"

In 1970, in response to numerous attempts by the Israeli government and court system to force him out, Avivi declared the independent state of Achzivland. *Protekzia*, knowing somebody in the right place, is too often the real law of the land, and Avivi had so many contacts in successive governments, many of whom had enjoyed the countercultural pleasures of the place as youths, especially the nude bathing, that he always knew which string to pull. The penniless beach bum had turned himself into an alternative institution, illegally charging entrance to the beach, flying his own flag, and singing his own national anthem. His state's constitution warned, "Every nationalist is welcome except for churls, thieves, cads, and misers." Young Israelis, for whom foreign travel in those days was mostly a dream, loved to get their passports stamped with the elaborate brown emblem of Achzivland.

When Avivi told me he didn't have any children, I made the mistake of asking what would happen to Achzivland after he died, which, given his coughing spasms, seemed imminent. Rina got up and walked away, and Avivi suddenly launched into a furious loud tirade that made birds rise in alarm from the carob tree. "I know I won't leave it to the government! Anything but that. Not after how they tortured me! Everything I had to fight for!" he yelled, throwing his arms around to encompass the landscape. "When I came here, there was nothing, nothing for miles along the coast. I built it all. Then one day they came with a bulldozer and they started to bulldoze my home. My home! How could they do that?!"

It seemed relevant but, because Avivi was already struggling for breath, ultimately pointless to point out that he built his home on a bulldozed Arab village. "I took my gun and said I'd shoot them. I ran to Jerusalem to stop them. I've been here fifty-five years. Fifty-five years!" He paused to wipe his brow and placed his hand on his chest, as if to demonstrate his sincerity, or maybe to feel for heart palpitations. "Every year they take a bit more of my land. I love Israel but I hate the government. All the governments. I fought for this country: I joined the Palmach when I was fourteen. I was a commando, I fought the British, I fought the Arabs. And now they've destroyed everything." I leaned forward and patted Avivi's arm, trying to slow him down. I didn't want to kill the guy. "Israel was so beautiful," he added, "the rivers so clean that I could drink from them. Today, they are polluted or they've all dried up!"

He paused to sip his tea and catch his breath. I saw Rina pop her head around the door of the office to check on her husband. I checked my recorder to make sure it was still running. Then Avivi asked, in a calmer voice, "What about you, are you married?"

I smiled. "Yes, my wife is Israeli."

"What's her name?"

"Hagar." I waited for his response. My wife's name sometimes sends rightwing Israelis into a rage, furious that Jews could name their daughter after Hagar, Abraham's slave wife who mothered the Arab race. But the mention of Hagar prompted an entirely different train of thought in Avivi, he of the thousand and one nights. "Hagar, ah, Hagar. I remember Hagar very well."

"It isn't the same Hagar," I said. "At least, I hope it isn't."

"Hagar," Avivi said wistfully. "I had a girlfriend called Hagar, from a kibbutz. Dark like a Yemenite."

I shifted uncomfortably. My Hagar is from Kibbutz Ashdot Ya'akov in the Jordan Valley, and she's half Yemenite.

"A bit different," he continued, "special sort of girl. From the first second I saw her, she went naked. There was an army position on the hill, and all they did was look at her through their binoculars. She ate rice with her fingers. A very special girl."

Uh-oh, I thought, sounds familiar. No, it can't be . . .

He nodded happily and his tired eyes sparkled. "She was always naked. In the kibbutz, she served in the dining room naked, and the kibbutz had a meeting and threw her out. A beautiful girl, dark hair, beautiful body, sixteen years old, she became my girlfriend. In Jerusalem, she met a man who said he was the messiah, rode a white donkey, she behind him, the two of them, they became famous, they burned the Torah, then they got religious. Today, he's a rabbi, and she's a rabbi."

Phew.

Avivi broke into coughing, then smirked again. "When she married this guy, the messiah, she told him how we made love in one of my rooms and that I took hundreds of naked photos. So he came one day and said he wants the photos, he wants to destroy them, but he looked at the album a million times and said, 'Don't destroy them.'"

"So now the rabbi has the album with the naked photos?" I asked.

"I'm not stupid," Avivi said. "I didn't give him all the photos." He chuckled until another fit of coughing.

"You must have had many girlfriends . . ." I prompted, enjoying the glint in the eyes of this feeble old lecher. Even now he had a wicked charm, and as tourists in bikinis strolled by, he didn't fail to ogle the cute ones.

He grunted loudly. "King Solomon didn't have as many girlfriends as me. He had a thousand. I had many more. And the photos, the naked photos! I didn't have to tell girls I wanted to photograph them. They asked me. And they showed them to their friends and they came too. You don't know anything about women. They can do anything. Thousands of girls."

Avivi invited me back to his house to see his photo collection, and to hear more stories, but I said maybe another time. I felt I had tired him enough. Certainly he had tired me. A friendly man, I thought, who from nothing built a hedonistic lifestyle many would relish, financed by renting out other people's destroyed homes that he had turned into holiday chalets. But how obtuse can a man be, I wondered, as I strolled among his cottages and admired the purple and yellow bougainvillea blossoms that spread over the looted olive presses and tombstones, lending such an authentic air to the approach to the beach. I thought of the Arab refugees whose home this once was. Most live in Lebanon but some, Israeli Arabs, now live nearby in towns like Nahariya and Acre. When I had asked him what the Arabs thought about him living in their homes, he had answered that they were happy. "They think I'm looking after their homes for them," he had said. "They are sure they'll come back."

"And will they?" I asked.

He flicked his hand. "Believe me, I don't know. I hope not, but who knows? This Israel is more and more in danger. There are many Arabs in the Knesset, they're against Israel, they're in offices, you see Arabs everywhere, everywhere, they can take over one day."

Incredible, I thought: The villagers he had displaced didn't seem to concern him. In the mind of this gentle old hippie—a man who rhapsodized about freedom from the state, who in photos wore a white robe and a white beard, like a biblical patriarch—in his mind, the natives had been neutron-bombed. He was truly fulfilling the Zionist slogan of "a people without a land for a land without a people." But in the case of Al-Zib, it wasn't that there had been no people. There just weren't any people left. They had been chased away, and as Avivi himself feared, they might return to "take over one day." No wonder he preferred to talk about naked girls.

Before leaving Avivi to his midday nap, I asked him whether any of the refugees from the village came to visit the national park next door, which charges twenty shekels to get in. "Often," he answered. "I know some of them. We're friends."

"Isn't that a bit strange for them, to pay to visit their old village?"

"No," he answered, "if they used to live here, they only pay half-price."

YOU CAN'T TRUST ANYONE

I was about to leave Achzivland when I changed my mind and decided to pay a visit to Avivi's private museum. As I've mentioned, his collection of objects found in Achziv and in the sea is tastefully stored in the home of the old mukhtar, who I later discovered is an elderly man living in Lebanon called Ataya Husayn. It is a beautiful Arab home with twelve-foot ceilings, arched windows that overlook the sea, floors decorated with floral tiles, and walls covered with enough dusty artifacts to fill an arcade of antique stores. Each room leads to another and is packed with antiquities and interesting finds: marble columns, carved rocks and friezes, ancient wooden farming plows and hand tools, oil lamps of all sizes, bullets, hunting rifles and belts, an old British Bren machine gun, iron cannonballs (probably from Napoleonic times), birdcages, kitchen pots and pans from different eras, remnants of sculptures in stone and marble, heads without noses, arms without hands, torsos and legs, and display cases of beads, jewelry, and glass.

Nobody else cared about this stuff when Avivi arrived in 1952. Israelis were occupied with building a state, the Arabs had vanished, and the few tourists didn't come this far north. It was a beachcomber's paradise. But by rights, I believed, it all belonged to the state. I scanned the cabinets, spotting one full of old coins. Looking over my shoulder, I thought it would be easy enough to shove a handful into my pocket. They're all stolen, every item.[1] It stirred my juices; I'm a bit of a bandit myself. I decided to steal something. It seemed the right thing to do.

It wasn't every day that I stole from a private museum. I felt my heart beating. Peering nervously around the walls and out the front door, seeing no sign of security cameras, I went back and tapped on the case labeled BYZANTINE GLASS. Avivi nicked the lot, I reminded myself, to strengthen my resolve. I tried to lift up the case's glass top, and it rose halfway. I could get my hand in easily. Do it! I thought. Nobody'll ever miss it, and anyway, stealing from a crook is a double negative, which is a positive. I thrust my hand to the back of the case, where the best-looking piece sat by itself on a silken padded cloth. It was a perfect small glass jar, no chips or cracks, deep azure blue with an attractive patina of shiny shades of blue-green, with

earth still clinging to the rim and to one side. The label said it was Byzantine, but it looked like a Roman perfume bottle to me. They achieved that
deep blue by adding copper or cobalt.

Reassuring myself that my theft would not be witnessed, I closed my
sweaty fingers around the treasure and pocketed it. Heart racing, I saun-
tered out through the tall metal gate and headed for the path. I couldn't
walk to the beach through the national park and Club Med, as both
guarded their privacy with high metal fences. I passed through a clump of
eucalyptus trees along the disused and broken old British railroad and,
calmer now, sat on a rock. When I examined my loot, I realized that it was
either a rare and priceless example of early Byzantine or Roman art—a
pristine museum piece, worth a small fortune—or else it was an ink bottle.
Inside, I found congealed pieces of black and blue grit. Old ink? Surely not.
Detritus of time? I hoped so! Wait a minute, I thought, could this be a
stamp? I made out the letters "KB," which I googled the next time I got my
computer going:

> Robert N. Steffens sat down to develop a new fast drying
> ink. He had no ink or chemical training, but he dove into
> the study of ink-making and KB Ink was created. It is not
> the only water ink in America today, but it pushed other
> ink manufacturers to make a competitive product. The re-
> sult is that today as much as 99% of the ink used in Amer-
> ica is water ink.

How did a KB bottle end up in Avivi's inadequately sealed display case
of alleged precious Byzantine glass? I don't know. I didn't go back to ask
him. It sits behind me on my bookshelf as a reminder that you can't trust
anyone. I didn't go back to see Avivi's naked photos, either.

I did go back, though, to find some of the Israeli Arabs who had lost their homes to his dream of paradise, to the national park, to Club Med, and to the neighboring Kibbutz Achziv that had been built on their village land. I wanted to ask the Arabs what it felt like to pay half-price to visit their own home. But if Avivi turned out to be more complicated than I'd expected, the first Arab refugees from Al-Zib whom I found, the allegedly hostile and resentful "enemy within," turned out to be equally surprising. They were more loyal to the State of Israel than Avivi himself.

I DECIDED TO BECOME A JEW

The numbers are disputed, but the best assessment is that the former village of Al-Zib is one of 450 Arab villages[2] destroyed within the State of Israel in 1948. About half the Arab population lost their homes in the war they call the Nakba, the catastrophe. United Nations agencies counted 720,000 Arab refugees, while the new Israeli government put the number at 550,000, and the Arabs claimed 900,000. Today, the number of Palestinian refugees and their descendants for the purpose of the peace process and their potential return or financial compensation has grown to around 4.5 million, about a third of whom still live in UN-administered refugee camps. In 1948, a further 120,000 Arabs remained within the borders of the new state of Israel, about 17 percent of the country's population, a proportion that is roughly maintained today. These became the Israeli Arabs, who now number about a million.

In many places, the first Israeli directive in 1948 was to destroy the suddenly empty Arab homes, for much the same reason Saladin destroyed the Crusader castles along the coast a thousand years earlier: to make sure the inhabitants couldn't return. But there was such demand for homes for Jewish refugees flooding in from Europe, now that the British were not there to stop them, that a new order was issued: Stop destroying the Arab houses and let Jews live in them. This was the logic that allowed Eli Avivi to set up home in the ruins of a house that had once belonged to the Sa'adi family of Al-Zib. And as I set out to find some of the Sa'adis who had been chased away that day in 1948, it turned out that a few of them still lived nearby, inside the ancient walls of the old city of Acre, only ten miles away.

In 1950, under one of Israel's earliest pieces of legislation, Israeli Arabs such as the Sa'adis officially lost their land—not like most Arabs, who were classified as "Absentees," or refugees who had left the country, but as internal refugees, people who lost their homes but lived nearby. Under the law, the term for Hussam Sa'adi, a stocky ex-fisherman from Al-Zib, was "Present Absentee." Who came up with that phrase, I wondered? Shouldn't it be "Absent Presentee"? Orwell and Kafka would have been proud. The term conjured up a phantom, a body without form, a disembodied victim, not here but here.

None of this applied to the man I met, introduced to me weeks later, after I had finished the trek and was researching my stories. An Arab friend of a friend didn't know him well but thought he would be a good spokesman for the refugees. How wrong can one be? "Meet me in the home of Captain Sami," Hussam Sa'adi had said on the phone. I followed his instructions through the cobbled alleys of the Acre casbah to a small house facing the city wall. And if anybody was more surprising than Hussam, it was his nephew Sami, a lecherous curtain designer nicknamed "The Captain."

The first hint that something was askew in my search for the Arab side of the story came when I entered Sami's living room and saw a big Israeli flag covering one wall, and above the sofa, a photo of the Hasidic leader, the white-bearded Lubbavitcher Rebbe. Then I saw another photo, of Sami in an Israeli army colonel's uniform. Sami is the most un-Arab Arab man I have ever met. While washing the dishes, cleaning the floor, ironing and folding clothes, and serving us coffee and lemonade, Sami loudly and frequently interrupted my conversation with Hussam, trying like a child to bring attention to himself, often by attempting to show me photos of shapely Russian hookers lying on his bed, until finally he erupted: "I want to get married! It's time! Find me a wife! I'll do the dishes, wash the floor, do the ironing, I'll have the baby!" He wore black shorts with an apron and was bare-chested, revealing a muscular frame and strong forearms. I grinned dutifully.

Across the small kitchen table, Hussam, sixty-seven years old, with a tanned face and crinkly white hair, also attempted a smile. Later, he whispered that we should meet again, so that we could talk in peace. His droopy eyes and plodding voice reminded me of a man desperate for a comfortable bed, but he was constantly alert and didn't miss a thing. They were an unlikely couple, and I wondered what the link was, beyond blood. Sami, who spoke only in loud, shotgunlike bursts, shouted, "Don't be taken in by him. He's a world-class fucker!" Hussam shushed him wearily and tried to answer my question about Eli Avivi living on his family's land.

"I don't blame Avivi; in fact, I still visit him sometimes," Hussam said, sipping from a small cup of cardamom coffee. "I gave him food and water when he had nothing. It isn't his fault; he just wants somewhere to live. He didn't take it, the government did. But it's the Arabs' fault. They ran away. The Iraqis and the Jordanians. And we were stupid! The Jews came in tanks, and we tried to stop them with the spikes of cactus plants." He jerked a finger forward, in a stabbing gesture, narrowly missing the coffee cup. "Avivi? He came as a guest. We didn't think he would stay, that he would own everything. It was painful for us to see him living without food and without heat in winter, so we helped him." Hussam's voice slowed to a mumble. He made a flicking motion with his wrist. "He didn't fight us. I'm not angry; we surrendered . . ."

"Tell the truth!" Sami shouted from the kitchen sink, where he was washing the dishes. He waved one hand with a glass in it and banged the counter with the other. "They stole everything. I love that land! It's my grand-, grand-, grand-, million-grandfathers' land, and if we want to go there we have to pay for it. We want to swim, we want to picnic, it's a lovely place, and we have to pay like everyone else! Good luck! Good luck!" Sami was so agitated that he had dropped the glass, smashing it on the tile floor. "Good luck!" he shouted again.

"Why are you so angry?" I asked Sami.

Now he was bellowing, furiously wiping his hands on his apron: "Why am I angry? I am angry at my people, they are dying for nothing. I am angry at everyone. They kill children. Who said that suicide bombers go to heaven? No way! They are not fighting in God's name. They are killing civilians. Jews, they are bastards, they kill more."

"Are you angrier with the Jews or with the Arabs?"

He shouted even louder. "I am an Arab, and I will die a Muslim!" He rushed to the window and shouted it into the street for all to hear: "I am an Arab and I will die a Muslim!" From my seat by the window, I could see groups of tourists hurry by with nervous glances at the shouting coming from our room. Cars tooted at the pedestrians as they crossed the narrow street. Sami added, more softly, "But I don't like their behavior. So I became a Habadnik."

What!? Did I hear right? Now Sami had a huge smile, as he referred to the Hasidic Jewish sect. That's where the photo of the Lubbavitcher Rebbe on the wall came in.

"Excuse me—you're a Habadnik?"

Sami launched into a tirade about how the only people who do good with no ulterior motives are Hasidic Jews. They, he asserted, are sweet and good and lovely. "They will feed anyone—Fatima or Sara, Esther or Susan. If Fatima doesn't come one day they will say, 'Aah, where's Fatima, she is sick?' And they send food to her home." They had helped Sami once. And so he considered himself one of them. Another roar: "When I die, I will give my house and shop to Habad!"

This is an Israeli Arab, I thought—the enemy within? The only evidence was the heavy bitter aroma of the Arab coffee and the penetrating, ululating songs from the transistor radio. Just while I was coming to grips with this loudmouthed Arab being a Habadnik, he threw me a curveball. "You don't know that Yohanan is a Jew? He's been Jewish for thirty-five years."

"Who is Yohanan?"

"Hanan!"

I was confused. "Who is Hanan?"

"Him," Sami said, pointing to Hussam, who looked calmly at me. "My uncle."

"You're Jewish?" I asked Hussam. He shrugged. Sami pointed to the army photo on the wall. "A colonel. An honored colonel." Now I had no clue what was going on. "Isn't that you?" I asked Captain Sami.

"No, it's him. Like two drops of water, we looked so alike."

"Really?" I said to Hussam. "You're a Jewish army colonel?"

He nodded. "My name is Yohanan, in Arabic Hanan, but my original name was Hussam."

"So what should I call you?" I asked.

"Hanan."

Sami instructed me to turn off my digital recorder, which I did. "Will you tell him what happened?" he said to Hanan.

"I'm definitely going to record this," I said, turning the recorder back on. I had come to hear the time-honored narrative of, "They stole our land and we hate the Jews." I had wondered to whom these refugees would relate more closely: to their Arab relatives in Lebanon, to Palestinians in the neighboring West Bank, or to other Israeli Arabs. I didn't expect them to relate best to the Jews. The plot was thickening dramatically.

Hanan had spoken calmly and rather feebly, but now his voice changed and he spoke with the passion of a much younger man, staring at me across the kitchen table as he talked. "You want to know why I became a Jew? Not because of the religion! I was seven years old when the Jews attacked Al-Zib. They tricked us, and we ran away in the middle of the night, my father and one of his wives, and we didn't stop until Lebanon. We thought we would go back soon, but years passed. It was hard for us there. They didn't respect us. They said to us, 'You sold your land, you ran away from the Jews, you have no honor.' If they saw a donkey, or a dead mouse in the street, they would say, 'Why, you look like a Palestinian refugee.'"

He paused, as if to recover from the painful memory. "And then this is what happened. When I was ten, my mother sent me to a shop to buy some fireworks. There was a wedding. I didn't know it, but it was the day a Palestinian assassinated King Abdullah in Jerusalem.[3] When I asked for the fireworks, the shopkeeper, Abu Marouk—you see, I still remember his name, it was sixty years ago—he said to me, 'You are celebrating, you have a feast today, your mom sent you?' And in front of everybody, this son of a bitch slapped me in the face. I was ten years old." Hanan put his hand to his cheek, as if he still felt the sting.

"I ran home. I was humiliated and angry. There was no reason to beat me. I felt then as if he'd stabbed me with a knife. There was no difference between slapping me and stabbing me. I cried a little, I don't remember the details. I ran away, back across the border, back to my home in Al-Zib. It was empty. I found my real mother in Mazra'a and I lived with her. But I never forgot that man and how he slapped me. I was just a child. I was not guilty of anything. I dreamed of him. For many years, I dreamed of revenge."

"And what did you do?" I asked when he paused again. Even Sami had finally shut up and was listening intently.

"I decided to become a Jew, join the army, find that man who slapped me, and take my revenge," said Hussam, who became Colonel Yohanan. I looked at the photo on the wall. He had been a handsome young officer with thick black hair and a proud bearing.

"And did you get revenge?"

He nodded. "One day, I was in that village again, as an Israeli soldier. And I found him. He was an old man, and he was sitting on a chair in his store."

"What did you do?"

"I went up to him. I said, 'You need something from me.' He said, 'What do I need from you?' And I said, 'Do you remember me? When I was a little boy, I came to buy some things in your shop, and you asked me if I was happy and you slapped me. Now you need from me a slap.' And I slapped him."

"Did he fall down?"

"No, he was sitting on a chair. I felt good. All those years, I thought about that moment. I took my revenge. That's why I became a Jew."

I shivered as I heard this tale made for Hollywood. A few weeks later, when I proudly related Hussam's story to a friend, Dov Shimon, a prominent Israeli heart surgeon and entrepreneur, and a rational man, his response floored me. "That can't be true. Arab boys get slapped every day; otherwise their mother isn't doing her duty. It wasn't like that. Otherwise, why want revenge for so many years? The storekeeper didn't slap him. He raped him. And when he went back, he didn't slap him. He killed him. If it's true at all."

I chuckled at his cynicism. Dov continued with a question: "What unites Arabs everywhere?"

I threw up my hands. "Honor? Or the opposite, shame?"

He shook his head. "No, they can't separate fact from fiction. They say it, they believe it. It doesn't matter if it happened or not. They believe it, so it's real."

That sounded to me like a racist stereotype. But as I thought about it, the difference between fact and fiction, myth and logic, is at the core of the Israeli-Palestinian conflict. Twenty-five hundred years ago, Plato came up with the labels of *mythos* and *logos* to describe competing worldviews. *Mythos* emphasizes honor and shame and constructs a community version of events. This version fits the community's needs, and the community then acts upon it. *Logos*, by contrast, emphasizes the facts and only the facts, an idea that is the basis of Western legality and its concepts of right and wrong. Hussam's version of boyhood humiliation may not correspond strictly to the facts, or even loosely, but it certainly dictated his emotion and, to him at least, explains his life. It may not be the true story, but it's his story. Likewise, both sides in the Jewish-Arab conflict, these desert cousins, base today's logic on what they believe is the same ancient truth; they each believe in the divine promise of the same land. God gave me the land. No, he didn't, he gave it to me. Did not! Did! Take that!

With some additional digging, I found a different account of how Hussam returned to Israel from Lebanon. Years earlier, he had told another writer that he had been holidaying in Lebanon when the war broke out, and the family stayed there to wait out the fighting, believing it would last a week or two. After several years of life as refugees, unable to return, his father, a strong swimmer, rescued a downed Israeli pilot in the Mediterranean one night, and as a reward his family received an entry permit to Israel.

So which story is closer to the truth? When still later I ran them by some of Hussam's other relatives, they said they'd never heard these stories before, and then ordered me not to mention the name of "that Jew" in their house. What is indisputable is that Hussam, whose family lost all its possessions, became an honored fighter for Israel, or, from the Palestinian perspective, a cursed collaborator. When I asked him what he had done to reach the rank of colonel, I hit a blank wall. He wouldn't say. Nor would Captain Sami. Later, back home, I called Eli Avivi to ask him. After all, he and Hussam had known each other since 1952. I needed to understand what would drive an Israeli Arab, a refugee whose family lost everything, to join the Israeli army and fight against his own people. Because if it wasn't all some tall tale invented by Hussam to justify his betrayal of his people, then maybe it wasn't a betrayal at all, and there were more like him, many more. And that would mean that Israeli Arabs could well accept the loss of their land and be loyal citizens, posing no threat to the country. But when I mentioned Hussam's name, Avivi interrupted me abruptly. "Don't ask me. I don't need more trouble. It's security stuff. I can't talk about him."

Hussam had admitted only one thing to me: that he had been involved in Israeli prisons. One of the prisoners he had been responsible for was Ahmed Yassin, the paraplegic founder of Hamas. "I should have killed him when I had the chance," Hussam said. However, one of his other escapades did become public knowledge, and it turned out that Hussam was indeed a key figure in Israel's underground fight against the Palestinians. Thanks to an unguarded aside from Hussam mentioning early 1971, I found a newspaper reference, and then a detailed account in the Middle East section of the 1971 *Yearbook of the United Nations*.

On January 15, 1971, Israeli forces killed at least ten Palestinians and wounded dozens more in an unusual raid against a Lebanese village, Sarafand, twenty-six miles north of the Israeli border. In answer to Lebanon's complaint at Israel's attack on its sovereignty, Israel claimed that it had captured six fedayeen divers who had come by boat from a terrorist base in that village to kill Israelis, and that they had divulged information about attacks being planned from Lebanese soil. The Israelis even put one of the divers on TV. But the Lebanese counterclaimed that an Israeli double agent had tricked the Palestinians into sending the divers into an ambush, in order to justify Israeli attacks inside Lebanon. Israel's aim: to force the Lebanese government to crack down on the growing Palestinian terror structure in Lebanon. Given the legendary success of Israel's dirty tricks department, the Lebanese claim had the ring of truth.

The UN report said that the Lebanese army had tracked an Israeli agent who had infiltrated the Palestinian camp in Sarafand, and that the

Lebanese had warned the Palestinians about him. But the Palestinians preferred to believe the man, who then turned out to be an Israeli agent after all. His name—Sa'adi. And when the Israelis attacked a few weeks later, they had a guide on the ground—Sa'adi.

By phone, Hussam did not deny the story. So now I knew one of his more dramatic exploits, yet I was still no closer to understanding why he had turned against his own people. And from this, another intriguing question had emerged: Can an Arab be a loyal Israeli without betraying his own people? It was growing clear that Hussam and Sami were not going to give me the answers. Of all the million Israeli Arabs, I had fallen upon possibly the most reviled, and his buffoonish nephew.

DON'T MENTION HIS NAME IN MY HOUSE!

I couldn't leave with Hussam and Sami as the only voices of the refugees from Al-Zib, so I tried to find a more typical representative who could also fill in the blanks of Hussam's story. It wasn't hard. I was directed deeper into Acre's casbah, toward an old Ottoman merchant's house. Fading sunlight streamed upon the tall roofs, while shafts of light pierced the hazy cobbled alleys. A pleasant aroma of ground coffee lingered. The ground was wet and slippery, since the merchants had just washed the alley after the market had closed for the day. The muezzin's call to prayer echoed through the Old City, and on almost every wall there was a poster with injunctions from the Koran, white letters on a green background: "The best of wisdom is to fear God"; "Begin your prayer before death"; "Prayer is the pillar of organized religion, and to stop praying is to demolish religion."

I passed through a stone arch, walked up some marble steps polished to a shine by centuries of use, and asked a weathered old woman peering through a metal grill in her door if she knew where Um Mohammed of the Sa'adi family lived. She pointed upstairs.

I knocked on a thick wooden door, and moments later Um Mohammed opened it herself. She was eighty-three years old, a mother of eleven and grandmother of fifty-three. She had the classic features of a Grimm's fairy-tale witch: long, bony, drooping nose that reached her thin lips, small hooded eyes, and hair wrapped in a tight black kerchief. She even rubbed her hands together as she talked. Yet to me, she seemed proud and becoming. Her eyes were gentle. And also, I suppose, witches don't cry.

At the very mention of Achziv, Um Mohammed's eyes teared up. "Ah, Al-Zib!" she said. "The Bride of Galilee. We had all kinds of fruit in our land, apples, apricots, grapes. We were rich, we owned land, so much land we couldn't plant it all. Not like this!" She glanced around at her modest apartment and started sobbing. Her son Samir handed her a tissue.

We were sitting in a long narrow room, almost a large corridor, with ceilings eighteen feet high and grand wooden carvings etched in fading pastel green. Three other rooms extended off it. The crumbling living room wall went straight down the middle of the original space, and on the other side was another apartment with another family. Wistful photos of sunsets and sea views decorated the walls, next to Koranic inscriptions. "There were fruit trees everywhere," she continued. "Everything we wanted, we had. Ya-Allah." She indicated from her wrist to her elbow, referring to the gold bands that women wore, carrying their wealth on their arm: "We had gold from here to here."

I was party to a timeless scene: a deeply wrinkled old woman, sitting on her chair with her son at her side, in a darkening room, telling of the past. "Women couldn't go to school then," she continued. "We couldn't read or write, so we couldn't send letters to boyfriends. Nobody asked whom we would marry. One day Father brings a man, and that's that." She began to cry again. "I was engaged, but the Jews killed him before the war. So I married his brother. What weddings we had then! Seven days of eating and dancing, meat and rice, changing dresses every day. He was my cousin. So was my fiancé. He fell sick and died."

Turning sharply to me, Um Mohammed asked where I was from. When I said England, she wanted to stop talking to me. Shaking her finger, she said, "Allah will take revenge on you. What did the British do for us? What did the Arabs do for us? What did anybody do for us? Nothing. I listen to the news. What will he do for us?" she asked, meaning me.

Samir soothed his mother: "He isn't guilty, it's not his fault."

She thought about this. And then, with tears still streaming down her face, she continued her story. "One day, the Jews came and started shooting. They killed a man and his son while they were feeding the cows. The wife started shouting that the Jews are here, and everyone ran away. Some of them ran to other villages like us, and most went by boat to Lebanon. The Jews came to our house and killed my father. I was twenty-one then. My mother hid with me in the chimney. We hid until dark and the Jews had gone, and then we left Al-Zib. They destroyed our life." Her son advised her to be careful of what she said, but she continued. "I don't care, I am telling the truth, what are they going to do to us? They took our lands and everything we had. What more can they do to us? And that's that. What else can I tell you? To talk more about our disaster so you can write about it?" She stopped with an air of finality and wiped her eyes with her rough old hands, pursing her lips as if sealing up the torrent of words.

I asked about her cousin, Hanan Sa'adi, the Israeli army colonel, and her face hardened as she turned on me. "Don't even mention his name in my house! Dirt! Jew! Nobody speaks to him."

Okay, I thought, so much for him. I decided to take a different tack. I asked Samir, her thirty-year-old son, whether he saw peace one day between Israel and the Palestinians. "After all," I said, "you are an Israeli Arab, an Israeli citizen."

He made a dismissive, tutting sound: "Tsuh! No. We wait. Nobody knows what will be. One day, something will happen." After a few more questions, it turned out he had been in jail for a security offense, but he wouldn't say what. I asked him if he had ever come across Marwan Barghouti, a leader of the second Intifada. Barghouti was seen by many as the most credible Palestinian leader; he had been sentenced to five consecutive life terms for murder. I thought Samir's answer would indicate how serious his own offense was. "Yes!" he laughed. "I was in the cell next to him. I said to him, 'You're so small! And you cause so much trouble!' Nice guy. We didn't talk politics, just the sun, flowers, family. They move him around every few months."

I asked Samir about Hussam's slapping story. "Dirty liar! I never heard that before." But about Eli Avivi living on their land, his reaction, and Um Mohammed's, was as generous as that of Hussam and Captain Sami had been. "Eli Avivi is a nice guy. He didn't take the land, the government did. He's okay. He declared his own state. He got a state before we did!"

"But you have a state," I pointed out. "Israel. You're a citizen. You're an Israeli Arab. You have a passport, a home here, your children go to school here."

Samir just laughed. At that moment Raheli, Samir's wife, entered with their little son. As if the tale needed another twist, this slim and appealing woman was born Jewish. Now that she was back, little children suddenly emerged from all the rooms. "It was easy to become Muslim," she said. "I just went to an Islamic court and said, 'I witness that there is no god but God, and Mohammed is the prophet of God,' and that was it. The rabbis were furious. They asked if I was being blackmailed. I said, 'Leave me alone, just sign the paper.' My sister is Orthodox. She won't talk to me."

She performed her military service in an air-force base in a secret unit involved with antiaircraft fire. She related with relish that the air force was furious when she converted to Islam to marry Samir. He laughed and said, clearly not for the first time, "She is the occupation. She bombs us!"

I asked Raheli, "Can there still be peace between the Israelis and the Arabs?"

A brief smile flashed across her face, like a fleeting memory. "Leave me alone. I'm too busy with the children."

WILL YOU DIE IN PEACE?

Although I understood the visceral, almost organic connection of Arabs to their land, I still didn't understand why Um Mohammed and Samir could not come to terms with their new lives. Yes, they lost their land, but did they really need to fight for generations and generations, just to move ten miles back to their old apple trees? And although I now knew what other Arab refugees thought of Hussam, what an outcast he was, I still didn't know why he had changed his religion to join the Israeli army. So I called Hussam one more time, and we arranged to meet at his old village, Al-Zib, where the rocks form a semicircle on the beach, and water laps gently in a little lagoon. I thought, If I get him alone, away from Sami, in the embrace of his land, in the shade of a fig tree, he may relent and explain.

Today the village entrance is just a dusty parking lot at the water's edge with a warning sign, DANGER, NO SWIMMING. But for Hussam, every rock held a memory. He caressed the rocks with his feet in his leather shoes. He pointed at a bush where the coffeehouse had once stood, and he looked in vain for the two stone steps. He walked over and kicked a low ridge covered in shrub and yellow flowers. "This was where our gas pump stood; it was a good business." He peered up at the fenced-off hill with all the mounds of earth, which was the cemetery, and where there was only one gravestone left standing: "That is my uncle." The rest were smashed or collected to decorate Eli Avivi's museum.

I followed Hussam as he walked along the Kziv creek, which gave its name to the village. It had once been an important water source, one of three that had sustained settlement here for thousands of years, but we were walking on pebbles and smooth rocks, lined by tall reeds; all that remains is a stagnant puddle of smelly, dirty water.

Two hundred yards on, we came to the wooden bridge that the Palmach fighters had tried to blow up. They had died in the attempt, the start of the villagers' problems. It isn't even clear what killed them. It could have been the Arabs. Or the British. Or a stray bullet could have hit their explosives, causing a blast. Nobody knows. There were no survivors. Above the creek, the white-and-blue Israeli flag fluttered over a war memorial to the fallen Jews.

Hussam looked around glumly. He trailed his fingers down the wooden bridge support and gently rolled a stone with his foot. He took in the view beneath the bridge, the flag above, the reeds, and the dry riverbed. "I never came here, I never brought my children here," he said sadly. "Since 1948, this is the first time I have seen this bridge. They fixed it up for the tourists." He read the memorial plaque aloud in Hebrew, then pointed. "There's the old police tower. There's another lookout post. The British army camp was behind those trees."

He fell silent, the moment heavy. He was lost in his memories. After two minutes, my reporter's instinct told me that the time had come. I interrupted him, gently, with the question that had brought me back. "Tell me, really, why did you become a Jew?"

At first he just stared at me, and then he shook his head and pursed his lips.

I persisted. "Your own family calls you a traitor. They say you killed your own people. What really happened? Why?"

Still he didn't respond. He looked at me, his droopy eyes narrowing further. I saw his body stiffen and he shook his head slowly again. Then he turned around to walk back to his car, dismissing me. But there was another question I just had to ask. It would sum it all up. It would have been cowardly not to ask. I felt the need to touch the heart of this lonely man who had led such an unfortunate, extraordinary life. I wanted to understand his soul, which was so at odds with the soul of his family, and of his people.

I caught up with him, and after a moment walking by his side, I said, softly, "Hanan, we all die in the end. Tell me, when your time comes, will you die in peace?"

And this elderly Arab, who killed his own people for Israel, who waved away all questions about his past, who never acknowledged his pain, who had told me he had never visited a doctor and slept well every night—this man visibly slumped, like a punctured balloon. His eyes reddened and moistened and he quickly turned his head as if not to show his tears. He shuffled down the dry riverbed, picking his way over the stones in his black shoes, his shoulders bent, alone. I stood and watched him until he disappeared behind the tall reeds.

I waited. Alone again at the creek, I climbed a grass verge and reached the manicured memorial to the fallen Jewish fighters, a circle of squat graves lined up as if on parade. Tall cypress trees pointed toward the sky; as they say here, guiding souls to heaven. As I walked along the headstones, reading the names and ages, I glanced up at Rosh Hanikra, on the border with Lebanon, only three miles away, and saw green hills ending abruptly in white cliffs that dropped sharply to the sea. When I had begun my journey up there, the view across this fertile plain had been pristine, almost innocent, a Garden of Eden. But the view from up there was not the same as the view from down here. I heard Hussam's car start up and watched him drive away. That was the last I saw of him.

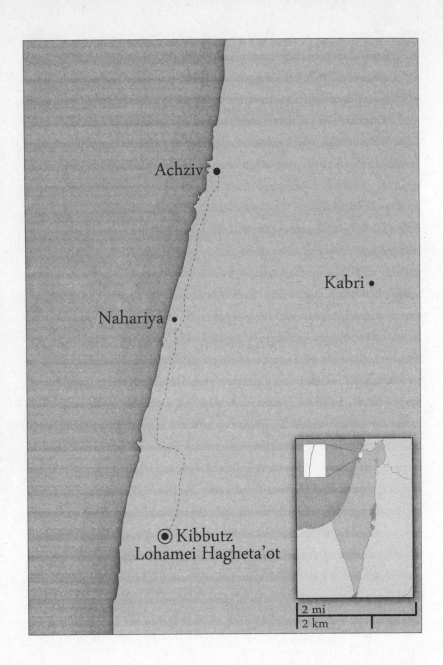

Achziv •

Kabri •

Nahariya •

⊙ Kibbutz
Lohamei Hagheta'ot

2 mi

2 km

3

Revenge of the Jews

ACHZIV TO KIBBUTZ LOHAMEI HAGHETA'OT

Trucks thunder past and the siren of an ambulance screams and fades as I run across Highway 4, the long coastal road. This is a busy and ugly stretch lined with factories, workshops and foundries. I head for the calm of Kibbutz Lohamei Haghetao't, just off the highway; the metal gate is open and unguarded. The stone arches of an Ottoman aqueduct, blanketed in purple and white bougainvillea, rise from brown fields, merging with the modern kibbutz amphitheater. A sign guides visitors to the guesthouse and the Tivol factory, whose vegetarian burgers, frankfurters, and schnitzel provide a comfortable existence for about a hundred and fifty families; their modest homes are spread around green wooded lawns. But it is the Holocaust memorial, Israel's first, for which the kibbutz is best known, as well as the kibbutz's new addition, a tribute to the one and a half million Jewish children killed by the Nazis. One can only wonder what burden it imposes on a child to grow up in a home whose address is apartment 7, Kibbutz Warriors of the Ghetto.

After leaving Eli Avivi with my stolen Byzantine perfume bottle/modern inkpot, and reassuring myself that the police weren't on my trail, I spent a pleasant night sleeping on the beach just south of his spread. The next morning, I swam in the warm water and luxuriated in the shade of a grove of eucalyptus trees. I felt I was beginning to adjust to my new leisurely pace away from the world of "breaking news." After a midday siesta, I pulled myself together and walked a few meandering miles along sand and rock from Achziv to the most northerly coastal town, Nahariya. Old couples were enjoying the late-afternoon breeze, while young parents played with their children in the gentle eddies of the waves. I tried, according to plan, to delve deeper into the hearts of Israelis by engaging strangers in conversation, but already I was discovering a conceptual flaw at the heart of my journey. I'm lousy at talking to strangers. I'm English and need to be introduced. Each time I did try to strike up a conversation, I was met with sudden recoils and looks of alarm. I could see their point. An old, unshaven Brit with a backpack and grimy shorts lurching toward you, speaking poor Hebrew, would be enough to scare anybody's kids.

By the time I reached Nahariya, the sun was setting, so I sat down on a rock and stared blankly at the horizon. Hagar, my in-house Zen Buddhist yoga teacher and general practitioner of all things good and healthy, had given me, in addition to dried fruits and nuts, strict instructions to sit cross-legged on a rock and watch every sunset, meditating with my arms at my side and my palms up, reciting a mantra of my choice. I tried, I really did. Yet after a few minutes, my knees stiffened, my back ached, my mind wandered repeatedly, and I found myself beseeching the sun, a vast fiery ball on the horizon, to hurry up and set already!

When I couldn't stand it any longer, I got up and stretched my legs, massaging my knees. Unwinding was harder than I had thought, even after my leisurely start. Two days into this experiment, and I was still in news mode after all. My steps quickened and my thoughts returned to more familiar territory: terrorist attacks. Nahariya is known in Israel as a holiday town, a northern beach resort whose seaside bars thump at night, yet I had visited only when terrorists attacked or Katyusha rockets fell. Now, instead of identifying wildflowers from my newly purchased botanical guide and looking for the sand tracks of Yigal Sela's nesting loggerhead turtles, I found myself reflecting on one of Israel's grisliest and most infamous terrorist attacks, which I had covered here years earlier.

In 1979, Arab terrorists landed from the sea by night and took hostages in an apartment building. They shot a father to death in front of his four-year-old daughter and then smashed her head on a rock. The mother hid in a crawl space above a door in her apartment as the assailants searched from room to room. To keep her two-year-old daughter from making a sound, she clamped her hand tightly over the child's mouth and unwittingly smothered her to death. It was an appalling tragedy, and the nation wept with the mother, twenty-seven-year-old Smadar Haran. She survived and was immediately taken into the nation's bosom.

I knew from earlier meetings over the years that Smadar's mother had made it through Nazi labor camps while her family had died in Auschwitz. Since Smadar and I had never gone beyond her own story, I wondered now how her mother dealt with her daughter's tragedy. My own mother lost her family in the Holocaust, as my father lost his. What would they have felt if anything had happened to my family? Or to me, on all my dangerous trips covering wars around the world? Unless you've been there, it's impossible to conceive the existential terror felt by people who have lost everything once. Nahariya was a fun town, but my mind had turned to grimmer things. My idea for this walk along Israel's coast had been simply to follow my thoughts, in the hope that they would be more interesting than usual, and that I would turn my reporting in new and different directions. So now I sat on a rock and pulled my cell phone from my backpack. I got Smadar's number through directory assistance and phoned her. She promptly invited me to tea.

I headed toward her house, walking up the beach to the concrete boulevard that runs its length. Maybe it was the pavement's sudden hardness after the sand, its uncompromising nature, but for some reason, seeing the path and the wall aroused additional, very clear memories of the hard conversations Smadar and I had shared. Smadar had become Israel's iconic terror victim. When Prime Minister Yitzhak Rabin traveled to Washington to sign the Oslo Accords with Yasser Arafat on the White House lawn in 1993, he invited her to accompany him, to represent Israeli victims of terror. Smadar declined. Despite her trauma, which she had described as "an abyss of pain," she refused to dwell on the past. Smadar mourned and remarried and raised a new family. Her story has been told many times; but what she doesn't say, unless prompted by her second husband, Yaacov Kaiser, a psychologist, is that the social worker who helped her through her traumatic encounter with Arab terrorists was himself an Arab. Smadar's eyes reddened easily, but she smiled as she recalled the first two social workers, both Jewish, with whom she had found no common ground. Then she was offered the Arab. "We still have a good relationship, he is a very nice person, very smart and wise," she told me once. "The truth is that from the beginning I decided that what happened to me won't make me anti-Arab or racist. I wasn't one before. We must relate to people through what and who they are, not through race."

I marched along the festive boardwalk, past gaudy black and white leather sofas in the beach bars, past the early evening strollers. I continued straight to Smadar's smart, leafy street, pondering all along how she could remain so balanced in the face of her despair. It seemed relevant to Israel's fight with the Palestinians today: Both peoples remain stuck in the role of victims. Palestinians cannot break free of their calamity in 1948, when they lost much of their land, while Israelis fear another Holocaust. Yet Smadar, the ultimate victim, was a poster child of restraint and decency and elegance. And her mother, I also knew, lived quietly as a nurse on a kibbutz. Didn't either of them ever want revenge? How long can you just sit back and take it? Were they not "fighting Jews"? Or was their restraint and reason Israel's true strength and a beacon for hope?

I'M DOING MY BEST

Smadar's street ends at the sea, from where the terrorists came, not far from the rocks where her first husband and daughter were killed. She chose this location deliberately. "They can't chase me away," she told me once. "If I run, I'll never stop." Her home is one of Nahariya's most historic, seventy-five years old, yet tastefully modernized with glass walls and large windows. Smadar led me through an open lobby, by her gaunt etchings hanging on the wall, to a bright living room where large glass doors opened onto a neatly tended garden. Everything was orderly, mirroring the psychological order she had reclaimed in her life. Smadar was petite with cropped black hair and a wistful smile. Her husband brought herb tea and rich chocolate brownies before sitting down to join us. Smadar kept looking to him as she talked, as if seeking his support. Her face was leaner than the last time we met, and now her black hair was flecked with gray. As we talked her eyes glistened, warning of tears.

Smadar did indeed talk of revenge, but not of killing. "My mother lost everyone, but my mother's revenge, the Jewish revenge, is to build a family and build a life. From one generation to another, we know that we must put strength into developing and building our minds, our hands, our ideas—to be creative." Smadar had been an art teacher, but after the terrorist attack she became a helper—a social worker and then campaigner on behalf of victims of terror. Now, after twenty-nine years, it was time to return to art. Describing her own healing process, she said, "I think what happened to me gave me a very strong perspective about what it is to be a human being, how brutal it can be, and yet how people can have so much kindness inside them. I encountered the whole range of people, and I learned from them, from my friends and people I met. Maybe I taught something too, but I learned that the human spirit, my spirit maybe, is almost unbreakable. If it breaks, it will be from me, not from someone on the outside. Surviving is not enough; survival is just the beginning. You have to become something, to be a caring person." Yaacov smiled and took her hand.

Smadar caught me glancing at her squiggly figure drawings on the wall. She had once taught drawing part-time in the evenings. "But the most important thing I created is my own life again, as an artist, as a wife and a mother and a daughter, sister, friend, social worker, whatever. I'm doing my best." Here Smadar paused, dark emotions rising. If this were a TV interview, I would have glanced at the cameraman to make sure he was zooming in close in case the tears began. But now I found myself swallowing hard and hoping she would not cry. I was afraid I would cry myself. I felt very close to her pain, as if my own family's pain was hovering over us. Many dead people seemed close, watching and listening. My mother and father had done their best too, and it wasn't always enough. After a moment, Smadar regained her composure. She looked with wet eyes at Yaacov and went on. "Family is the most important thing, the basis for going out into the world and doing other things. That's what I want to tell other victims of terror."

And you have earned the right to tell them, I thought. And so has your mother.

I remembered that Smadar's mother, like Smadar, had hid in a small space, a hole in the ground, but from the Nazis. When I asked about it, Smadar replied, "My mother had a lot of revenge. She built a kibbutz, she was a nurse, she did the best she could for everyone, she helped build her country, she built a family. We're good citizens, we have a good life. This was her revenge. It's Judaism; it's something good in the way we were brought up. We always knew that our answer is to build and rebuild. I think I learned from my mother."

It's what I would keep hearing as I talked to Holocaust survivors; despite everything, despite their fantasies of revenge after their liberation, nobody, not one person I would speak to, said he ever really wanted to kill a German.[1] The real revenge, everybody said, is to live and raise a family. But as I listened to Smadar, in the fading light, I kept coming back to the same sad thought—in my own family there were no survivors. For us there was no question of revenge, of any kind. Everyone who went to a camp perished. The burden this placed on my mother and father was unimaginable; as a child I had had no clue. What is it like, I wondered, to imagine the worst, and discover that reality is even more terrible? I asked Smadar, "And did your mother ever find comfort?"

Her answer again reminded me of my own mother. "I don't know," she said. "My mother didn't talk. She is from the generation that doesn't talk. A big part of her generation doesn't talk."

Smadar told how her mother last saw her family when they were sent to Auschwitz; she spent the war sewing German army uniforms in a labor camp. Beyond the factory walls, friends dropped dead every day. After she was liberated, Smadar's mother trudged back to her hometown in Poland and prayed six months for any family member, however distant, to show up. None did. So, aged nineteen, she joined a group of "lone" survivors and emigrated to Israel. Yet the loneliness continued. There was no healing. "Nobody talked about the Holocaust in Israel," Smadar explained, "it wasn't done. There was no room for feelings. There was a sense that we have a country to build, a war to fight. People didn't want to dwell on the past." Smadar's little frame suddenly shook with a sharp intake of breath followed by a huge sigh, a loud expulsion of air that surprised me. "Anyway, whenever my mother does talk about it now, she feels sick and gets depressed for weeks. So we still don't talk about it."

That sounded familiar. My mother never said a word about what happened to her family, beyond the barest reference. And if I asked my father, his eyes would moisten, and he'd walk away. So I knew about pain. And I knew about that empty, aching place of not knowing what happened to your grandparents, wanting to know but fearing to hear it, fearing even to ask the question. Ultimately, even the questions get suppressed. You move on, but not really.

I asked, "Do you talk to your mother about the killing of your first husband and children?"

"No," she answered. "We can't talk about it."

And there I had it, two survivors from two generations who used selective silence to cope, and who rose from the wreckage of their lives to build good new ones. As I took my leave and retraced my steps to the beach, heading for Nahariya's main boulevard, I thought that surely this is the strength of this nation. Israel's Holocaust survivors thirsted not for further brutality against the perpetrators, but for life. Their retaliation was to raise families and build a state. This thought took me back to something else Smadar had said. "During all the suicide bombs, I always heard the justifications of the Arabs: 'My brother was killed,' 'the army beat my father,' 'this is my revenge, I'll kill twenty, I'll kill thirty.' I never thought I should kill a family or ten families, never for an instant it occurred to me. I lost my family, and now I have a new one."

HOLOCAUST TABOO

When the United Nations partitioned Palestine in 1947, to create Jewish and Palestinian states, Nahariya was part of the Arab state, although it had been founded by German Jews twelve years earlier. Israeli fighters seized the town in Israel's War of Independence, and Nahariya has been staunchly Israeli ever since. Today it is 98 percent Jewish, and walking beneath the towering eucalyptus trees that dominate the main drag, Ga'aton Boulevard, I couldn't help chuckling at the sights and sounds that were so utterly Israeli. It was night now, and crowds of boys and girls shouted and shoved their way toward the bars and ice cream parlors. A gaggle of girls flounced toward me, followed by a large friend in a short, tight, strapless black dress with folds of stomach pinched and protruding. She tottered by me on very high heels, and I could hear her short, sharp breaths as she muttered to herself. I turned just as she plumped herself down on a low concrete wall and shouted to her friends, "Stop! Wait! I can't walk anymore, my feet are killing me!"

I stopped for cold cherry soup and grilled fish in a small Hungarian restaurant. It was located in a quiet square that had been half destroyed by a Katyusha rocket during the 2006 war with Hezbollah. The waiter, whose arm was in a sling, informed me that the cook was off, and that I should look only at items on the menu that could be cooked with one hand. When I asked him if he was glad he'd immigrated to Israel, he answered, "I'll tell you at the end of my life." A woman at the next table, hearing my British accent, asked if I wanted to buy her house. And a couple of hours later, when I found a room in a run-down motel around the corner, the receptionist asked why I wanted to stay there with much nicer hotels nearby. I liked the people in Nahariya.

My heart sank, though, when I saw the dismal room on the first floor, overlooking a rather sad garden. I should have listened to the receptionist. There were no sheets or towels. There was a laminated list of motel regulations, though, which I used for much of the night to slap mosquitoes. As I reviewed my notes from the day, one phrase from Smadar struck me strongest: "Nobody talked about the Holocaust in Israel." And that reminded me of something the Israeli architect who designed Club Med in Achziv had said when he was asked much later what he felt about the Arab villagers displaced by his thatched holiday huts. He had answered, with crushing honesty: "Few Israelis then thought much about the Arabs' history. I must say that at the time, it was a kind of taboo. It was not really in our conscience." Then he added, as if trying to be fair, "The Holocaust was also a kind of taboo then."[2]

I lay awake with mosquitoes buzzing in my ear, puzzling over the notion that in Israel's early days the Holocaust had been a taboo subject. My thoughts drifted to Smadar's mother and other Holocaust survivors, and I wondered how they must have lived with the knowledge that their fellow Jews weren't interested in knowing of their lives in Auschwitz, Treblinka, and Bergen-Belsen. I could understand why postwar British people wouldn't be interested in the hard-luck stories of Jewish refugees and survivors like my parents, but wouldn't Israeli Jews have wanted to hear what happened to their fellow Jews? The next day, I intended to head for a nearby kibbutz called Lohamei Hagheta'ot, meaning "Warriors of the Ghetto." It houses Israel's first Holocaust museum. I had never seen the new children's wing, but now I had another reason to go, to answer a question: Wasn't the lack of empathy for the survivors a travesty, a moral failing on the part of the Jews? And it wasn't just a historical issue. If Jews in the 1940s couldn't sympathize with their own people, so soon after the slaughter, how could they be expected to sympathize with the Palestinians' plight today?

I woke before dawn and left the sleeping town of Nahariya. Picking my way through the night debris of broken beer bottles, discarded cigarette packs, and overturned beach chairs, and passing by young couples sleeping it off on benches, I walked along the beach toward the village of Shavei Zion, an upmarket collection of homes that lines the beach two miles to the south. On the way, I chanced upon Manny Sokolowsky, the local mayor, who was out for a swim. He told me he had first come here as a soldier, lying in ambush on the beach for terrorists like the band that had attacked Smadar's house. "Samir Kuntar, the terrorist who killed her family? He was caught. He should never have made it to jail," Manny said. "One 5.56 bullet and it would have all been over." It happened to be the subject of the week. There was talk of releasing Kuntar, who had been in jail for twenty-nine years, as part of a prisoner exchange with Hezbollah, and indeed he was freed a few weeks later.

Farther on, I climbed a slight sandy hillock, and saw, low on the horizon, pink morning light flashing on the roofs, steeples, and minarets of Acre, the ancient port city that had changed hands more often than Jerusalem. The buildings were gleaming white, and surf crashed onto the city walls. With its violent Crusader past and its modern calm, the clashing calls of the muezzin and the church bells, the cramped structures of the boisterous bazaar and the fish restaurants on the beach, Acre is one of my favorite places in Israel. I was eager to get there, but it would have to wait until after the Warriors of the Ghetto.

I tried to pick up my pace in the heavy sand, past the Golani army base and dozens of trainees sweating and shouting after a night march ("There it is, boys, not far to go!"). I stopped briefly at a memorial to navy commandos who had been ambushed and killed in Lebanon—twelve giant concrete slabs, one for each soldier, each slab resting on another, like frozen dominoes, the last falling into the sea. Two miles beyond Shavei Zion, I stopped at a café for my favorite breakfast: hummus, salad, and black coffee with grains of cardamom. Then I had a quick swim in the warm sea. As my shorts dried in the sun, I called Hagar to tell her what I needed for my visit to Kibbutz Warriors of the Ghetto. She called back within minutes with a list of people to call; it turned out a friend of hers had been born there.

The first lady I dialed was home and said she would wait for me. I told her I would arrive around noon. I pulled on my shorts, almost dry now, and continued happily down the beach. Then I hung a left through the dunes and dry shrub, scanning for snakes, and reached the main road, which I followed all the way to the kibbutz, trucks and buses whooshing dangerously close.

RESISTANCE FIGHTER

The Israeli poet Chaim Guri called Lohamei Haghetaʼot "the center of the culture of remembrance," because unlike Jerusalem's Yad Vashem Museum, people here live among the memories. It is certainly pretty and well maintained. Purple and white bougainvillea climb the walls of an intact Ottoman aqueduct that extends almost into the Holocaust memorial, spanning the centuries. There are huge trees with thick foliage and lush lawns. The quiet when I arrived was broken only by the mellow warbling of kestrels in the eucalyptus trees. Following the instructions of Havka Folman Raban, the kibbutz founder I had arranged to meet, I entered by the main gate and headed straight to the health clinic, about two hundred yards inside the kibbutz. Across spacious lawns, small low houses with tended gardens spread out in neat clusters. In front of most, little electric carts were parked to help the old folks get around. When I knocked on the door

Havka had described, I heard a frail voice calling what I thought was "Come in," but I hesitated and knocked again. This time there was no mistaking the boom that followed: "I SAID COME IN!"

Havka was a tough old bird. She had a sturdy farmer's body and a firm, determined look on her face. It was hard to imagine this formidable eighty-four-year-old lady, who lounged in her black leather armchair, legs up, hair coiffed, ordering me to a seat, as a child in the Warsaw Ghetto. Moreover, when I asked her what her strongest memory of the Holocaust was, she lit into me. "Huh! Typical question of a journalist! So many interviews, you all ask the same question. What, in schools for journalists you study this question? This question I don't like. It shows you have no idea, what was the Holocaust." I shifted uncomfortably and stammered a few words, but she brushed them aside. "So many times I was one minute from death. You cannot understand. In six years, there were so many difficult moments, it is impossible to choose one."

This striking old lady had been a key figure of the resistance in the Warsaw Ghetto. Her tale was not unique. Others did what she had done, or tried. But few lived. Those who survived and helped build this kibbutz in memory of their fallen friends can be counted on the fingers of one hand. Literally. Five.

"Only about five of the founders had fought the Nazis in the ghetto," Havka recalled. "Building the kibbutz gave us a goal, a reason to live, a way to forget, to be normal for a few hours at least." About eighty people founded the kibbutz with Havka. Some of the others had fought elsewhere—in the Red Army or with the partisans in the forests. Some were children who hid with Polish families. But all were Holocaust survivors. "We wanted to be like everyone else," she repeated, "to be normal."

This gave me a chance to ingratiate myself; I was still smarting from her outburst. I said, "Someone said that if you survived the Holocaust and are normal, you must be crazy." Havka laughed, a great sudden boom. "That is probably true, but I was drunk with happiness. I worked in the fields; I was so excited by everything. I was very, very happy. My dreams of freedom, of life close to nature had been realized." I looked around her home. It was large for a kibbutz, with several rooms and all the conveniences of a modern home. "You like?" she asked. "We started in tents!"

Aside from being survivors, the founders of Lohamei Hagheta'ot were unique in another way, too. They were adopted by the leaders of the Jews in Palestine in a way most survivors were not. Even today, Havka smiled at the memory with what seemed like pride and fondness. "Yitzhak Sadeh, the founder of the Palmach, he drove me himself around Tel Aviv and Jaffa, he showed me the fortifications. I went to his home. And Yigal Allon, the Palmach commander, he became foreign minister, a true Sabra, he took me everywhere." She summed up her welcome simply: "I felt wanted, because of what I had done."

After Havka had nearly bitten my head off, I had to phrase my next question carefully. I knew she would not admit to having done anything special—her type never did—but I did want to know exactly what she had done that merited such exceptional treatment. If the Holocaust had been such a taboo subject in early Israel, why not in relation to her? True to character, her first response was "I wrote a book. What, you didn't read my book? It's all in my book!" After I promised to buy her book at the museum store, she described her wartime experience in a crisp, matter-of-fact way, each sentence falling like a hammer blow:

"I was seventeen, blond and pretty, and I had false papers. I went in and out of the ghetto. I traveled across Poland. I delivered messages, documents between other ghettos, and I gathered information. I was stopped many times and questioned. We had heard that Treblinka was a death camp, but we were not sure. So I went there. I smelled the burning flesh. So we knew it was true. That was one of the reasons we decided to fight back, while we could, before it was too late. I was waiting once at a railway station, and I saw Jews rounded up and forced into freight cars; I saw them being murdered. I could not do anything except tell the resistance."

With her false papers and Aryan looks, Havka could have easily fled the country, but for two years she slipped in and out of the Warsaw Ghetto, carrying forbidden papers and weapons, until one day the Gestapo caught her. "They tortured me for weeks, but I didn't tell them anything. I will not tell you what they did to me, so don't ask. Finally, they sent me to Auschwitz." I looked at the tattoo on the outside of her forearm, in faded blue, like varicose veins: 32291. "I was in Auschwitz-Birkenau for two years. Then I was on the death march to Ravensbrück."

Havka was proud, with good reason. And Israelis were proud of her and her friends. Later, I read more about Lohamei Hagheta'ot and discovered that it had long played a key role in Israel's understanding of the Holocaust. On Remembrance Day in the 1950s, it hosted the leading memorial events in Israel. Israel adopted its founders' story of resistance as part of the new Jewish narrative of a nation of fighters and builders. "Only later on," Havka would write, "when the memoirs of many survivors were published, did I learn that the welcome I received was an exception."

The writer Primo Levi, a Jewish medical orderly in Auschwitz, offered this nauseating image to describe the liberation of his fellow survivors, as they crawled out of the camp gates to freedom: "ragged, decrepit, skeletonlike patients . . . dragging themselves everywhere on the frozen soil, like an invasion of worms."[3] When these emaciated and traumatized victims finally landed in the arms of their Jewish brethren, they were regarded as unwelcome reminders of the "lambs who went to slaughter," an embarrassment, just as Jews in Israel were reinventing themselves as farmers and warriors, as fighting Jews. True, their bodies were welcomed. New immigrants from Europe contributed half the Jewish fighters in Israel's War of Independence, and a third of the dead. But the part of them that most needed help, their souls, was ignored and silenced.

Israel's Declaration of Independence stated on May 1, 1948: "Survivors of the Nazi Holocaust in Europe . . . assert their right to a life of dignity, freedom, and honest toil in their national homeland." But nothing was written about their right to therapy or even sympathy. Israel's mover of mountains, the first prime minister, David Ben-Gurion, a legend of bluntness, famously lumped Holocaust survivors and immigrants from North Africa into one dismissive phrase: *avak adam*—human dust. He wondered what they did to survive and once said that the best had died.[4] He was no less condescending, and wrong, when it came to the Arabs. Supporting moves to force Arabs from their homes in 1948, Ben-Gurion predicted in his diary: "The old will die, and the young will forget." As we now know, such arrogant nonchalance, coming so soon after the Jews' own tragedy in Europe, augured ill for Israel's future.

EMPATHY IS CHEAP

Havka was a great old lady and a heroine, but I found her smug, and I left feeling angry. Her kibbutz was wealthy, its residents had all they required, and they had done it all themselves, but did she really discover how other survivors were treated only when she read their memoirs? Had she and her fellow resistance fighter heroes been so wrapped up in their cocoon of acceptance that they hadn't known what others had gone through? Couldn't they have used their own exalted status to help those less fortunate? Thinking about this as I hiked back to the beach, I realized that I was projecting my own experience again. My own parents didn't get a jot of help from anybody. When my mother, who was a nineteen-year-old refugee in London, and who worked three jobs including repairing stockings, saved enough money to buy the first refrigerator on her street, her English neighbors gossiped and jeered. "Of course," they said, "what do you expect, those Jews have lots of money." They didn't mind depositing their torn, smelly stockings at the grocery store for my mother to pick up each evening, leaving a measly threepence for the repair the next morning. And nobody asked if she needed help in the new country.

During the summer of 2008, after I had completed my trek along the coast of Israel, I continued my research into the travails of the Holocaust survivors, partly because my parents belonged to that sad group, which made it personal, and partly because the poor reception that survivors met in Israel seemed so contrary to the state's ideals. I started calling elderly friends and meeting them in cafés, and they introduced me to their friends, and so on. One man told me, as an afterthought, that during the war he had spent two years in a hole in the ground with his sister. It wasn't too bad, he said, apart from the rats. And the cold. And the damp. When German tanks rumbled through the town, and the earth shook, they thought the walls of their hole would collapse on them. But the real problem, he said, was that he went into the hole when he was fifteen years old, and kept growing, so he had to bend over more and more. He still imagined he had a stiff neck. He was eager to talk, but others declined. One man said he hadn't said a word about Bergen-Belsen for sixty years, and wasn't about to start now.

As I met old men and women over coffee and cake, I was reminded of the truism that Israel can thank the Holocaust for its existence, and I thought, with some bitterness, didn't Israel have an obligation to honor the survivors, even when times were tough? Then I found I wasn't the only one wrestling with the treatment of Holocaust survivors. I came across a recent newspaper column written by the retired journalist Yehudit Winkler about her mother, a survivor who had been ignored. "There is a great degree of pretense on Holocaust Martyrs' and Heroes' Remembrance Day," Yehudit reflected bitterly.

> Not because there is no intention of remembering it, but because a separation is made between the Holocaust as a general concept for the horror, and the people themselves:

My mother, her friends, even the survivors who are forced
to humiliate themselves in the face of the insensitivity of
the governments and leaders of Israel, in order to merit, for
example, crumbs of financial assistance. They are humiliated not only because their voice has faded and their elbows
are weak, but because in the roots of the Israeli consciousness, their place is missing, because they scratch the false
collective image of the new Israel.

Affected by Yehudit's intensity more than sixty years after the war, I
phoned to arrange an interview with her and her ninety-five-year-old mother.
"You are welcome," she said, like everybody else I called, and we met the following week.

It was noon when I arrived at her modest apartment in a quiet Tel Aviv
side street near the sea, and I was encouraged by the table laid out with
wine and cookies. But Yehudit said, "I'm sitting shiva.[5] My mother died
two days ago." We sat on her brown leather sofa, and as we leafed through
photos that showed an elegant white-haired lady with a cultured air, who
could have been a fine European in any smart café in Vienna or Budapest,
Yehudit said, "She died a happy woman. She always seemed happy. She
was a survivor. Physically. But inside, mentally, like her friends, she was
broken; she just hid it well. Really, there were no survivors. They survived,
but not really. But she was my hero. She saved my life so many times."

Yehudit's mother was smart. When Yehudit was six years old, her
mother placed her in a convent in Budapest, where the little girl learned to
pray like a Christian. One night in 1944, Yehudit's mother had a bad feeling and told the nuns she would take her daughter for a short walk. "She
put me in a boat and paid a fisherman a lot of money to take us across the
Danube, because we broke the curfew. She always had hunches, which
saved us. The next morning, the Germans came and took all the nuns and

the children and shot them dead because someone told them there were Jewish children there."

Yehudit excused herself and stood by the kitchen door, smoking, until I said the smoke didn't bother me and she should sit down next to me. Yehudit brought her ashtray and lit another cigarette. "When we came to Israel in 1949, she put me in a kibbutz, Gan Shmuel, a socialist kibbutz of Hashomer Hatzair. I was one of four children from the Holocaust, out of twenty-four kids. They called us soap."

"Really?" I asked, and immediately regretted my knee-jerk reaction. The catcall was a reference to the myth that the Nazis used oil from Jewish bodies to manufacture bars of soap. I had heard of these kinds of names before, but putting a face to the nickname gave me a chill.

"It was terrible," she continued. "They didn't know how to deal with us. Kids don't come up with ideas and words like that; it came from their parents and even the teachers. We were scared, terrified. We were not like them. There was no sense of, 'Let's help these poor children.' No sense that we came from a hard place and suffered traumas. I was the only one with a parent. The other three were orphans. All the kibbutz cared about was to make us good socialists. Stalin was the sun god. We studied and worked by day and by night there was nonstop indoctrination. They were paid by the Jewish Agency to keep us there, to give us housing and schooling. Boys and girls lived in the same room, washing and bathing together, till age fifteen and sixteen, till after we became men and women. I rebelled. I refused. Looking back, I see that it was completely crazy, but that was the system. Two boys and two girls lived in each room. To come from where I came from to a place like this was like coming to a different planet. And they didn't care, they didn't understand. The attitude was—denial."

"But those were hard times for everybody," I said. "A new country, at war, so many immigrants, no money . . ."

"Empathy doesn't cost money," Yehudit interrupted sharply. "Empathy is a humane quality. Singly and collectively, it was the attitude. Even in the summer my mother's friends wore long sleeves to hide their tattoos."

FINALLY THE VICTIMS SPEAK

It took sixteen years to breach Israel's Holocaust taboo. In April 1961, a thin, balding, middle-aged man with poor dentures, poor eyesight, and a nervous tic at the corner of his mouth sat inside a bulletproof glass booth in a Jerusalem courtroom, compulsively sifting through his papers. He faced fifteen charges, twelve of which carried the death penalty. They included causing the enslavement, starvation, deportation, persecution, sterilization, and murder of millions of Jews. For two months, the most heartrending scenes occurred daily in the community theater turned courtroom, and these were relayed throughout Israel and the world. I went through the film archives to see the footage, and it was hard to watch. Holocaust survivors pointed, accused, cried, screamed, and fainted as they described their tortures.

The prosecutor at the trial of Adolf Eichmann, the architect of the Final Solution, asked witness after witness: "Why did you not fight back?" "Why did you not protest?" "Why did you board the train?" These were good, if brutal, questions that I remember asking my own parents. They were lucky—they escaped from Vienna in 1938, moments before the door slammed shut—but few others from their families survived. Now I know how painful my questions must have been. Indeed, my parents may have wondered the same. Questions like: Why did the victims actually turn up at the assembly points on time, dig their own graves, undress and arrange their clothes neatly in piles, and lie down side by side to be shot? My grandparents and their cousins, aunts, uncles, nephews, and nieces may have done that. These were indeed the questions that demanded answers.[6] The prosecutor, Gideon Hausner, in his direct, provocative manner, was not seeking to prove cowardice. On the contrary, he let the answers build a picture of how impossible it had been to resist. The genius of the Nazis had been always to leave the victims with a glimmer of hope.

During Eichmann's trial, the attorney general's office received almost ten thousand letters from Israeli citizens. They were equally divided between young people asking bitterly why so many Jews went meekly to their deaths, and Holocaust survivors spilling their hearts, many for the first time. Hausner wrote later that he was overwhelmed by survivors asking to testify. His instructions were unequivocal: No detail, however grotesque, should be omitted. Listening, he said, should be torture. In his opening statement, Hausner himself set the tone: "In a cell for those sentenced to die of hunger, a dead prisoner was found with a second prisoner slumped over him—also dead—who had managed to tear the liver out of the dead man's body. Death came to him as he consumed a human liver."

The survivors found their voice, and Israel listened in horror. The nation huddled around their transistor radios for hours, every day. Buses brought groups from the whole country to the trial, including Havka Folman from Lohamei Hagheta'ot. Ariana Melamed, a little girl playing under her father's chair at home, later wrote that it was the first time she saw her parents cry.

One witness, forty-five-year-old Rivka Yosselevska, spoke softly but nobody missed a word. The record shows that her description of what happened after she was rounded up in Belarus's Pinsk ghetto was so painful that even the judge had difficulty listening. What follows is an edited transcript of her testimony. After so many testimonies like this, Israel could no longer look away.

Witness: When I came up to the place we saw people, naked, lined up. But we were still hoping that this was only torture. Maybe there is hope—hope of living. One could not leave the line, but I wished to see: What are they doing on the hillock? Is there anyone down below? I turned my head and saw that some three or four rows were already killed—on the ground. There were some twelve people among the dead. I also want to mention what my child said while we were lined up in the ghetto. She said, "Mother, why did you make me wear the Shabbat dress? We are being taken to be shot." And when we stood near the dugout, near the grave, she said, "Mother, why are we waiting? Let us run!" Some of the young people tried to run, but they were caught immediately, and they were shot right there. It was difficult to hold on to the children. We took all children not ours, and we carried them—we were anxious to get it all over—the suffering of the children was difficult. We all trudged along to come nearer to the place and to come nearer to the end of the torture of the children. The children were taking leave of their parents, and parents of the older people.

Presiding Judge: How did you survive through all this?

Attorney General: She will relate it.

Presiding Judge: Please will you direct the witness.

Witness: We were driven; we were already undressed; the clothes were removed and taken away; our father did not want to undress; he remained in his underwear. We were driven up to the grave, this shallow ...

Attorney General: And these garments were torn off his body, weren't they?

Witness: When it came to our turn, our father was beaten. We prayed, we begged with my father to undress, but he would not undress, he wanted to keep his underclothes. He did not want to stand naked.

Attorney General: And then they tore them off?

Witness: Then they tore off the clothing of the old man and he was shot. I saw it with my own eyes. And then they took my mother, and we said, "Let us go before her." But they caught Mother and shot her, too; and then there was my grandmother, my father's mother, standing there; she was eighty years old and she had two children in her arms. And then there was my father's sister. She also had children in her arms, and she was shot on the spot with the babies in her arms.

Attorney General: And finally it was your turn.

Witness: And finally my turn came. There was my younger sister, and she wanted to leave; she prayed with the Germans; she asked to run, naked; she went up to a German with one of her friends; they were embracing each other; and she asked to be spared, standing there naked. He looked into her eyes and shot the two of them. They fell together in their embrace, the two young girls, my sister and her young friend. Then my second sister was shot and then my turn did come.

Attorney General: Were you asked anything?

Witness: We turned toward the grave and then he turned around and asked, "Whom shall I shoot first?" We were already facing the grave. The German asked, "Whom do you want me to shoot first?" I did not answer. I felt him take the child from my arms. The child cried out and was shot immediately. And then he aimed at me. First he held on to my hair and turned my head around; I stayed standing; I heard a shot, but I continued to stand and then he turned my head again and he aimed the revolver at me and ordered me to watch and then turned my head around and shot at me. Then I fell to the ground into the pit among the bodies; but I felt nothing. The moment I did feel, I felt a sort of heaviness and then I thought maybe I am not alive anymore, but am feeling something after I died. I thought I was dead, that this was the feeling which comes after death. Then I felt that I was choking;

people falling over me. I tried to move and felt that I was alive and that I could rise. I was strangling. I heard the shots and I was praying for another bullet to put an end to my suffering, but I continued to move about. I felt that I was choking, strangling, but I tried to save myself, to find some air to breathe, and then I felt that I was climbing toward the top of the grave, above the bodies. I rose, and I felt bodies pulling at me with their hands, biting at my legs, pulling me down, down. And yet with my last strength I came up on top of the grave, and when I did I did not know the place, so many bodies were lying all over, dead people; I wanted to see the end of this stretch of dead bodies but I could not. It was impossible. They were lying, all dying; suffering; not all of them dead, but in their last sufferings; naked; shot, but not dead. Children crying, "Mother," "Father"; I could not stand on my feet.

Presiding Judge: Were the Germans still around?

Witness: No, the Germans were gone. There was nobody there. No one standing up.

Attorney General: And you were undressed and covered with blood?

Witness: I was naked, covered with blood, dirty from the other bodies, with the excrement from other bodies which was poured onto me.

Attorney General: Mrs. Yosselevska, after they left the place, you went right next to the grave, didn't you?

Witness: They all left—the Germans and the non-Jews from around the place. They removed the machine guns and they took the trucks. I saw that they all left, and the four of us, we went on to the grave, praying to fall into the grave, even alive, envying those who were dead already and thinking what to do now. I was praying for death to come. I was praying for the grave to be opened and to swallow me alive. Blood was spurting from the grave in many places, like a well of water, and whenever I pass a spring now, I remember the blood that spurted from the ground, from that grave. I was digging with my fingernails, trying to join the dead in that grave. I dug with my fingernails, but the grave would not open. I did not have enough strength. I cried out to my mother, to my father, "Why did they not kill me?" What was my sin? I have no one to go to. I saw them all being killed. Why was I spared? Why was I not killed? And I remained there, stretched out on the grave, three days and three nights.

After two months of such harrowing testimony from more than a hundred witnesses, the real mystery that remained for Israelis, as the writer Hannah Arendt noted at the time, was not why so many Jews failed to resist, but how any survived at all. The collective disaster of the Holocaust, which had been reduced to a concept and set aside, suddenly had names and faces that could no longer be ignored; they were neighbors, parents, teachers, the bus driver with the number on his arm. Given Israel's tendency toward extremes, as they could no longer be ignored, they were finally embraced. Women with tattooed arms wore short sleeves again. They starred in the projects schoolchildren did on their family roots, complete with show-and-tell items such as striped concentration camp uniforms and the yellow stars Jews had been forced to wear. Survivors accompanied school trips to the concentration camps in Europe and wept with the children at the crematoria. At Auschwitz's elaborate metal gate, one survivor kept entering and leaving the camp. When a student asked him why, he answered, "You can't imagine what it feels like to walk out of here!"[7]

The trial was the therapy that survivors had been denied. But like most therapies, its success was only partial. I had left Smadar and the motel in

Nahariya with the idea of tracing the path of the survivors to full accep-tance. But as I discovered, many were still traumatized, and even to this day they lived in poverty, forced to fight like anybody else for their rights. A 2008 government report stated that 87 percent of all people over eighty years of age living in poverty were Holocaust survivors. This astounded ev-erybody. Holocaust survivors were competing with all other pressure groups for a share of the budget, and they were falling short. Now that they were old and weak, didn't they deserve special attention?

THE FIRST HOLOCAUST DENIERS

My trek down the coast of Israel had already taken something of a detour. Instead of walking and meeting interesting people and taking it easy, I found myself deeply involved in painful questions that I had rarely consid-ered as a news reporter. I had spent three hectic decades living among Is-raelis and writing about their trials, yet I was surprised at how little I had engaged them emotionally. Now, with the help of Smadar, Havka, and Ye-hudit, three strong women who had suffered enormously, I was coming to grips with the steel strand that binds Israel's Jews.

I had entered a dark place in Israel's history that challenged one of the country's founding myths—its moral superiority. This realization led to further questions. Today Holocaust survivors are admired and even feted. But what was this like? To be ignored and even disdained, and then to be held up as an example of strength and determination, must be a neck-snapping change, even if it took decades. What did the survivors think of the society that treated them in this way? Did they feel vindicated or an-gry? Maybe they didn't think about it at all? Or did it encourage more of them to empty their hearts of the demons from the camps? Michal Havazellet, a therapist friend, called the survivors the first Holocaust deniers because they couldn't talk about it. In a sense, they had come full circle: victims of the Holocaust and then victims of silence, until finally they found a voice, and an audience. But did that help them?

Somebody mentioned a new place called Café Europa, where survivors could meet and were treated with affection and respect. So one Sunday I joined them for the afternoon, and there I met Moshe Rothman, a dapper gent who uttered the most memorable line I have ever heard.

Café Europa is a large room in a community center in Ramat Hasharon near Tel Aviv. Social workers had wanted to do something for the survivors who lived locally, so they asked the old folk if they would like to meet once a week to relax together and maybe chew over old times. They said yes, we'd love to meet, but definitely not to talk about the past. What would you like to do? the social workers asked. Dance, they said. We want to dance!

And dance they did. It was a pleasantly chaotic scene, with fifty pensioners shuffling on the dance floor and another fifty at the tables, leaning across one another and shouting into hearing aids. The room had been decorated like an old Viennese café. Large photos of 1930s café scenes adorned the walls, and the tables were laid out with pressed red tablecloths, drinks, and cookies. A social worker, Miki Horowitz, directed me toward a tall man, saying he had been a prisoner of war in Syria. He was having a rare old time, this tall, nimble, seventy-nine-year-old called Moshe Rothman: waltzing dreamily with his wife, Miriam, then tangoing with a cute lady with gray hair and a thirties-style green flowery hat with feathers and silver bangles, and then back with Miriam, doing the cha-cha, all the while giving lingering pecks on the cheek to any passing female, including the young Girl Scouts who volunteered to serve the old folk coffee and cakes. Dancing next to him was a tiny, shrunken lady with straight red hair and smudged red lips, embracing her young female Filipina caregiver. People clapped to the Gypsy violin music and sang along with the singer, who beamed and called for requests. When Moshe took a break from his exertions, I asked to join him at his table. With an expansive wave of his arm he invited me to sit, and with some ceremony poured me tea. As we nibbled poppy-seed cake, I could see him eyeing the ladies, so I cut to the chase. "How was it to be a prisoner of war in Syria?" I asked.

Moshe's reply was numbing: "Hah! It was like a sanatorium after Auschwitz!"

I was stunned for a moment. I smiled at Moshe and he smiled back and winked. "So what was Auschwitz like?" I asked. I instantly regretted the inane question, remembering how a similar one had upset Havka. But Moshe was made of different stuff.

"I'll tell you," he said, "but not here, not now. Here, I dance!" And with a flourish, he brushed the crumbs off his shirt, downed his tea, and went back to the floor. It was a Gypsy tune, and he jigged and twirled with a new lady on his arm.

A week later, at his home nearby, Moshe told me that he hadn't spoken a word about his tortures for fifty years. Then ten years earlier his grandson, who was writing a school project on his family's roots, asked him about Auschwitz, and for once he answered. He didn't know why, beyond a feeling that it was time to tell. Miriam, hearing it all for the first time, couldn't stop crying. Moshe said he had felt as if, by finally unloading his burden, he had reclaimed his soul.

With a flick of his wrist, Dr. Joseph Mengele had selected Moshe, a strapping sixteen-year-old, and his elder brother, Pinkhas, to work, and with another flick he had sent their mother and sister straight to the gas chambers. After months of hard labor in the snow, Pinkhas fell sick with dysentery and left Auschwitz the only way Jews did, as the guards taunted, "through the chimney." Moshe carried one-hundred-pound sacks on his back from dawn till dusk. He suffered from frostbite. Guards whipped him and beat him. "I had open wounds, lice were eating me alive. I lay there like a dying dog. For months I smelled. So one night I went out and lay naked in the snow and used the snow as soap. A guard saw me and set a German shepherd on me. But I was faster and the barracks was near. I got away. If not . . . I ate what the pigs left, I ate with the pigs. When the Russians came, the Germans took us to Schottenburg. Barefoot. Who fell, they shot. Again I was lucky. My friend helped me. I had no strength left. There the Russians freed us. I weighed ninety pounds." He showed me a photo taken three months later: a bony, forlorn boy in shorts, sitting on a chair in a room, staring knowingly at the camera, shadows darkening the wall.

In Palestine, the young man worked as a construction laborer, until war with the Arabs came, and he volunteered to fight. Despite the mythology of heroism that grew from this war, with tiny Israel defeating six Arab armies, Moshe's experience was different:

"They sent me to the Jordan River. I was there a week with fifty men, shooting, everything okay. One day, thousands of Syrians with tanks came. Two guys with a Bren machine gun said, 'We'll go around and surround them,' but they ran away. My officer ran away. I was alone, with a lousy rifle. The Syrians were behind me, they said, 'Put up your hands . . . alfayidak!' I did. They beat me, but I had nothing to say. They gave me cigarettes and wanted me to work for them, but I refused. I was stubborn and proud. They sent in an Arab as a prisoner who spoke Hebrew to get me to talk, but I didn't fall for it. Then they beat the Arab to scare me. Idiots! They should have beaten me! I was there for nine months; then they sent me back."

Moshe married, worked in construction, raised a family, and lived modestly. "I was always an optimist. My father taught me that the heart is so small and the ass is so big, so why put everything in the heart, much more room in the ass!" He laughed and slapped me on the knee. "What has the pessimist got? Nothing, just the nose down. Optimist is always okay, he sees things rosy, it'll be okay, so it is better. I don't think too much about the past. Enjoy what you have, the family, I've always done that. The past is dead."

In 2005, Moshe returned to Auschwitz-Birkenau for the first time, accompanying the school class of his grandsons, who are twins. He said Kaddish, the Jewish prayer for the dead, for his mother. "I say it every year, but that was the first time I could say it on the spot. It was important to me. I had the feeling that she was listening to me." Moshe paused to wipe his eyes, and he continued, as if she were with us in the little computer room and not merely a faded black-and-white photo on the screen: "'Here I am, your son, saying Kaddish for you.' It made me feel good. With all the pain, it was good. 'I want to tell you hello, not good-bye, I'm happy I could at least do this for you.' I was the smallest, and the closest to Mommy. I helped her bake cakes. She looked after us like a hen with the chicks. We all slept together in the bed. A good mommy." The last time he saw his mother, Moshe said, she was standing naked outside the gas chamber. Of a hundred family members, ten survived.

Back in Auschwitz with the schoolchildren, Moshe was the eyewitness, the respected survivor who brought the past to life. He pointed out the barracks where he lived, the bunk he slept in, where Mengele sat, where Pinkhas dropped his heavy loads when he was sick, where a friend was beaten to death. "The guide hit his forehead and asked, 'How can you remember?' and I answered, 'How can I forget?'" Moshe became the children's hero. "One sixteen-year-old girl wrote me that until now she never had a grandpa—now you're my grandpa!" Moshe proudly showed me a folder thick with notes of gratitude and appreciation. The girl's letter, written in a strong young hand, read:

It's important that you know you are now my grandpa. You are a great person. When I arrived at the gates of Auschwitz, I had tears in my eyes. But when I saw you enter, I was a little confused because I didn't really understand what I was going to see. But you, with your twins, confident, strong,

I was overwhelmed with pride. Who can know what you did for me then? I really believe that it was important to hear your experiences. We asked questions, you answered everything. Each day we visited a camp, each night we talked about it. Grandpa, I tell you personally that my children will know what happened, and I will not forget what happened. With love from me, Ravit Khaze.

When Moshe showed me Ravit's letter, I was touched, and I congratulated him. If ever a note showed how the survivors had reached their deserved place in the nation, this was it. Their experiences were no longer to be repressed and forgotten, but exposed and remembered. "You are part of the good news story of the Holocaust survivors," I said, pompously. "You are an example to the young, of somebody who overcame his problems and never gave up." Moshe smiled, calm, gentle, and knowing. He is a man of few words. "I'm okay," he said. "Many aren't."

THANK YOU

I liked Café Europa. It was a lovely place and an example not only of how far the survivors had advanced in acceptance and respect, but also of how much Israel's self-confidence had grown, allowing it to accept the weak as well as the strong. There was so much to learn from these old dancers. Moshe escaped death many times in the Holocaust, he was a prisoner of war in Syria, and his children and their children were still fighting the Arabs. Yet he insisted he has no hate in his heart. "Young Germans are not guilty," he said. "If I hate them, they'll hate me. Hate breeds hate, hate doesn't heal. Hate is healed by love. I don't hate Arabs. They're human too. A bad Arab is a bad Arab, but an okay Arab is an okay person. I have no hate in my heart." I liked Moshe, too; there should be more like him on both sides. Maybe the conflict with the Palestinians would look different.

On Moshe's eightieth birthday, his family gathered in the large garden of his daughter's imposing villa a mile from his house. I was surprised at how many people came. Some cousins had survived too, and they had children and grandchildren, and their spouses had large families. It was a noisy, happy affair with a waiter carrying a silver tray with bottles of gin, rum, whiskey, and vodka. As I watched, I thought of my own little family in London, which consisted of my mother, my father, my brother, and me. When we had a family gathering, that was it. I wondered once again why nobody from my family had managed to survive the camps. Some were gassed, others died of typhoid, one had a heart attack, and most just vanished from the pages of history. Would I have survived, I wondered, had I been there? Who knows. It was mostly luck. Moshe did, and here he was, a fine, uncomplaining, gentle, strong old man. He sat under a lychee tree that burst with red fruit as one of his volleyball-playing grandsons led the tributes. The whole team turned up and presented Moshe with their shirt. On the front was written "Moshe Rothman." On the back was his team number: 80. One after another his wife, children, friends, and relatives praised him. A photomontage ended with these words: "It is a great honor for us to be part of your life's journey and your world. We are your victory."

I studied Moshe as he listened. He sat serenely with his arms folded, a true patriarch, Miriam at his side in a smart cream suit and a necklace of pearls. He was savoring his family's adoration, but there was something distant about him too, like a boy staring out the window in math class. His face appeared to me to be too fixed, his eyes too steady. He wasn't really there. Maybe I imagined it, but it seemed that he was remembering rather than listening; he wiped away tears at banal comments and didn't respond to emotional moments. I thought of the title of Havka's book, *They Are*

Still with Me, and wondered, Maybe he's thinking of his elder brother, Pinkhas?

Now Moshe rose to speak. He eased himself up and stood silently before his family and friends, as if lost for words, elegant in his cream shirt, khaki slacks, and light brown leather loafers. His grandchildren stopped running around and gazed up at him. A nice family, I thought, a big one, a lucky guy.

"My turn has come," Moshe said. "Thank you for coming and sharing my celebration. It's hard for me to talk, but I'm going to say thank you. Who would have thought that I would reach this age, that I would survive after all that I have been through? This is a sign that there is a God."

And then Moshe sat down. What else was there to say?

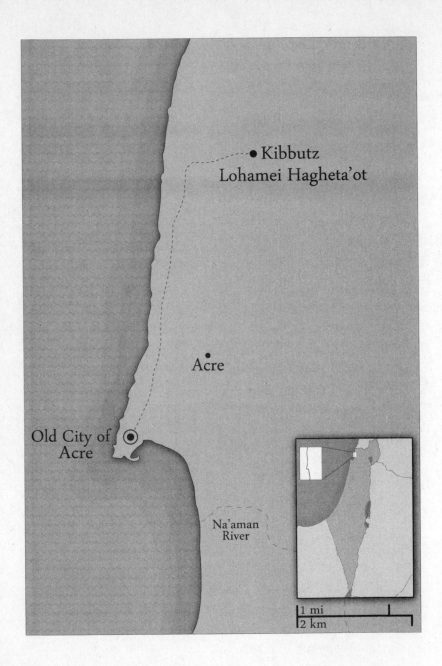

Kibbutz
Lohamei Hagheta'ot

Acre

Old City of
Acre

Na'aman
River

1 mi
2 km

4

Four Faces of the Truth

It all comes together in Acre's Old City, where church bells mingle with the muezzin's call to prayer. Entering the city from the north on Hahagana Street, you find a faded green door with a big blue Arab Hamsa, a ceramic hand that wards off the evil eye. Next door stands a small Baptist church, a low building with a modest stone cross above the entrance and metal gates carved with sheep and the Crusader cross. The next house, with arched windows and tall wooden doors, offers a jarring sign, a white-on-green exhortation from the Koran to "begin your prayer before death." On the next corner is the Baha'i house, with signs nearby pointing to St. George's Church and Haramhal Synagogue. Everyone has a place in this five-thousand-year-old town. The gnarled dark faces of the bleary men sipping coffee and puffing on the day's first water pipe seem from another age. On the terrace of an old-age home facing the sea, wrinkled women in shawls doze in wheelchairs or play backgammon and smoke. No matter what time it is in the Old City of Acre, it always feels like the end of the day.

As I left Kibbutz Lohamei Hagheta'ot at dawn, I found myself wondering whether my journey was taking me in the right direction. When I had set out three days earlier, I had hoped to find a lighter side of Israel, but so far I found myself concerned with conquering Israelis, displaced Arabs, and Holocaust victims—business as usual for a news reporter. Now, as I headed to the beach across Highway 4, the coast road that runs from Lebanon to Gaza, I wondered: Maybe it's my fault. Are these the kinds of people that I, as a journalist, seek out? Who said I should go to Lohamei Hagheta'ot and find Holocaust survivors? I could just as easily have gone to the neighboring Kibbutz Regba and investigated the international success of its custom-made kitchens. But even there, I would have probably been more interested in another angle—the collapse of the entire kibbutz enterprise. Let's face it, I thought: I'm programmed to seek the bad news and not the good. But perhaps there's hope: If I meditate at sunset and eat all my fruit and nuts and keep walking along the beach, maybe my priorities will change.

Only a few miles down the coast lay one of my favorite places in Israel, the ancient port town of Acre, with its fascinating Old City, a UNESCO World Heritage Site. Acre, settled continually for five thousand years, is known to-day, despite its calamitously violent history, for its peaceful relations between

Jews and Arabs—so peaceful, so removed from Israel's conflict with the Palestinians, that in three decades of reporting from Israel, the only stories I have ever done there were on the annual theater festival. No suicide bombs, no mass attacks, only rare ethnic clashes. Chaim Yavin, Israel's Walter Cronkite, said to me once while he was working on a documentary about Israeli Arabs, "Acre isn't a story for me, it's too quiet, it's boring. They live together in coexistence." That was exactly why I liked to visit the place, and why I yearned to visit it now. Enough with the heavy stuff.

After emerging from an alley between two factories, I reached the sea and saw Acre, bold in the distance, its fortress walls jutting like a fist into the surf. Faint early sunlight sparkled on the rippling waves like a flashing mirror. Kicking off my sandals, I splashed in the cool water, my feet tingling pleasantly. I hadn't had breakfast, yet already my stomach juices were preparing for my favorite dinner: grilled fish of the day, green salad, hummus, and tehina in the old port with a glass of dry white wine, the whole consumed while watching the red sun ball sink into the glittering Mediterranean. In such a lovely setting, I had often wondered why Acre, surrounded by so much tension, a city whose own history of war goes back thousands of years, had become such a pleasant, peaceful backwater. Now that I had time to linger, I wondered whether there wasn't a lesson here for the rest of the region. I couldn't even remember seeing a policeman or a soldier in the Old City. Everyone just wandered around minding his own business, and in this part of the world, that's an exception worth investigating. But there I go again, I thought, falling into journalist mode. I still couldn't quite suppress my nose for the story, only in this case the story seemed to be the utter lack thereof.

WHEN MEN WERE MEN

That turned out to be not quite true. Although I had visited the city's historic part many times, I had always driven through the modern town straight from the highway. Now I was arriving by foot from the north along the coast through the poor suburbs, and it wasn't pretty. This was not the haven I cherished. For one thing, there was the pollution. The closer I got to town, the more unpleasant the sea became. In the waves I saw compressed flashes of light that I thought were schools of flying fish. That excited me; I love to see them shoot in graceful arcs across the bow of my catamaran at sea, their gills flashing in the sun. But as I approached, I saw these were just lots of plastic bags, floating on the water and fluttering in the wind. I had been enjoying stamping through the water, yet now there were so many strips of plastic bags and plastic bottles and so much scummy debris washing onto the shore that I retreated higher onto a nearby path. The water here reminded me of the only line of poetry I remember from high school, from Samuel Coleridge's *Rime of the Ancient Mariner*: "Yea, slimy things did crawl with legs, upon the slimy sea." Then I started to smell tangy urine, which a mile on became even stronger, a stink. I passed the leaking sewage pumping station, which was next to a cell-phone repeater tower; smell and radiation, two dead-cert signs of a nearby town. I was taken aback by the dinginess of the approach.

The first strollers and swimmers appeared. Without exception, the women were fat and pale, wearing loose, bulging bathing suits and tight swim caps, like Michelin women. They swung their arms like weightlifters. The men were thinner, with muscles and pinched features. These early risers could only be Russian immigrants from Acre's closest suburb, a collection of drab apartment blocks that wouldn't look out of place in Moscow. All were impervious to polite greetings. When I ventured to one man, "Good morning, you're quite far out of town . . ." he answered, without looking or slowing, "Close, far, who cares?"

I walked through deserted streets with overflowing trash cans and abandoned, looted cars. I shifted the weight of my backpack from one shoulder to the other and hurried on. Then I got scared. Before a large building, a very aggressive-looking bunch of beefy bald guys in jeans and T-shirts with shades on top of their skulls were shouting and slapping each other's backs, as if celebrating a bank robbery. I had to walk by them, and I knew that any hesitation might encourage them. I walked within a yard of the men, my heart racing. Two had pistols on their hips. Others had bulges in their shirts. Then I saw the police station sign. They were plainclothes cops, and they piled into two dusty unmarked cars and drove off, still shouting. I laughed at myself and went on. A tough old guy was doing push-ups against a bench. I attempted another cheerful "good morning," and he ignored me too. Well, I thought, it wasn't as bad as New York, where Hagar had said good morning to a homeless man and he had told her to get lost.

By now I was thirsty, because I had forgotten to bring water for this portion of the trek. Breakfast would be nice. I passed into the Old City in search of my beloved hummus and quickly cheered up. On my left was the wide, deep moat and the first massive city walls, built by the Ottomans in the eighteenth century on Crusader foundations from the twelfth. As Isaiah called for swords to be turned into plowshares, here they turned the moat into basketball courts. Way down in the moat, a dozen boys were whooping and yelling, jumping and competing for the ball, their noise muffled by the moat and the thick city walls.

Otherwise, it was quiet at eight a.m. The Old City is a sleepy place, with little to do and nowhere to go, which is half its charm. It is a place to sit, drink tea, and daydream. And there is so much in Acre to daydream about. I loved losing myself in Acre's long and turbulent past—I would sit in cafés reading about the Crusades and then amble along the fortress walls, conjuring up the battles. Those were simpler times, when men were men and respect was won by the sharpness of the sword. Christian Crusaders fighting for God, Muslims battling the blasphemers. Alexander the Great blasting through on his way to conquer the world, Napoleon's army crashing against the walls. Marco Polo resting here as he journeyed the Silk Road to China, Queen Berengaria nursing her sick King Richard the Lionheart back to health, while his Crusader knights caroused with their whores. I could almost hear their horses clatter and slip on the shiny, time-polished stones of the cobbled alleys.

MY TWO-STATE SOLUTION

I had been walking for three hours and was now seriously hungry. I hurried to Hummus Sa'id, a famous eatery crowded with Arabs and Jews. Hummus is best eaten with both elbows on the table while talking loudly, and most here complied. It seemed that everybody was shouting. I finally found space at a table with strangers and dug into the creamy hummus ful: chickpea paste and beans with olive oil and tahini, fresh tomatoes, olives, and extra onions on the side. It is the world's healthiest fast food, shoveled in with warm, fresh pita bread. There was a commotion outside with men running by, so I went to look. They were chasing a mouse among the food stalls, laughing and shouting, "Good Luck!" I smiled at a waiter as I returned, and he smiled back. I didn't need to ask how he was because I knew his answer: "Thanks God!" Christians, Muslims, Jews—in the Old City of Acre, the answer was always the same.

As I tore off some pita, mopped up the last of my hummus, and sipped cardamom coffee, I looked around at the photos of the Humus Sa'id soccer team on the wall; at the raucous youngsters; at the placid older folk staring blankly as they ate; at the Jewish men with the skullcaps and the Arab women with headscarves, some covered from head to toe. This is how it should be, I thought. Contented people, living in peace. And this thought led the irrepressible journalist in me to a revelation about the peace process. I had solved the problem. Yes, there should be a two-state solution for Jews and Arabs, but not one for each race, because the radicals on both sides would always stymie it. Instead, one state would be for those Jews and Arabs who want to live together in peace. Its capital could be Acre. The parliament could be in Humus Sa'id. God bless them. And there should be another state, for all the others who want to keep fighting. To hell with them.

I paid my fourteen shekels, about three and a half dollars, and ambled through the alleys, which were now filling up. I enjoyed the friendly bustle and the mingling scents of coffee and fish and a hundred colored spices. At one point, the sharp, sweet smell of roasted garlic dominated, an instant later musty cardamom. Even the canned Arab music did not grate too harshly. I looked at the stands of musical instruments, the ouds and the drums, and fingered velvet dresses and embroidered caps. I sipped my favorite drink, cold pomegranate juice squeezed on the spot. At the clock tower in Venice Square, I eavesdropped on a tour guide talking to his Israeli clients. This man was a stocky, strong Arab in his mid-thirties, about six feet, with a black goatee resembling that of a duke in a medieval Spanish painting. He wore shorts and carried a backpack, and he was pointing up at the face of the clock on top of the crenelated tower. "Built in 1906 for the Turkish sultan Abdul Hamid," he informed his Israeli clients. "But look at the numbers—what do you see?"

They looked up, craning their necks. "The time?" one asked.

And then another said, rather nastily, "It's in Arabic. Why is it in Arabic? Why isn't it in Hebrew? This is Israel!"

The guide grinned and then, embarking on what was clearly his shtick, said, "Exactly! You are looking at just one face of the truth, for there are other sides to every issue. Come look." He walked around the tower. The tourists followed, and so did I. "See?" he asked, pointing. "There are four faces to the clock: north, south, east, and west, and each one has different numbers—Arabic, Hebrew, Roman, and Indian—but the time is always the same! So, no need to be angry." He playfully tapped the shoulder of the

Israeli who had complained. "Whose truth are you seeking? Whose truth do you find?" The Israeli was lost for words. The guide chuckled, pleased with himself. "It just depends where you stand!" I chuckled, too, loving the Arab's corny payoff, and feeling that it rang true.

Thinking he could tell me a thing or two, I requested and received the card of Abdu Salvatore Matta, Tour Guide, Storyteller, and Christian Arab. I visited him that very afternoon, and to kick things off I complimented him on his clock story. He laughed with a great roar, as if I'd found him out. In truth, he said, it was a lousy clock, since each face told a different time and they had to be corrected twice a day. "But still," he said, stroking his goatee, "this is my way to teach. Everybody is suspicious here, and through my tour I show many illusions and stereotypes that we suck from our mother's breast. Part of my tour is also ideological: to show Jews and Arabs that there are many common things and less separating things."

A CITY OF BROTHELS

It was another sweltering summer day, but comfortable in the shade of a grape arbor along the side of Abdu's house outside the Old City. Abdu heated an old black kettle on a gas flame and we sipped herb tea and ate bourekas and fruit for hours as he told me of his family and the city. Like most Christian Arab families, Abdu's had come from abroad, in their case from Greece around 1730. They were jewelers, brought over with other craftsmen to help in the Ottoman reconstruction of Acre after five hundred years of decay. "It was a ghost city. For five centuries never more than three hundred people at most lived in the ruins of Acre—fishermen, pirates, and monks . . ." Abdu was off on his tour-guide narration, which he recounted with flourishes, even breaking into song, and I admired his show as he proudly produced maps and books and old photos to illustrate his recounting of Acre's broader history.

Acre's past amounted to a succession of military victories and defeats, the sheer number of which bore out Abdu's observation that "the only lesson of history is that we don't learn from history." Generals from Alexander the Great to Napoleon all brought their armies for the same reason: control of the coastline, the gateway to the interior. They dressed it up with stuff about trade routes or religious heritage or who was here first, but as Abdu noted, it always boiled down to the same thing: land, which all called holy. It is no different today.

Reflecting on this months later, I considered that Acre's history could well stand as a synecdoche for that of Palestine as a whole. From the Romans and the Jews, Richard and Saladin, the Ottomans and the Syrians, the Jews and the Palestinians today, each clash, each war, seems to replay an earlier one, only with fiercer weapons. That lends a certain resignation to events here, as in: "It's always been like this, so why get excited about it?" Jews and Arabs fighting about the land? Okaaay . . .

Abdu was just as erudite on the seamier side of Crusader life. Today, 9,000 people live inside the square mile of the Old City, and it's cramped enough. But in the eleventh and twelfth centuries, between 25,000 and 60,000 people crowded in and around the city walls, giving themselves over to every urge and desire. I could relate to the frustrations of the bishop of Acre in the late twelfth century, who railed against his wicked Crusader flock: "Hardly one in a thousand takes his marriage seriously. They do not regard fornication to be a deadly sin. From childhood they are pampered and given to carnal pleasures."[1] It sounded like fun to me, especially as I observed the beautiful Arab women of present-day Acre, Christians no doubt, in shimmering gold tops and tight jeans. But the twelfth-century bishop was beside himself:

Almost every night people are openly or secretly murdered.
At night men strangle their wives if they dislike them, and

wives, using the ancient art of poison and potion, kill their husbands to marry other men. In the city there are vendors of toxins and poisons, so that nobody can have confidence in anyone. The city is full of brothels, and as the rent of the prostitutes is higher, not only laymen but clergymen, nay, even monks, rent their houses all over the city to public brothels.

At least they were still Christian. As for the Jews, in the twelfth century there were only about two thousand in all the Holy Land, but they appear to have grated beyond their numbers. The bishop snarled: "They have become weak and unwarlike even as women . . . The Arabs among whom they dwell hate and despise them more than the Christians. They work with their own hands at the vilest and lowest trades. . . . The Lord keeps them for a time like a log from the forest to be burned in winter, they are like an evil vineyard, that brings forth only wild grapes." Then the prelate's coup de grace: "For they remind us of Christ's death."

The stench and the overcrowding in medieval Acre can hardly be imagined, especially during the periodic sieges that lasted months and even years: so many people wearing flea-infested clothes and living in such narrow alleys and small dark rooms, in terrible heat, with almost as many horses and livestock as people, and no real sewage system or enough fresh water. To make life tolerable, rules of decorum were critical. Only the highest-ranking men had their own plates and cups, while everybody else ate in small groups, licking their fingers and plunging them into the common bowl. So it was agreed: It was no longer good enough to clean hands the usual way, by spitting on them; hands had to be washed in water before meals. In 1290, the Italian Fra Bonvicino da Riva laid out some no-no's in one of the first known books on etiquette: "One should not put the fingers in the ears or the hands to the head, nor should a man who is eating scratch his private parts."[2] Blowing one's nose at table with one's fingers was out, too.

Abdu described all this with gusto, waving his arms and washing his hands in the air, narrowing his eyes, his voice rising and falling. He was in full flow, and I enjoyed him immensely. I found the bishop's perceptions of the Jews entertaining, but only by virtue of being so ancient. Less funny was that extremist Arabs and Jews speak about each other in similar terms today. Given that modern reality, I felt that the old bishop's hatred carried a critical warning: that beneath the charm of these ancient alleys can lurk great danger. I shouldn't get carried away by the beauty, and events would soon show why.

It was getting dark, and I began to wonder how much I should pay Abdu for his time. But then he started off on a more recent and intricate bit of history, one that would help me put Kibbutz Lohamei Hagheta'ot and Israel's founding narrative in new perspective. I couldn't help but stay and listen.

RIGHTFUL HEIRS OF PALESTINE!

Around 1720, a man named Daher el-Omar became the governor of Acre, whereupon he rebuilt the city walls and restored commercial life. Daher was considered a gentle, tolerant man, and craftsmen from around the Mediterranean flocked to benefit from the new prosperity, among them Abdu's ancestor. Unfortunately, Daher was assassinated, and something of the subsequent Ottoman ruler of Acre, Ahmed Pasha al-Jazzar, can be surmised from his nickname: "The Butcher." His chief adviser was a Jew, Chaim Farhi, who became so powerful that a contemporary observer exclaimed in wonder: "A Jew is ruling over Muslims and Christians, high and low, near and far, without any limits." There must have been some limits, though, because in 1794 al-Jazzar put out one of Farhi's eyes and cut off one of his ears and the tip of his nose, for reasons today unknown. Once recovered from his dreadful wounds, Farhi nevertheless continued as al-Jazzar's trusted adviser, a comment on the era's casual cruelty.

Then Napoleon entered the story. Laying siege to Acre in 1799, he got more than he bargained for. The defenders were well fed and determined, while his own men were hungry and sick. And that damn Jew Farhi was rallying the Muslims to fight as if God were on their side. Some historians believe that it was a desire to get Chaim Farhi to switch sides that prompted Napoleon to issue the first call for a Jewish homeland in Palestine, under French protection, anticipating Britain's Balfour Declaration[3] by 118 years. Napoleon's support for a Jewish state rarely gets a mention these days, but it is significant as another early recognition of Israel's right to exist. Napoleon was even ahead of the Zionists.

Napoleon's call was published in Paris as "Letter to the Jewish Nation" in a government newspaper, *Le Moniteur*, on April 20, 1799, a month after the siege of Acre began and a month before it collapsed. It read as follows:

BUONAPARTE, COMMANDER-IN-CHIEF OF THE ARMIES OF THE FRENCH REPUBLIC IN AFRICA AND ASIA, TO THE RIGHTFUL HEIRS OF PALESTINE.

Israelites, unique nation, whom, in thousands of years, lust of conquest and tyranny have been able to be deprived of their ancestral lands, but not of name and national existence! . . .

Arise then, with gladness, ye exiled! A war unexampled in the annals of history, waged in self-defense by a nation whose hereditary lands were regarded by its enemies as plunder to be divided, arbitrarily and at their convenience, by a stroke of the pen of Cabinets, avenges its own shame and the shame of the remotest nations, long forgotten under the yoke of slavery, and also, the almost two-thousand-year-old ignominy put upon you; and, while time and circumstances would seem to be least favorable to a restatement of your claims or even to their expression, and indeed to be compelling their complete abandonment, it offers to you at this very time, and contrary to all expectations, Israel's patrimony! . . .

Rightful heirs of Palestine! . . .

The great nation which does not trade in men and countries as did those which sold your ancestors unto all people (Joel 4:6) herewith calls on you not indeed to conquer your patrimony; nay, only to take over that which has been conquered and, with that nation's warranty and support, to remain master of it to maintain it against all comers. . . .

Hasten! Now is the moment, which may not return for thousands of years, to claim the restoration of civic rights among the population of the universe which had been shamefully withheld from you for thousands of years, your political existence as a nation among the nations, and the unlimited natural right to worship Jehovah in accordance with your faith, publicly and most probably forever (Joel 4:20).[4]

Nothing came of Napoleon's historic proposal because Farhi didn't bite and Napoleon lifted the siege soon afterward. On May 5, 1799, when Napoleon's troops finally battered their way through the fortress walls, surging forward to destroy, loot, and pillage, they were stopped short by another unexpected and quite massive wall. Farhi's men had been working around the clock, erecting a hidden second line of defense, and now they poured fire into Napoleon's soldiers who were trapped between the two walls. The French quickly retreated, suffering great losses, and with another two thousand men dead from bubonic plague, Napoleon called it quits. Thus ended his ambition to conquer the world. Napoleon reputedly said later that if Acre had fallen, "The world would have been mine." It isn't recorded if he blamed the Jews.

After hearing this story, I took my leave of the erudite Abdu, thanking him for his time and hospitality. He refused any payment. The next day, he showed me a plaque on one of the destroyed city walls. It praised the Jewish adviser Chaim Farhi for saving the city from Napoleon. During my many previous trips to Acre, I had never spotted the plaque or indeed had any idea of this part of the city's past, let alone a Jew's contribution. My visits to Akhziv and to Lohamei Hagheta'ot raised questions about the moral underpinnings of Israel's founding narrative, yet here in the Arab Old Town of Acre I had found some unlikely support for the notion of a Jewish state. Farhi's service to the Muslims in Acre, and Napoleon's recognition of his pivotal role, were not even footnotes in today's history books, but nevertheless they were part of a long Jewish narrative of belonging to this disputed land.

SHE CALLED ME HER JEW

Shortly after I had finished my walk down the coast, Abdu phoned in great excitement. "You won't guess who I met today," he shouted. I had no idea. "David Farhi! Chaim Farhi's great-great-great-great-et-cetera-grandson! He was my client, him and his wife. I showed them the plaque, everything. We stood in Farhi Square and they took photographs."

"Really?" I said. "Did you show them the clocktower and ask what truth they were seeking?"

He laughed. "Do you want to meet them?"

"Sure, I'd love to."

By this time, I was following up on many of the people I had met on my trek, and I thought that maybe Farhi's descendants would have an interesting take on Jewish coexistence with the Arabs. After all, their ancestor had lost half his face and still lived in peace with them. Abdu gave me David's phone number, and I called him immediately. I was in luck; it was the last day of his vacation in Israel.

David was indeed a direct descendant of Chaim Farhi, and he later sent me a comprehensive family tree that charted the scattering of his family through Syria, Lebanon, Jordan, Egypt, Turkey, the USA, France, Italy, Brazil, Bulgaria, Romania, Argentina, and New Zealand, as well as Israel. David's surname had changed along the way to Galante, and he was married to Lucy. They were in their early sixties, cloth merchants living in Milan. Now we shook hands and they invited me into their small holiday apartment on Ben-Gurion Street in Tel Aviv, near the beach. The high point of their holiday had been their trip around Acre with Abdu. "We are like pilgrims in Acre," David said. "There's a plaque to Chaim, but they have to cut a tree, it's covering it." He had another gripe: "An Arab lives in his house on Farhi Square. He told us he wants to sell the house! He got it when other Arabs left in 1948 and he was a refugee from a village nearby. The government committee for abandoned houses gave it to him. Cheek! Our family could get together and buy it back. Maybe we could turn it into a museum of family history. Abdu gave us the idea."

David Galante was a kind-looking man with a gentle, quiet voice. Lucy listened respectfully, every now and then suggesting a better word in English, Hebrew, French, or Italian. Before Milan, they had lived in Damascus and Beirut. They were a patrician couple, at ease with themselves, descended from a long line of bankers, community leaders, and philanthropists. I liked them immediately. Later, back at his grape arbor, Abdu had the best word for them: "noble." If it was left to Jews like David, Abdu said, there would be peace between Jews and Arabs. "Why?" I asked him.

"Because they are Arabs as well as they are Jews. They lived with us, they understand us, they know the subtleties. A European cannot understand. Their culture is too different. Understanding comes from culture, nothing else. It's very personal. If you haven't lived in Arab countries, you can't understand. A Jew who has, he understands. He has the same sensi-tivities."

But maybe David understood too well the role of Jews in some Arab countries. "When the Muslims walked on the sidewalk, Jews had to walk in the streets," he had said. "In towns, Jews could only ride donkeys, not horses or camels."

Lucy, his elegant wife, had tried to show me that the Arabs would never rest until they had regained superiority over the Jews. "When I grew up in Lebanon," she said, placing her fingertips together and smiling, "I had an ex-cellent Sunni Muslim friend. Intellectual, clever, her family was crème de la crème. We were like sisters. We agreed on everything. Her name is Asma. In the Six-Day War, she cried, 'What will happen to me and my Jew?' That's what she called me to her friends, her Jew. I called her my Muslim." She paused to smile and see my reaction. "After Israel won, I felt bad for her. I wondered how I would be able to get on with her, as I was now a bit superior. Then I traveled and after ten years she came to see me in Italy.

"I left my family for three days, and Asma and I talked endlessly. I asked her, 'Why isn't there peace? I'm a Jew, you're a Muslim, we're both interested in religion, we're both married, children, we've trod the same path.' And she said to me, 'You're crazy, it doesn't work like that, you don't understand anything.' She brought me so many presents I felt bad. So much money. A beautiful Lebanese tablecloth, hand-sewn. Mosaic back-gammon. Two superb photographs. And so much food! The least thing was for me to give something back, but she didn't accept. She stayed with me a week, but that didn't account for so many presents. I felt uncomfort-able. So I invited her to a big dinner, and she said, 'No, you can't pay for me, there is something stronger than me that prevents me from taking your favors.' 'I don't understand,' I said, 'I can't pay for a coffee?' 'No,' she said, 'it's stronger than me, even with a great Christian friend, I must pay.'"

David slowly nodded, anticipating the story and confirming the message to come. He added, "And she is a clever woman—director of the Arab League library, at the American University, too."

Lucy went on: "So I dropped it. When Asma left, I didn't listen to her. I paid for a great dinner; it was the least of things. She was angry and said, 'You'll regret it.' At the airport, she said she had left something under the mattress." Lucy paused for dramatic effect, and raised her eyebrows knowingly at me, as if I would never guess. "It was the cost of the dinner. And I understood that Jews and Arabs can never make peace because Arabs always have to be superior, however slightly, even though we were such great friends. To be equal, no. They don't accept that."

David said, "You see, that's why there is a conflict among Arabs. Some accept us, but most don't and never will."

Lucy went on, "After the Six-Day War, Asma said to me that the Arabs will never accept defeat. They must have the impression they won. After we parted, we wrote and we said we'll see each other again in another ten years. But there were wars and it went cold. Our friendship changed. She won't talk politics, now it's just how's your family, I remember your father, et cetera. Totally superficial. I understood we can be so close but the Arabs must feel superior; equality, never. It's the culture, it's too strong."

And yet, I thought, earlier you said that Israel winning the Six-Day War made you superior. Now here you are, claiming that Arabs need to feel superior. Maybe, I thought, you both need to feel superior, and that is another source of the conflict. David interrupted my thoughts. "It's from the Koran. All religions must bow to Islam. Muhammad is the last prophet, so all the others must obey him."

PEACE IS FROM THE FAMILIES

When I related this story to Abdu, the Christian, on my next visit to Acre, he wasn't impressed. "Why?" I joked. "Because Christians are superior?"

He said it isn't about superiority, but friendship and trust, which he said goes some way to answering my original questions: Why the conflict, largely, was absent from Acre's Old City, and what the rest of the region can learn from this.

"When most people fled in 1948," he said, "their homes were taken over by other Arabs, and by Jews, too, mostly new immigrants from Arab countries like Morocco. We all lived together. We celebrated their holidays, and they brought presents when we had a baby. We worked together. Arabs built synagogues, Jews built mosques. Then the Jews began to move into new buildings outside the Old City. But when they had money, so did the Arabs. We knew each other, it's a small place, fifty thousand people in the whole city. We had common interests, like business. We all wanted to succeed and we worked together. In 2000, when the Intifada began, it broke the chain. We lost trust. But outside, the fighting lasted years. Here, after two months it was peaceful again. Why? The families. Trust between the families. And their common interests. Nobody writes about that. They only write about violence, but peace is from the families."

Not that everyone was totally happy in Acre. Tensions mounted over the Old City's growing gentrification, and over the influx of religious Jews to a new yeshiva study center near the walls, which convinced many Arabs that the Jews would eventually deport them all. The Arabs complained that their schools and social services were far inferior to the Jews'. But Abdu joked—at least, I think he was joking—that it was critical for Acre to have more Jews than Arabs, because that way the Arabs knew they would get a decent city budget.

Then on Yom Kippur, 2008, several months after I had completed my trek, something happened that both challenged and confirmed Abdu's thesis. On this holy Day of Atonement, the most solemn day in the Jewish calendar, the entire country shuts down. No work, no television broadcasts, no travel. Nobody drives a car, except in emergencies. But in Acre, an

Arab, Tawfik Jamal, had decided that he could not wait to pick up his daughter from a friend, so he drove his Honda Civic into a Jewish neighborhood. He said later that he drove slowly and carefully. Jews said his car radio was blaring, and he tried to knock them over. Either way, they attacked him, inflicting light wounds on him and his son and trashing his car. Within minutes, a mosque's loudspeaker was ringing urgently around the Old City: "The Jews are attacking us." Hundreds of Arab youths carrying clubs and rocks surged through the walls of the Old City and smashed cars and shops. The chaos continued for hours, even though Jamal had long since been resting quietly at home. A frightened Jewess, Silvi Vaknin, told an Israeli newspaper reporter: "The girls woke me up at two a.m. and said there was a gathering of Arabs calling 'Itbah el-Yahud'—Kill the Jews."

When Yom Kippur ended, it was the turn of the Jewish youths. Hana Sa'adi, an Arab, lives down the road from Vaknin. "I have lived here for eight years," the Arab lady told the reporter, "always in coexistence. My children went to mixed kindergartens. Yesterday, dozens of religious Jews came into the yard, shouted 'Death to the Arabs,' and demolished my car."

The number of cars burned and shops damaged ran into the dozens. Several people were lightly injured by stones, including a man and his dog. In the grand scheme of Mideast violence, not too bad. But the next day, a Jewish member of Parliament who lives in Acre managed to cram most of the hate slogans into one short paragraph, railing against "the Crusades against the Jews," "the pogroms," and "the Inquisition against the Jews in the Diaspora." A prominent Arab resident lamented in the local newspaper, "My dear city has been dealt a mortal blow," and an overwrought reporter concluded, "A wall of fear and hatred now crosses the mixed city." The future foreign minister Avigdor Lieberman whipped up passions further: "The pogrom in Acre symbolizes the start of an Intifada in the heart of the country." Dozens of mounted riot police gathered near mosques for the end of Friday prayers, the traditional powder keg. Seven hundred additional police were brought in, including police special forces. Television crews swarmed to the battlefield.

Putting on my news hat, I called Abdu: "Should I come up?"

"The mayor called the imam of the mosque," he said. "He told him to calm things down. And the families told the boys to stop. So they did. It's over. Stay home. Next week is the Acre theater festival. We all need the business."

Arab business needs, however, didn't carry much weight among the Jewish youths, who waited until dusk to continue their rampage. Israeli Arabs feared the violence would spread to other mixed towns and, for the most part, tried to lower the rhetoric. Outside the country, Hezbollah in Lebanon congratulated the Arabs of Acre and hailed their "heroic resistance aimed at protecting land and honor . . . from the violent and barbaric assaults by the Zionists." A government-affiliated newspaper wrote in Syria, "This is additional proof that Israel hates Arabs and wants to purify its territory from all Arab presence."

I checked in again with Abdu. "Are you okay?" I asked. "And your family?"

"We're fine," he answered, but he was upset. Two tour groups had canceled their visit, and the mayor had canceled the theater festival. That surprised him and hit him where it counted—in his pocketbook.

"I don't get it," I said. "An Arab was stupid enough to drive his car on Yom Kippur, that's all. Why the riots? What happened to Acre?"

"It's crazy," Abdu said, "but it's all been happening in a small, poor neighborhood where about thirty Arab families live among the Jews. Those Jews are making us crazy. They hate us, and it was bound to happen sooner or later. This place is waiting to explode."

I was surprised at his emotion. "That doesn't sound like you," I said.

"What, you think I'm different? We never spoke politics, that's all. Come back, I will tell you my ideology. I am Christian, Israeli, Palestinian,

Arab. My government is fighting my nation; that is my feeling. I am part of it all. Just give me respect, and my children, that is our heritage."

I didn't want to get into all that. I had enough politics at work. "How was it in the Old City?" I asked.

"Very quiet. Nothing happened. Just like I said. It was all outside."

I doubted that. I thought that maybe Abdu didn't want to scare away tourists, who after all were his bread and butter. But then I thought: Could it really be true that I was actually right for once? That the Old City really was isolated from the troubles, as I had always felt?

To double-check, I called Jenny Moore, an American drama therapist I had met at a hotel in the Old City. She was preparing a show for the theater festival and was devastated that it had been canceled. She had been in the Old City throughout the five evenings of rioting, and she agreed with Abdu: "Nothing happened here, it's true. I heard some shouting, that's all. It was all outside."

Thank goodness, I thought.

When the rioting erupted, I had selfishly thought, Oh no, there goes my peaceful if imperfect retreat. But it was the opposite. The Old City's isolation was confirmed. Maybe it was the physical separation of the walls, or the heritage of so many cultures and peoples, that gave the place its soporific nature, or indeed, the strength and influence of the families, as Abdu believed. That took care of the Arab side. As for the Jews, when I asked Abdu if he feared they would attack the Old City, as some had threatened, he snorted with disgust. "No, because they know that if they do, they won't get out again. Nobody ever does." I wasn't sure if that was Abdu the historian talking, or Abdu the storyteller.

The story of the five evenings of rioting, in which nobody was seriously hurt, ended in a way that perfectly matched the mixed message of Acre—a peaceful place on the surface, but with a legacy of violence and hostility that can explode at any moment. When the offending driver, Tawfik Jamal, was questioned, he offered to have his head cut off if it would repair the damage he had done. He was inconsolable. He said all he wanted was for things to go back to the way they were. "I always worked for coexistence," he told police investigators. "I helped found a community center thirty years ago. We invented coexistence. The last thing I want is trouble in my city." Since the Jewish New Year was approaching, Jamal, the man who had inadvertently torn away Acre's veil of coexistence, wished the Jews *"Chag Sameach"*—Happy Holiday.

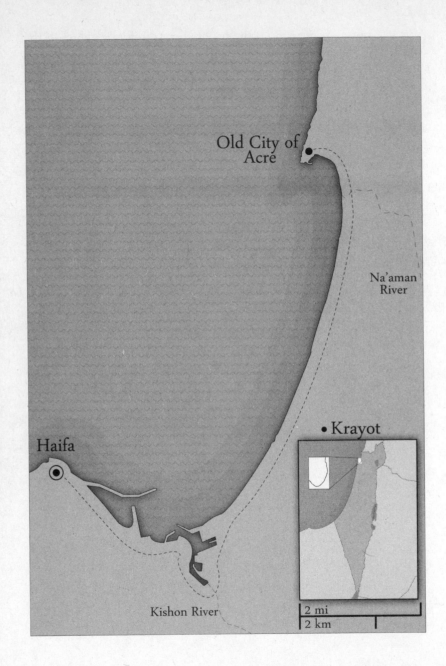

Old City of
Acre

Na'aman
River

Krayot

Haifa

Kishon River

2 mi
2 km

5

The Cream Arabs of Haifa

Haifa, Israel's garden city, lies spectacularly atop the Carmel range, overlooking the Mediterranean Sea. The streets are steep and lined with trees, and for the most part it is a quiet place. The gleaming dome of the Baha'i Temple sits like a golden crown atop terraces of manicured lawns and flowerbeds that tumble down the hillside like the Hanging Gardens of Babylon. Haifa's 270,000 residents make it the country's third-largest town— testament to Israel's small size. Yet what they lack in numbers they make up in complexity; Haifa is home to Jews, Christian and Muslim Arabs, Druze, Carmelite monks, and Baha'is, all with their own shrines, cultures, and values. They live a life of mostly calm coexistence. Despite the small numbers, Haifa's Arab markets and midtown shopping streets seem dense and confined. The streets are narrow, and for much of the day, they lie in shadow. Hills and buildings block the sun, which elsewhere wraps the country in its glow.

From the minaret of the mosque of Jazzar Pasha, the haunting call to prayer drifted across the dark roofs of the Old City, echoed around the ancient walls and through the stone alleys, and woke the faithful. It stirred me, too. I walked from my bed to the window and gazed at the cool moonlight reflected in the Mediterranean's somber waters. Shadows hurried along the cobblestones, Muslims answering the muezzin's promise that prayer is better than sleep. It was dawn in Acre, two days after I had first met Abdu, Day Six of my trek, and for me the penetrating summons was a call to hit the road again. I couldn't wait to begin the next stage of my journey, ten miles around the bay to Haifa—a walk through time as much as space.

As the centuries slipped by and ships grew in size, Acre had swapped roles with Haifa, its deepwater neighbor. The Crusader city of Acre declined into a pleasant backwater for fishing craft, while the little Arab fishing village of Haifa grew into Israel's major port. In 1948, about sixty thousand Arabs fled, or were forced to flee, and Haifa became predominantly Jewish. Today, like Acre, the city is held up as an example of coexistence. And like Acre, that doesn't tell the whole story, for Haifa is largely divided into three clear sectors: The remaining Arabs live at the bottom of the hill, the Jews on top, and in the middle are the more recent

Russian immigrants, mixed with a smattering of poorer Jews and some Arabs. The division has kept the town peaceful enough, but it has also contributed to its lack of real integration. An Arab friend who lives in the Arab section of Wadi Nisnas told me when I arrived in Haifa later that day, "The Jews come here to eat hummus and falafel, and that's coexistence."

That sparked my interest in another issue relating to Jewish-Arab relations, the gap between perceived coexistence and real integration. Plenty of Arabs in Haifa reached the top of their professions, but if even the educated, secular elite of Arabs could not truly live side by side with the Jews, then what Arabs could? As I would discover, educated secular Arabs in Israel often took their social cues from the secular Jewish way of life. But there was one problem: A Western lifestyle assumes equality. And that often proves more elusive than many Israelis would like to think.

THE MIGHTY BELOS

I had left Acre's Old City at daybreak but then had quickly gotten lost among the silent side streets of the predominantly Jewish areas, where the green Koranic inscriptions and Arab street names gave way to avenues named Weizman, Ben Yosef, and Pinkas. I was daydreaming again. In my mind, I wasn't going down Ben Ami Street toward David Remez Street but following in the footsteps of Richard the Lionheart and Napoleon Bonaparte, whose armies followed the same sandy plain and sweeping dunes south of Acre, around the glistening bay of Haifa, and into the Carmel range. I would soon see its wooded foothills sloping gently into the sea some ten miles on. I was armed with eyewitness accounts of the escapades of Crusader knights, as well as chronicles of Napoleon's flight from the Holy Land, and I also looked forward to seeing the Israeli coast through their ghostly eyes, a parallel journey through time. I trusted I would not become as tired on my trek to Gaza as Napoleon's grenadiers, as described by a smug English commander: "The utmost disorder has been manifested in the retreat, and the whole track between Acre and Gaza is strewed with the dead bodies of those who had sunk under their fatigue."[1] But where the Frenchies were running for their lives from the plague and Muslim horsemen, the greatest problem I faced was where to stop for lunch.

Jolting me back to the present was a knot of sullen Jewish youths that I now encountered. They were blocking the pavement, smoking and drinking, and in general offering up the hangdog intensity of boys who had been out all night. I felt a tinge of urban terror, as an old guy with a backpack may when approaching a rowdy crowd in hoodies and jeans. Since I was lost, I had no choice but to ask directions to Haifa, my next stop. I had misjudged them. A friendly discussion ensued on whether I should take a bus or train. When I told them I was walking, they couldn't believe it. They laughed in wonderment, for they had never heard of anybody walking to Haifa.

I regained the beach and pressed on along the coast. It was now around eight in the morning and uncomfortably hot. I imagined I was a scribe, with quill and parchment, following a dust cloud of Napoleon's twelve thousand troops. The weather would have been similar, for they retreated from Acre on May 20, 1799, and I left the city on June 27, 2008. I was in better shape than they. I wore shorts and a T-shirt and carried two bottles of mineral water in a small backpack, while the French were starving, parched, and boiling in thick European cotton vests beneath ninety pounds of armor. Half were sick, too. As they had laid siege to Acre, where sixty inhabitants a day were dying of bubonic plague, their British enemies had been delighted to see the feared fever and blood poisoning seep through the walls to infect the French, which they saw as divine retribution. A British commander gloated, "The heaps of unburied Frenchmen lying on the bodies of those whom they massacred two months ago, afford another proof of Divine

Justice, which has caused these murderers to perish by the infection arising from their own atrocious act."[2]

As I adjusted my sunglasses, I thought of the bright sun glaring off the sea and bouncing off the white sand that would have blinded the feverish and wounded French soldiers. I removed my sandals, hung them from a loop on my backpack, and splashed happily through the shallow water that lapped onto the beach. The wet sand slurped through my toes. I was looking forward to reaching the mouth of the Na'aman River, whose fine yellow sand, I had read the night before, had been treasured by ancient Persian goldsmiths. But it had another great claim to fame: The Phoenicians discovered glass there five thousand years ago. The Jewish and Roman chroniclers Josephus and Pliny tell the same story: A horrendous storm forced sailors ashore, where they lit a cooking fire on the banks of the Belos, as the Greeks called the Na'aman. As it was just a sandy beach, with no rocks on which to rest their pots, they had brought some of their cargo, lumps of natron, a mineral used for mummifying bodies.[3] The heated natron melted into the sand, and the combination produced something clear and transparent that they had never seen before. From there it was but a small step to double glazing.

I continued along the beach until a six-foot-wide current of smelly, excrement-colored water disgorged from bracken and undergrowth, carving its own channel through the sand and into the sea. I had encountered pollution on my way into Acre, but this was much worse. I kept my distance, wondering whether to jump over, wade through, or walk out to sea to get around it. Two strollers arrived from the opposite direction. "Good morning," I said. "Can you tell me how far it is to the Na'aman River, please?"

"You've arrived," one said, pointing at the grunge. "This is the Na'aman." I looked down at the legendary waters and felt more than a pang of disappointment. "It's waste from factories at Karmiel," he added. "Same with the Kishon farther south."

I knew about the Kishon, another river I would pass on the way to Haifa. It had been a sweeping torrent, celebrated biblically in Judges 5:21 as the waters that defeated the enemies of the prophetess Deborah: "The river of Kishon swept them away, that ancient river, the river Kishon." But I had been told to avoid it like the plague. Today's Kishon is so polluted with cobalt, strontium, thorium, and radium, as well as other factory waste and sewage, that in the last forty years three hundred navy commandos developed cancer there and died, according to Lieutenant-Colonel Yuval Tamir, who headed the diving course of the Israeli navy special forces unit Shayetet 13.[4] He himself suffered skin cancer and colon cancer and now heads a campaign to compensate the victims' families and to stop naval training there. Before he learned of the water's toxicity, he would discipline his trainee divers by ordering them to fill their fins with the filthy water and drink it.

"Yuck!" I grunted on the phone when he told me, but I couldn't suppress my reporter's instinct. "What's it taste like?"

"Like gasoline and soap," he answered, "and it stank, too."

W. C. Fields famously said he didn't drink water because fish fuck in it. Yuval had given me another reason not to go near the waters of the Kishon, or the Na'aman, for that matter. Nodding at the two men, I threw my backpack across the dirty stream, walked back ten yards, broke into a sprint, and leaped across, landing heavily and jolting my back.

The first man pointed and said, "Well done, but you can only walk another few hundred yards; there's a wire fence that goes into the water. You're not allowed past it. It's Rafael, the weapons factory. You can't walk on the beach anymore. You'll have to go to the road and walk around." He added, rather maliciously, "Now you'll have to jump back again." So I did, but because I had hurt my back, I landed right in the middle of the muck, which splashed onto my lips. It tasted foul and I spat in disgust.

I retraced my steps along the beach and made my way to the busy coastal highway. Then I walked eight miles past the industrial area of Acre toward Haifa. I couldn't help compare the pristine bay the Crusaders and Napoleon described with what I saw around me. Much of the bay area is now known as Krayot, the little towns, an ugly industrial and residential conurbation that stretches most of the way from Acre to Haifa. It is the worst of urban blight: blocks of neon-lit strip malls, run-down garages, and decrepit metal shops, followed by miles of Soviet-style apartment blocks with air conditioners and clothing rails sticking out from the verandas like boils. The closer I got to Haifa, the more bitter and acrid the smell became, especially from the oil-based factories—olfactory pollution. I felt hot, sweaty, and nervous as I walked along narrow stretches of sidewalk, fearful that I would soon be hit by a bus.

Eventually I reached Kiryat Haim, a more pleasant collection of boulevards on Haifa's periphery. I hung a right, and twenty minutes later I found the crowded seaside boardwalk. I had been walking for five hours, most of it along the noisy road. I stripped down to my underpants and collapsed into the sea. As the cool waves lapped over me and the heat drained away, I began to smile. I tried to catch tiny fish as they darted by. Sunlight played in ripples on the surface. A plastic bag stuck to my face. Then suddenly I knew, just knew, that somebody was stealing my backpack. I jerked my head up and in the same motion leaped to my feet, ready to lash out. But I was wrong. Couples were strolling by, infants splashing in the water, and all was well.

I lay happily in a deck chair, my backpack securely between my feet, and ordered a large, freshly squeezed orange juice. I received a fizzy orange soda instead. Sipping it with my eyes closed, I listened to the children playing and thought of my late father, who loved to sit and watch children. He spent many happy hours at the playgrounds in London's Hampstead Heath and Regent's Park, enjoying the antics of the infants and talking to them. But it wasn't the same here. Apart from the fact that today he'd probably get arrested, he didn't meet the kids in Kiryat Haim. They ran, screamed, and came to blows over plastic boats. A boy who came up to my waist ran by, shouting, "F@#k your mother's c#$t!" His friend, a little girl, screamed back, "Up your ass!"

I paid for the soda and walked the rest of the way to Haifa.

A THOROUGHLY MODERN MARRIAGE

Some flatter Haifa, or at least try to inflate the sagging real estate prices, by comparing it to San Francisco, Rio de Janeiro, and Cape Town. Like these cities, Haifa sits in verdant hills above the sea and enjoys spectacular views. Yet Haifa lacks their flair. Busy roads cut the hillside off from the sea. And even when you cross them, you can't reach the beach from the town center because warehouses, factories, and navy docks occupy the coast. Haifa is no Rio. There's not a thong in sight.

This sad lack was pointed out to me some months later by Ala Hlehel, a young Arab writer I met in the garden of one of my favorite restaurants, Fattoush, an Arab place on Haifa's popular Ben-Gurion Street. The street slopes up the hill and is crowned by the golden-domed temple, the world headquarters of the Baha'i faith. We sat under a tree in the early evening, with dim lamps hanging from the branches, candles on the tables, and Arab music playing over the loudspeakers. Ala is an intellectual in his early thirties; with his dark hair and knowing smile, I imagined him easily in La Coupole in Montparnasse. He insisted on filling the table with a dozen small plates of Arab salads, bread, and meat. He was writing a novel: "It's about a shipload of prostitutes sent from France to Napoleon's troops that was seized by British warships off Acre. So the French get sent to the local Arab villages to kill the men and steal the women. But the girls were so hot and beautiful that the French soldiers stayed. They fell in love with Arabia."

I could see why on another occasion, when we were joined by Ala's wife, Abir, a beautiful young lawyer with dancing eyes. She was slim and angular with fine, sharp features and short black hair that offset perfectly her white sweater and tailored jacket; she could star in any TV courtroom drama. They had a rare old time recounting the beginning of their love affair, teasing each other, patting arms and laughing. I was fascinated by their open display of affection as well as by their story—so different from the stereotype of traditional arranged marriages among Arabs. Today, the move from rural to city life gives young Arabs opportunities to get together that had never existed before, and once they meet, they can do what they want. No more stilted conversations in formal living rooms and shy, furtive glances while Auntie glares. The genie was out of the bottle, and he was a sexy dude.

Ala said he had just started working at Abir's legal aid office in Haifa. "She wore jeans," he remembered, patting her leg. "I said, 'You look great,' she said, 'Please write about it. Write about my jeans.'" He turned to her for confirmation. "That happened, yes?"

Abir laughed in delight. "Yes! He wrote a masterpiece—a conversation between him and my jeans. Compliments, fashion, amazing . . ."

Ala continued, and it was clear that he could still hardly believe his luck. "I must tell you, I thought through this text I'd get a one-night stand, and suddenly this one-night stand became a relationship. She's good, authentic, honest, sexy, pretty, and she turned me on."

"Some jeans!" I said, meaning, some ass.

"Do you still have those jeans?" Ala asked.

"Yes, of course, but I got thinner."

Ala went on, smiling and taking Abir's hand. "I wrote her every day, every day, twenty to thirty text messages, so she loved me. We had sex one night, she had a court hearing in Beersheba, she told her parents she was sleeping over because of work and she stayed with me and we had sex and it was good. And I wrote passionate e-mails. She had a fantasy to be with a writer."

Again, Abir confirmed: "Yes, from age fifteen, I dreamed that my husband would be a writer."

"She found her fantasy," he teased, with more than a hint of male smugness. "It was the Haifa way to meet. I had a flat, we had an open relationship with sex and everything, quite impossible in the village."

Abir added: "Haifa facilitated our relationship."

That was what I had wondered about Haifa. Arabs and Jews live so closely to each other that habits rub off, especially among students at the university. Twenty percent of the students, about 3,500, are Arabs, and for many, student life is their first exposure to an alternative lifestyle, away from prying parents and, for the girls, possessive brothers who may well kill their sisters if they stray. Some newly arrived Arabs are shocked at the crowded bars and intimate parties, but many embrace them. Ala grew up in a small village near the Lebanese border, while Abir grew up within the walls of Acre's Old City, both home to extremely traditional Arab cultures that tend toward insularity. Abir's family, like those of her childhood friends, looked down upon outsiders, especially if they came from a small, distant village. "Today we can laugh at it," Abir said, "but at first my parents were not happy with Ala. He was from a village, with a heavy accent, badly dressed..."

Ala added, "Smelly..."

"Yes, smelly." Abir laughed. "And dirty!"

But Abir was more accepting, and she also became more open. "I think Jewish secular life in Haifa influenced me very strongly, even if subconsciously. I envied Jewish girls for their ability to live with their boyfriends. But nothing else. I was satisfied with my studies, my work, only I thought, Lucky you, you can live with your boyfriend without being worried about being caught by your parents. I dressed and talked as I like, and I became less racist. We lived with Jews; they are normal for me."

CREAM ARABS

Ala had previously known Jews only as his employers; he had often helped his father, a construction worker, in Jewish homes. But at university, where he met Jews socially for the first time, Ala was fascinated. He described this during our first meal together at Fattoush, without Abir. "The Jews came to school after the army; they were not stupid teenagers like us Arabs. They were grown men, responsible, they worked and studied at the same time. They possessed strong views of life. I was eighteen, while they were about twenty-six years old. I wanted to be like them—strong, independent, builder of my own life."

Ala told me that he came from a village with zero political awareness. As he developed such awareness in Haifa, his admiration for the Jews changed. There were demonstrations and arguments. "The first time I knew I was a Palestinian was when I came to university. I became very radical. I was trying to compensate for all those years as a stupid Israeli Arab, and suddenly I wanted to liberate Palestine."

That's when Ala began to regard his father in a new light. The arguments and tensions of the separation process, when adolescents establish their independence from their parents, are often suppressed in Arab life. When three generations share the same home, filial allegiance is paramount and calm is critical. But as is the case in many Arab households, the more Ala learned of the Palestinian struggle, the angrier he became with his father.

"I hated him," he said, offering me warm pita bread with zatar—sharp herbs mixed with sesame, salt, and spices—spread on top. When I declined, he wrapped it around a lamb kebab, added hummus, and chomped away. "We all started hating our fathers and grandfathers. We called them lousy fucking collaborators. One father worked for the Israeli government, another was just a fucking coward, you know, that was the atmosphere at university, and we took it back to the village. We shouted at our fathers, 'The Jews took your land, they took everything, why didn't you fight back?'" Ala trailed off, deep in his memories.

After a pause I asked, "What did your father say?"

Ala became agitated. "He didn't understand why I was so angry. He said, 'It's good for us here, we work, we eat, we have democracy, we can say what we want.' For him it was just about survival, keep your head down, mind your own business, raise the children in a quiet place; and in fact, they succeeded in this. But when I became involved in politics, he thought I would ruin everything. He wanted to throw me out of the house. I called him a coward. What rows we had!" Ala smiled, and then repeated ruefully, "How I hated him. But it's the age. I grew up."

He wiped his mouth with a napkin. "After a year or two I realized, this isn't really me. I'm not so radical, I believe in coexistence, I can live with Jews; I have a problem with Zionists, not Jews. Let's solve it. So I began to be more aware of who I am, and Jews became not people to admire and be fascinated by, but either the enemy or people with whom you have an issue that must be solved. And that's when I realized what it must have been like for my father. In 1948 his father lost his land and his home and he had ten children. They belong to a Jewish state, suddenly there's a military regime. If you leave your village without army permission, you get six months in jail. You need permission to work your land. You have to be a 'Good Arab.' They survived this period. They made mistakes, they accepted reality but they wanted to keep on living, because after '48 they knew that other Arabs would not help them. Israel was a fact, especially after '67. That was the hardest thing for Arabs. The '67 war was the end of the dream of Arabs inside Israel to finish Israel. So we had to adapt to our reality, even if we didn't like it. And other Arabs didn't like it either, that we were so accepting. They called us 'Cream Arabs.'"

Then Ala launched into a hilarious description. "That's what the Palestinians today call us," he said, "Cream Arabs. Because we're so delicate, nice, rich, not real Arabs. To them, we're just like the Jews. And sometimes it's true, although I try hard to eliminate these Israeli characteristics. We're becoming like them. We shout. In Amman and Cairo, they know right away we're Arabs from Israel. They say we're rude, greedy, we think we're God. They say we treat them like Bedouin, us with our light skin and smart clothes. Just like the Jews! And those Arabs, they treat us just like we're Jews. At a writers' conference in Cairo, we had a few drinks and they told me all this. 'You are rude and loud and drink and hate Arabs, so we hate you.' So I try to change. Not because I hate Jews. I don't, I like my friends. But I don't want this Israeli mentality or way of life."

I had laughed uproariously throughout Ala's account, but as he finished, I realized he was in a painful bind. Like many Israeli Arabs, or the 1948 Palestinians, as many preferred to be called, Ala had moved beyond his parents and their traditional culture and views, yet he had not reached full acceptance by Arabs outside Israel, nor by Israeli Jews. Israeli Arabs such as Ala were occupying an ethnic no-man's-land; they were in political and moral limbo, rather, it occurred to me, like the Wandering Jew.

Later, while writing up my notes, I decided to run Ala's account of his double bind by a couple of Arab friends. Mus, in Cairo, laughed too: "Cream puffs, we call them. I can recognize an Israeli Arab right away. He has a bald head, he wears shorts, he's noisy . . ."

And Moufaq in Amman became quite heated, mangling his English in his usual funny way: "In the healthy club, they don't put towel in basket, they throw him on the floor. No shower before pool! Annoying, don't talk nicely to reception, make problems, loud and rude, noisy . . ."

I got the message. Ala was right to be worried about becoming too much like his Jewish countrymen. It's an identity crisis that is common among many Arabs who live among Jews in Israel; they appreciate their life, but it changes their values and dents their pride. One man, Ali, a translator, told me, "This is a golden cage, but it is a cage." His twenty-two-year-old daughter Dina, a university graduate, added, "If the devil offers you paradise, he is still the devil."

More contradictions add to the confusion of many Arabs. Ala and Abir both come from uneducated and traditional families, while each is educated and modern. As Ala told me on another occasion, with his wife looking on: "We change on the outside, but inside we're the same as our father and grandfather." Then he cut to the chase. "A man can have as much sex as he wants, but those Arabs you see in a black BMW with loud music, if their sister has sex, they'll kill her. Today it's very common that a girl has a good life at university, drugs, lots of sex in the city, she lives like in Paris, then back in the village she has her hymen sewn up again to get married, and she's happy to be a teacher in the local school. Fifteen hundred shekels to fix the hymen. We call it 'closed,' not 'open.'" Ala brought his hand down on the table and his voice rose. I couldn't tell if he was joking or really was angry: "He wants blood? Give him blood! I say if the stupid fucking Arab wants some blood at night, give him blood!"

In his former role as editor of the newspaper of Balad, an Arab nationalist political party, Ala had been considered way out on the fringe of Arab social commentators, but nobody challenged his control of the facts. Abir nodded: "That's the way it is. It's very hard for me, too. At work as a human rights lawyer, I challenge the state every day; I fight for everybody's rights to be equal. I can go home at three a.m. after working on a petition for the Supreme Court, and my parents are proud. But if I told them I was out with a guy, no way! So I lied a lot. I suffered a lot. Why should I lie? So we married to save me!"

"And what about babies?" I asked. "You've been married for four years but no children yet. That's unusual, isn't it?"

"That's nothing to do with the Jews or their influence," Abir snapped. "It's education, career, we know what we want from our lives. We have the courage to stand up to the social pressure to have babies. From the first day we got married our parents started! Sometimes we think, Let's have one baby, just to stop the pressure. *Halas!* Enough! We like children but we don't feel this is the time for a baby. We're so busy, preoccupied, maybe next year. I may do a PhD, Ala has his career, the time isn't right ..."

They're not alone in their quandary, and Abir's hesitation to have children reflects two opposing forces: her parents' natural desire to have grandchildren, and the Israeli government's desire to reduce the Arab birthrate. From 1960 to 2007, the average number of babies born to Muslim Arabs in Israel dropped from 9.2 to 3.9, and to Christian Arabs from 4.7 to 2.1, while the Jewish birthrate dropped in the same period from 3.4 to 2.8.[5] One of the key reasons for this startling shift was highlighted in a policy planning document presented to the prime minister's office, which said that an effective way to reduce the Arab birthrate, critical to maintaining Israel's Jewish majority, is "by promoting the education of women and having them join the work force."[6]

When I pointed out to Abir that her reluctance to have a baby made her sound just like any other young professional woman in New York or London, or Tel Aviv for that matter, and when I wondered if that had anything to do with her education, career, and the influence of living in Israel, she interrupted me sharply. "Look, of course I am influenced by Jews, I can't deny it. I read Hebrew papers, see Israeli TV, theater, we're exposed to it, I don't live in a cave ..."

With dessert and drinks we moved on to lighter fare, and after three hours we shook hands effusively and went our different ways. I found them a delightful young couple, proud of each other and supportive. When Abir informed me that before Ala she had known lots of men, and seemed about to tell a story or two, Ala cut her off in mock alarm. "You don't have to give Martin the details!"

"Yes, you do," I leered, and Abir just threw her head back and laughed. Did she wink? Probably not. Ala had recently bought a bicycle with a basket to do the shopping. I could not imagine many Arab men pedaling home from the market with a basket full of tomatoes. Abir and Ala had a thoroughly modern marriage, and as professionals and intellectuals, they had thoroughly modern expectations for their lives. But they had still come up against a glass ceiling. They were Arab professionals but only within their Arab world. Ala was frustrated that Jews didn't read his books and essays, and Abir's work as a lawyer was largely confined to helping other Arabs. Ala had come to understand the dilemmas of his father, and sympathized with him, but he did not expect to experience them himself, and he certainly expected full equality for his children, *Inshallah*. In the end, though, a true sense of equality was still a long way off, even for such a couple as Ala and Abir.

WE LIVE IN A FUNNY WORLD

My plan for *Walking Israel* was to walk the coast, but not to limit myself to people and events on the coast; I would follow issues that arose wherever they should take me. So when I remembered the dilemma of another highly educated Israeli Arab, my old friend and colleague Khaled Abu Toameh, a journalist in his early forties who lives near Jerusalem, I decided to visit him. Khaled was accepted by Israelis, even to the extent of earning himself the enmity of some Arabs. I wondered how he really felt: Was he torn between the two sides, or did he just comfortably bridge them? Was he an example of how integration really can work, or was he simply a new generation of the "Good Arab"?

A writer for the conservative English-language *Jerusalem Post*, Khaled is the boldest, clearest-thinking writer on Arab affairs that I know. I have often phoned him, after yet another of his stories on Palestinian corruption, intimidation, or terrorism, and said words to the effect of: "Khaled, are you sure you can write that, isn't it dangerous for you?" His response is always a self-mocking, "I write the truth. And because it's in English, they don't care so much!" Apparently they do care, though, because senior Palestinian officials routinely reprimand him: "Khaled, what you write is true, but do you have to write it?"

If anyone can see Jews and Arabs for who they truly are, beyond the platitudes, it is Khaled. He has been scarred by both. He is as proud an Arab as any, but he has no illusions about his own people, and for good reason.

In 1988, Khaled's elder brother, Massad, an accountant, went for a two-week vacation to Athens and disappeared, feared dead, for fourteen years. "He enjoyed life, a simple guy," Khaled had told me once. "He never read a newspaper in his life, he liked to go to the pub, that was it." Khaled led the family search. "I had a war room," Khaled told me, "I never gave up." Sometimes he got calls from Arabs who extorted money, promising imminent news. "Many Palestinians deceived us during those years. I gave lots of money to many people." All were false leads. "Everybody feared he was dead—me, too—but we kept on hoping and looking." The breakthrough came when Khaled appealed to a relative, his sister's brother-in-law, who had just been appointed the head of bureau for the chief of the Jordanian secret service. Two months later, fourteen years after Massad had disappeared, and thanks to the intervention of the secret services of Israel, Jordan, and Syria, a call came from the Red Cross in the summer of 2002: Come to Amman and pick up your brother.

"At first I didn't recognize him," Khaled said, with a quiet chuckle. "I hugged and kissed the wrong guy, the guy from the Red Cross. Then I saw my brother. It was very emotional. We cried. Massad nearly collapsed."

I remember meeting Massad shortly after he returned. The three of us had sat in a café in the West Bank town of Tulkarm. Khaled was helping me report on the Palestinian uprising, and he had brought his brother. Massad's hands were constantly moving. He didn't stop smoking, and he drank cup after cup of extra-strong Arab coffee. His eyes shifted constantly, but they had no real life in them. He told me then that he had been imprisoned in an underground cell for fourteen years, without ever knowing why. I remembered his blunt answer to my rather silly question when I asked him how he felt. He had looked at me in some surprise and said, "How would you feel?"

Palestinians had befriended Massad in Athens, persuaded him to accompany them to Damascus, and then wouldn't let him leave. It turned out they were agents of the Palestinian renegade Abu Musa, who had his own small militia and a compound in Damascus, with twenty-five underground cells. Khaled believed that maybe they tried to turn his brother into one of their operatives, and he refused. Or maybe they thought he was an Israeli spy. Khaled didn't know, or didn't tell, the truth: "The fact that they didn't kill him, or put him on trial, or announce that they had him, means they didn't have anything against him." When four armed Palestinians, clearly from one of the militias, sat at the neighboring table, Massad looked at them nervously and stopped talking.

That day in Tulkarm, as we all sat around the table, I had asked Khaled whether his brother's kidnapping and his fourteen-year search made him look differently at his own people. "Of course," he answered, "hundreds of Palestinians disappeared, not only my brother. And Abu Musa is just a terrorist. The government jails are full, too."

"Israeli jails are also full of Palestinians," I said.

"Yes, but here you can go to a lawyer, the Supreme Court, human rights organizations like B'Tselem. In Syria, Jordan, there's nothing." Khaled laughed: "Even my mother says, 'Thank God we have the Jews here. The hell of the Jews is better than the paradise of the Palestinians.'" I chuckled and wrote it down, even though my recorder was rolling. I asked Khaled, "Tell me, do you know many Israeli Arabs who want to move to a Palestinian state, if there is a state one day?"

He laughed again. "If you find someone, send him to me, that will be the front-page story in tomorrow's *Jerusalem Post*. I never met one."

Khaled understands the Jews just as well as the Arabs. He grew up in the Israeli Arab town of Baka al-Gharbia, which he says had good relations with the neighboring kibbutzim. He went to a Jewish school in nearby Pardes Hanna. He graduated in English literature from the Hebrew University in Jerusalem. He could hardly be more Israeli, and in fact he felt that he had been fairly treated—until he worked at the state-controlled Israel Broadcasting Authority. "I worked there for nine years—as an editor, then an on-air Arab affairs correspondent, but they never gave me a contract. People came after me and got full-time jobs. Me, never. The editor gave lots of reasons. He even said, 'You didn't serve in the army,' which of course is another way of saying, 'You're an Arab.' Then we had another dispute, so I sued for discrimination. The judge agreed with me and awarded me a financial settlement."

It was Khaled's personal experience of the Arab's glass ceiling, and even after all the years that had gone by, he felt the pain. "I didn't feel like an Arab journalist or an Israeli journalist; I just wanted to be a journalist. That's still all I want. I don't want to see Arab this or Jewish that. I want to see democracy and liberty and good government, and certainly no discrimination." Unfortunately, Khaled's aspirations are a long way from fulfillment. Even Israel's then prime minister Ehud Olmert, complained in Parliament of the "deliberate and insufferable discrimination" against Arabs, especially in the public sector.[7] Senior Arab diplomats can be counted on one hand. The Israel Electric Corporation in Haifa, with thirteen thousand workers, employs little more than a hundred Arabs. And while Israel has been a construction site since its inception, not a single Arab town has been built. In an effort to appease Arab frustration, a new law mandates that by 2010, 8 percent of all civil service jobs had to be held by Arabs, and by 2012, 12 percent. As a man with no illusions about either side, Khaled is the perfect person to ask: How integrated can an Arab truly be? How much can an Arab ever feel at home in Israel?

We met up in his spacious home in a Jewish area on the Jerusalem outskirts. Proudly showing me around, he laughed, "The owner, a Persian Jew, had to get permission from the rabbi to sell the house to an Arab!" Khaled's charming wife, Ghadir, served her favorite soup, blended sweet potatoes and pepper, and kept up a flow of fruit, cookies, coffee, and tea. Nowhere beats an Arab home for hospitality. But Khaled was blunt: "This gap between Arabs and Jews—it's getting worse, and more dangerous. There is growing frustration among young Israeli Arabs who don't accept automatic discrimination. This is a new generation, and that's what Jews don't understand. These are not the mukhtars and the elders who accepted everything, the 'Good Arabs.' The new generation are more enlightened, more educated, more aware of their rights, and they're prepared to fight. They are going to fight, and they will instigate the next intifada, which will be inside Israel. The leaders are already pushing the Israeli Arabs to revolt. It's boiling. It will explode in our faces. It's only a matter of time."

In all my research for this book, this has been the most common warning—Israeli Arabs have had it up to here. But Khaled has a warning not only for the Jews but for the Arabs, too:

"I always thought Israeli Arabs could serve as a bridge between Jews and Palestinians, but in the last ten years Israeli Arab leaders have put the Israeli Arabs on the side of the Palestinians, and that's a big mistake. We should have stayed more neutral. And that puts us into the hands of the Israeli right wing, like Avigdor Lieberman, who call us a fifth column, a cancer, because we came out with all these fiery statements. We tried to become more Palestinian than the Palestinians in the West Bank and Gaza. That's why many Israeli Jews don't trust us. They don't see the difference between Khaled, the loyal citizen of Israel, and Muhammad, the suicide bomber from Gaza. We are all a bunch of Arabs who want to destroy Israel."

"Do you?" I asked.

Khaled answered carefully. "It is true that most Arabs would prefer that Israel not exist. Many Arab countries still see Israel as an alien body, a cancer planted here in the Middle East. This is the general view. So for these people, it's not really about the '67 borders, Jerusalem, refugees, another illegal outpost. It's really about Israel's right to exist."

I nodded in agreement, and Khaled continued with the fear expressed by all Israeli Arabs: "I don't believe that the Jews really want to kick the Arabs out, but it could happen. It might happen during a war. That Israel will use security as an excuse to expel the Arabs. It could happen."

So Khaled had summed it up: Arabs have had it up to here, their frustrations may explode, and the Jews may kick them out. Each side lives in fear of the other. But here he is, a pioneer, in a sense, of coexistence, if not yet integration. Khaled had been the first Arab to move into his street; now three Arab families live there, and in the whole neighborhood there are two hundred Arab families, with more moving in. Khaled took great pleasure in pointing out the ironies.

The little town where he lives is called Pisgat Ze'ev. It is a Jewish settlement built on occupied Arab land. When he bought the house, he got a state mortgage plus a government gift of twenty thousand shekels, about five thousand dollars, because he was helping to strengthen the suburbs of Jerusalem, a border neighborhood. When he first saw the house, on Yacov Yehoshua Street, overlooking a desert wadi leading into the West Bank, he had hesitated to plunk down $320,000 because the real estate agent warned him against crime and theft by Palestinians. Khaled grinned. "He didn't realize I was an Arab." Then Israel began building the wall and fence that cuts off the West Bank from Israel. Two months after he first saw the house, Khaled came back. But because of the security the wall would bring, the price of his house had shot up to $420,000, which he paid. That was four years earlier. "Now, because of the wall, it's known as a quiet area, and the house is worth at least eight hundred thousand dollars."

Khaled grinned, just like any Manhattan yuppie, and he asked, "What am I, a settler occupying Arab land? Or an Arab reclaiming it? Or am I just a guy living in a house with his family? We live in a funny world."

WHO WILL FIX THE FRIDGE?

I thought of Khaled's quandary and of the larger issue of Arab-Jewish integration at an election rally a few months later in Haifa, just before the January 2009 election. The firebrand Avigdor Lieberman, whom Khaled had warned about, was hoovering up support for his scarcely veiled call to throw out the Arabs. He soon became Israel's foreign minister. His answer to the question of integrating Arabs was clear—the more of them that can be disenfranchised, the better. He wanted to lop off chunks of Israel with lots of Arabs and swap them for West Bank settlements with lots of Jews; that way, Israel would stay a Jewish state. It was a platform barely distinguishable from that of Rabbi Meir Kahane, a stigmatized former member of Parliament who was assassinated in a New York hotel in 1990. Anyone who doesn't swear an oath of allegiance to the State of Israel should lose his rights as a citizen, Lieberman demanded, and 400,000 Israelis, desperate for a strong leader willing to sort out the Arabs, flocked to his nasty campaign slogan, laden with a barely concealed threat: "Only Lieberman understands Arabic."

But it was only Russian that could be heard outside Haifa's Joseph and Rebecca Meyerhoff Theater that evening as rally organizers prepared for

Lieberman's arrival. Pretty blondes in tight jeans and white boots helped tattooed schoolboys stick up posters of Lieberman. He stared sternly and with confidence from the walls, trying hard to project power, with his dark suit, graying goatee, and green eyes. A big woman in a black dress and sour face blocked the door, barking out orders, like a Russian prison guard. "You can't come in," she seemed to be telling everyone.

"Who's she?" I asked a photographer.

"Haifa's deputy mayor," he answered.

Really? This is a deputy mayor? This Russian bruiser? With her ample body, Yulia Shtraim, elected to serve the people, all the people, barred the way to Israeli Arab reporters, while allowing in journalists from Japan and Bosnia. An Arab reporter complained, "Our taxes pay her salary and she won't let us in!"

Nearby, knots of police stood around, cordoning off a small area far from the entrance to corral the promised counterdemonstration by Jews and Arabs. A young man with cropped hair and muscles bulging beneath his tight "Vote Lieberman" T-shirt strode the courtyard as if looking for someone to pummel. He turned out to be a former professional boxer from England. Soon thirty demonstrators arrived, Jews and Arabs championing coexistence. They chanted, "Fascism, no, Lieberman, go!" and "Yalla, Yalla, Yalla, go back to Russia!" Police barred their way and stared stony-faced. One big Arab with a mustache was dragged away by police, and a Russian took a swing at him but missed.

Then I saw the boxer going head to head with a little lady half his height and a third his weight but with a voice like a foghorn. Hannah Saffron, who lived down the road, had come to see the action, only to get drawn into the thicket of it. Hannah and the boxer had attracted quite a crowd, including numerous television cameramen and radio reporters, all sticking microphones at them. The two were yelling at each other, and it seemed odd that the polite little lady had the louder voice. I could only make out bits.

Hannah: We need peace, we need to talk!

Boxer: Excuse me, who started killing! How many suicide bombs! Babies, children!

Hannah: If you kill we will continue to be killed.

Boxer: How many? How many? They want to kill us all!

Hannah: Lieberman is a racist, an anti-Semite!

Boxer: Who is the racist! Lieberman wants security, he will give us security.

Hannah: He will make us all die here. We didn't come here for that. We did not come here to be anti-Arab!

Boxer: They are anti-Jewish! We have to show them who is strong, this is our land!!

When their energy seemed to fade, I mischievously called out, "What about the refugees who want their land back?" "Refugee" struck a chord as they both picked up on this cue word, everyone's default key, this trigger.

Hannah: I was born here, my parents were refugees, who are you to—

Boxer: I don't want to be a refugee, we gave Gaza, they still try to shoot at us!

I left them trying to outyell each other, and later, after Lieberman had slipped into the hall the back way, and all the Russians and their supporters were inside, cheering and clapping so loud that we could hear them in the street, I found Hannah again. She was wandering the yard, still looking for action. "Weren't you scared," I asked, "nose to navel with that big guy?"

"Not at all," she said. "What is scary is that they don't want to discuss with the Arabs, just throw them out. Citizenship is at stake here, like in Germany for the Jews. They start with the Arabs, then the gays, then mainstream, that's how it always is. If we believe in human rights, then it must be human rights for everybody. Arabs, Jews, we are together, united. Arabs won't kill the Jews, and we won't kill them. We tried for so many years and it didn't work. The trouble is the young people, they don't understand history. Somebody comes along and says, we will kill them, we will fuck them. [Excuse me? I thought.] It's awful, it's really awful, but they listen to such a terrible man."

"Where are you from?" I asked.

"I was born down the road on Balfour Street. My parents came from Ukraine and Latvia."

"What about the deputy mayor?" I asked. "The scary woman in black?"

"Awful! She shows how well we have integrated our new Russian immigrants. And yet we can't find a way to integrate the Arabs who lived here before us. We must find a way. We must all live together."

"And if you don't?" I asked.

"It will be terrible. Lieberman wants to expel the Arabs. I don't know what will happen."

After the demonstration, I strolled back to my car, which I'd parked by a grocery store. I went in to buy an ice cream and found two men, Uri and Avram, joking with an Arab called Muhammad, who was fixing a fridge. "Don't worry, Muhammad." Uri was laughing. "We won't let Lieberman throw you out!"

All three threw their heads back, roaring with laughter.

"But you'll vote for him!" Muhammad said, and they slapped hands like basketball players.

"That's different, Lieberman knows how to take care of you Arabs!" said Uri, and again all three roared. It seems they know each other well.

"Anyway," Avram manages to say, "if Muhammad gets thrown out, who will fix the fridge?"

Uri wipes his eyes and pants: "Lieberman, of course!"

This breaks them up; they can hardly breathe for laughing. Muhammad is bent double, tears flowing from his eyes.

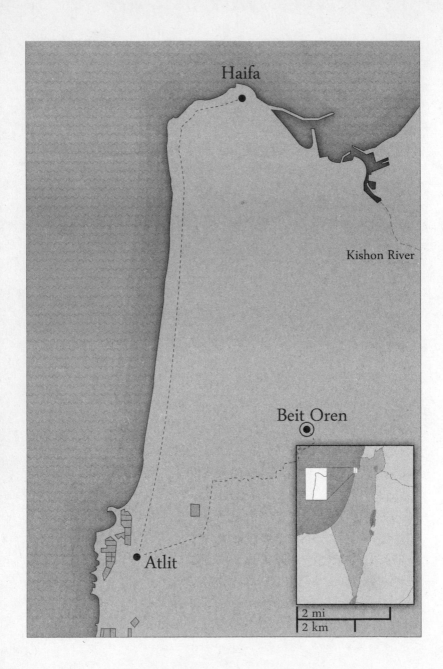

6

Remaking Utopia

HAIFA TO BEIT OREN

Israel bursts with overlooked gems, and one of them is the heart of the Carmel Nature Reserve south of Haifa, a web of woods, wildflowers, and cave formations that housed prehistoric man. Walking trails crisscross the forest, leading to natural bathing pools and ancient stone ruins. It is calm and beautiful. Near the western edge, a narrow tree-lined road ends abruptly at a small kibbutz atop a cliff, Beit Oren (House of Pines). All of nature seems to merge here. A sweet bouquet from plants and blossoms rises from the valley floor, and pine trees with nesting birds point to the sky. Eagles wheel, gently seeking prey. The Carmel range boasts many such quaint communities, well off the tourist trail, full of history and charm. Bat Shlomo (Solomon's Daughter), on Carmel's southern slopes, is a one-street village of fourteen traditional stone-and-wood homes, with art galleries and a café/museum selling homemade olive oils, cheeses, pita bread, and yogurt. Renovated stone homes nestle amid stands of pomegranate, fig, and olive trees at Ein Hod, a picturesque artists' village on Carmel's western slopes. Farther south lies the historic Zikhron Ya'akov, a cobblestoned wine-producing village established in the 1880s by Baron Edmond de Rothschild. At the foot of Carmel is the Atlit detainee camp, now a museum, with its more painful memories for the Jews. Here tens of thousands of Holocaust survivors found themselves behind barbed wire again, interned by the British as illegal immigrants to Palestine.

Seven days into my walk, and I'd covered less than thirty miles. As I'd taken vacation time for this trip, it occurred to me that I had better pick up the pace if I wanted to keep my day job. I hoisted my backpack and headed south once again, trembling in Haifa's dawn chill. I knew I would soon be cursing the heat; during Israel's relentless summer months, all the weatherman ever says is *"Ayn shinui"*—no change. Today I planned to walk ten miles down the coast to Atlit, a tiny town with a secret military base. Then I would take a little detour inland, cross the highways, and climb five steep miles through forest up to Beit Oren, a small kibbutz high in the Carmel hills. I already knew Beit Oren to be a stunning place, fragrant and alluring, with a priceless view stretching to the Mediterranean of craggy, wooded hills, green fields, and the glittering fish ponds of Kibbutz Ma'agan Michael by the ocean. But I wasn't tackling such a hard slog just for the beauty: I was interested in taking a new look at one of Israel's icons, its agricultural communes, or kibbutzim; for Beit Oren has its own peculiar claim to fame.

Founded in 1909, the kibbutzim played a critical role in the growth of the state of Israel. These little communities eked out a living in distant parts of the land, expanded the borders of pre-state Israel, led the secret

Jewish underground, and formed the nascent nation's moral and psychological backbone, giving the state an ideology of sharing and contributing that helped mold a motley collection of Jews from all over the world into a cohesive, determined whole. Although never representing more than 4 percent of the Jewish population, the kibbutzim took on a romantic aura as human foundries where effete European Jews took up arms and turned books into plowshares. Following the War of Independence in 1948, kibbutzim went on to produce some of Israel's most illustrious soldiers and statesmen, men such as Moshe Dayan, Yitzhak Rabin, and Shimon Peres. Even today, images of bronzed, muscled kibbutz workers dancing the hora in the banana groves with a rifle at the ready are as much a part of the Israeli psyche as circumcision and road rage.

But just as Israeli Arabs and Holocaust survivors have struggled to find their place in modern Israel, so, too, have the kibbutzniks. As early as 1952, *The New Yorker's* John Hersey wrote: "The kibbutz of today is suffering a mortal crisis . . . like a wild creature entering a new environment, the kibbutz has had to adapt or die." During the 1950s and '60s, the new state apparatus took on the nation-building functions formerly fulfilled by kibbutzim. Generational change, urbanization, and the development of Israel's capitalist economy also rendered the socialist kibbutzim increasingly irrelevant, while poor management practices ate away at their finances. The death rattle that Hersey identified lasted thirty-four years, until 1986, when Beit Oren became Israel's first kibbutz to go bankrupt. The commune's sixty families owed the banks $6.5 million, more than $100,000 each. The kibbutz movement advised members of Beit Oren to leave—the first such advisory it had given. But that was just the beginning. Two hundred and eighty kibbutzim accumulated debts of $4.25 billion, and they began to fall like dominoes. The kibbutz, possibly Israel's most popular calling card, was in disgrace. Thousands of kibbutz families flocked to the cities to try their luck, and it was a rare young person who returned after his army service.

What interested me about Beit Oren, though, was not the sad story of the kibbutz's decline, but the unlikely and inspiring story of its more recent rebirth. Over the past decade, kibbutzim have reinvented themselves and become much more viable financially. Today, young families are again flocking to join, children of members are returning, and outsiders are buying homes. Of course, "Saba," Grandpa, wouldn't recognize these new kibbutzim. Their plowshares have been turned into high-tech factories, and what farm laborers remain are likely from Thailand. More fundamentally, most kibbutzim have been utterly stripped of socialist ideology. The utopian collective, an icon of Israel, where everybody shared everything, including money, jobs, clothes, and responsibility; where days-old babies were separated from their mothers and reared in children's houses, with common rooms and showers for boys and girls; where shopping was done on a point system and everybody shared meals in a communal dining hall; where the most trivial decision was made by committee—all that is largely a thing of the past, replaced by individualistic, capitalist communities that nevertheless offer a unique alternative to city life.

Just as Beit Oren, founded in 1939 by Jews from Poland and Russia, was the first kibbutz to go under, it also turned out to be the place where the new kibbutz model was forged and tested. In a few short years, a handful of young visionaries took the demoralized elderly members of Beit Oren, their dilapidated houses and their bankrupt businesses, and built a thriving community that served as a model for the rest of Israel's failing kibbutzim. How did they do it? How was Utopia remade? More broadly, in our era of failing banks and governments sinking under debt, how can a spent, corrupt social institution find new blood? I didn't quite realize it when I set out, but what I was to find in Beit Oren over the course of the next several months amounted to a classic case study of how total economic collapse can inspire great innovation. Even more than that: It was a classic Israeli story of how a few good men and women with ideas and determination can reinvent the wheel.

HEART ATTACKS AND MELODRAMA

The thirteen-mile walk to Beit Oren was also a story, albeit of a very different kind. It started pleasantly enough. On the Haifa outskirts, upon passing the shuttered cable car that climbs from the sea to the Stella Maris monastery, I began to chuckle rather unkindly. I was remembering a windsurfer with his own survival drama. I had seen him being dragged from the sea right in front of me, here at the bottom of the cable car station, where the concrete columns reach the water. It was the summer of 2006, and I was hiding beneath the bridge from rockets fired by Hezbollah during its war with Israel. A commotion broke out at the water's edge, and I saw a number of people helping a big, burly young man with light brown hair. His legs hung limply, but he was conscious. They sat him down against a wall, and as he wrenched off his black rubber suit, muscles seemed to pop out from places, as Muhammad Ali once said, where most people don't have places. But this tough guy had just had the shock of his life, and he was babbling.

He had been catching a wave with a taut sail, experiencing a tremendous rush of speed, when he saw a dark flash. A missile landed in the sea with a giant splash and boom only meters away. Apparently a friend had persuaded him to go windsurfing during the war, so while most people rushed for shelter when the siren warned of incoming rockets, these two heroes were out ripping the waves. The man before me was angrier with his friend than with the Hezbollah fighters who fired the rocket. "I'll kill him! I'll slaughter him!" were the last words I heard before leaving the man in the care of the medics.

Now, looking up the hill and still smiling, it suddenly occurred to me that I couldn't leave Haifa without retracing one of my favorite tourist routes in Israel, which begins way up Mount Carmel. But I confess, to get there, I weakened. I don't know what it was, but I saw the steep streets winding to the top, a sharp incline of 550 meters, felt the weight of my backpack, and broke my coastal trek's golden rule: I hailed the next cab. In my defense, it was still early, I had already walked two miles, I hadn't had coffee, and the magnitude of the task I had set myself, to keep walking until the Gaza border, suddenly struck me, momentarily, as absurd. Anyway, I thought, who'll ever know? But to retain the moral high ground, and to maintain the integrity of this venture, I hereby admit: I took a cab, and it cost eighteen shekels. Believe me when I say that this was the entire transport cost for my hike along the coast of Israel. I regret it to this day. However, it beat walking up that hill.

Five minutes later, I crossed the stone threshold of the Stella Maris Carmelite Church and Monastery and admired the paintings and windows that make this one of the Holy Land's most beautiful Catholic churches. Imagine soaring pink marble walls and columns, paintings in a domed roof, and glowing images in stained glass, all showing Elijah flying on a horse-drawn chariot of fire. The sun streaming through the windows sends a rainbow of colors flashing through the nave. In the garden, an iron cross stands atop a simple pyramidal memorial stone. On it reads the familiar biblical text whose warning seems so pertinent to Israel's struggle with the Palestinians, when seen in the context of the many transient occupiers who have passed through this land. It still sends a shiver down my back: "How are the mighty fallen, and the weapons of war perished." If you depend on weapons of war, your days are numbered; better to make peace, for its price pales compared to the price of war. Beneath the stone is proof: the bones of two hundred French soldiers slaughtered by the Ottomans in 1799. When Napoleon retreated from Acre, he left them dying of plague in the care of the priests. As they shivered in their beds, Ottoman warriors fell upon them with their curved swords.

After the church, I took a dirt path down past the lighthouse. It quickly becomes a series of ancient stone steps that enter the woods. After walking for ten minutes, I came upon a rise and the entrance to Elijah's Cave. It is austere—a large rock cavern with walls of Jewish, Christian, and Muslim prayer books. The Bible relates that this is where the prophet meditated before defeating and killing the 450 pagans of Baal on Mount Carmel, proving that the Jewish God was the one and only. Later, Elijah hid here from the fury of King Ahab and his wife, Jezebel, and toward the end of his life he taught his disciples here. People of all faiths visit regularly to pray, read, and rest under the shady trees.

Since Elijah's Cave is only a minute from the coast road, I quickly made it back to the beach and walked an hour or so to Maxim, a popular gas-station eatery famous for being owned by Jews and Arabs. Unfortunately, that didn't stop it from being blown up by a suicide bomber in 2003. A female Palestinian law student killed twenty Israelis, including four Arabs. Taking stock of the past couple of hours, I realized that this is my usual kind of guided tour in Israel: a dab of history, a lesson from the Bible, and on to modern times—a rocket fell here, a suicide bomber blew himself up there, a car bomb down the road a bit. It was the eternal battle for survival and supremacy. Little did I know that now, after two hours walking, I was about to find my attention diverted—onto my own survival.

I had hoped to walk the coast much earlier in the year, during the cooler months of spring, but I didn't find time until June, and now, after barely two hours on the road, I was well aware that the physical effort of walking through heavy sand in intense heat may not be the smartest idea for an old geezer like me. I seemed to be tiring after a week on the road, even if I hadn't covered much ground. Leaving Maxim, I found myself becoming severely lightheaded. Despite my floppy hat and layers of greasy sunblock,

Martin Fletcher

View from Rosh Hanikra down the coast toward Nahariya.

Grotto in Rosh Hanikra.

Day one—setting off from Rosh Hanikra.

Chat with Eli Avivi, Achziv.

Eli Avivi, Achziv.

Martin Fletcher

Achziv Beach.

Martin Fletcher

Colonel Hanan Sa'id, Israeli Army.

Hanan Sa'id with "Captain" Sami at sink.

Moshe and Miriam Rothman, Café Europa, Ramat Hasharon.

Recruits training in Acre.

Acre.

Fisherman's Harbor, Acre.

Doron Horovitz

Russian immigrants near Haifa.

Hanging out with Arab friends near Bet Oren.

Campsite near Hof Dor.

Martin Fletcher

A shadow of myself, walking at dawn.

Martin Fletcher

Ya'Avoc Sa'Ar

Caesarea.

Beached shipwreck near Netanya.

Walking with Lora.

Tel Aviv seen from the hill of Jaffa.

Roger's café, Ashkelon.

Roger the Man.

Bat Sheva picking flowers, Kibbutz Yad Mordechia.

Rivkah Reicher, Kibbutz founder, Yad Mordechai.

Ben Schneider, my tour guide in Kibbutz Yad Mordechai Museum.

Statue of Warsaw ghetto hero Mordechai Anilevitch, at Yad Mordechai.

Herman Chanania

Martin Fletcher

Gaza City from near Israel's border.

my nose, neck, shoulders, and arms were red and itchy. When I entered the sea to cool off, the salt irritated the many scratches on my legs, which were also getting sunburned. And because so much of the beach slants down toward the water, I had blisters on the little toe and heel of my right foot, where much of my weight fell. To ease the pain, I sometimes walked on the flatter, deeper sand, but that was even more strenuous.

The beach here was wider and wilder than up north, with fewer interruptions. I took a long drink of water and opened my umbrella to shade my head. After a rest on a mound of sand, I kept on walking. My goal, Atlit, was just a haze in the distance, but I soon became giddy and faintly nauseous. A cold sweat gathered in my armpits, and as I walked, I placed my hand on my heart. I could feel it beating, hard and fast, and then I felt my heart beat even without my hand on it. Palpitations? I checked my left arm for numbness. What are the signs of a heart attack? I wondered.

I've been in my share of life-and-death situations. I've been bombed and shot at in wars across the globe, and let's not forget the mob attacks, car accidents, a near-drowning in the Zambezi River, and getting hopelessly lost in the Sahara Desert. Always, I've remained quite calm. This time, though, I found myself growing worried, maybe because I was older. It must have been well over a hundred degrees, and it wasn't yet ten o'clock. A breeze carried the sickly stench of a dead animal. Trudging along more slowly now, my head bent, my limbs heavy, I remembered twenty years earlier flying in a small plane low over the Namib Desert in Namibia, following a single line of tracks into the vast desert, wondering where the invisible animal could possibly be heading, alone and so deep into the wasteland. After twenty minutes' flying time, at the end of the tracks, at the foot of yet another sand dune, lay a bleached white skeleton. He must have dropped dead from thirst. Now I licked my parched lips and took another sip of water. I thought about stopping but decided against it. The coast road was only half a mile to the east, and I could easily find help there if I really felt bad. So I plodded on, hand on my heart, feeling sorry for myself.

A jeep raced by carrying two men and a dog. I thought of Napoleon's dragoons who had tramped the same way three hundred years ago, and the thousands of Crusader knights in their stifling armor seven hundred years before that, and I wondered how many of them had fallen by the wayside. I began to raise my hand to call for help but stopped myself. I didn't want to break my rule again; I'd already taken a taxi that day. So I willed my legs to stumble on, I drank lots of water, I rested a little on sandy hillocks beneath my umbrella, and finally—finally—I reached the secret navy base. The sign on its fence warned that any person passing this spot would be shot or arrested or something. I didn't write it down. I couldn't. All I wanted was to get out of the sun.

I found a shaded bit of fence and carefully sat down without removing my backpack. Why didn't I take this walk decades ago, when I had first thought of it, instead of waiting until the wrong side of sixty? In London, my hometown, I already qualify for a "Freedom Pass"—free trips on the bus and tube for seniors. Soon I'll be able to see a movie half-price in the morning, preferably a dirty one.

These were my lighter thoughts. After so many years reporting on wars and disasters, I am prone to nasty nightmares and vicious daydreams in which I wreak terrible vengeance on anybody who has upset me in the slightest manner. If a colleague mildly criticizes me, in my imaginings I pull his nose off and crush him with my heavily armored jeep. If a passing driver pulls ahead of me too abruptly, I picture myself slamming into him from the side until his car overturns a dozen times and its bloody passengers fly out the smashed windows, to be crushed by an oncoming bus until their heads pop open and their brains spill out and a dog comes to lap up the pulp and gristle. Next time learn to drive!

Of course, in reality, I wouldn't hurt a fly, because they, too, are sentient beings, but I think I do suffer occasionally from mild posttraumatic stress. And now, lolling against the wire fence in the partial shade of a meager bush, the sand burning my bare legs, I imagined the worst. It's been a good life, I thought, testing my left arm again for numbness and measuring my pulse. I never said no to any adventure, I always went the extra mile down the road to find the story, whether it was seeking the Khmer Rouge in Cambodia or a warlord in Somalia or the guerrillas in the Rhodesian bush. Several times, under Syrian shelling in the Golan Heights or caught in heavy gunfire in the no-man's-land between Greek and Turkish forces in Cyprus, I thought I really could die at any instant. And now, there I lay, defeated at last by a hot sun, expiring on a Mediterranean beach before lunch.

In my dreams, of course, I never actually die. The instant before experiencing a horrible, painful, tortured death, I always snap out of it. And so it was now. I felt much better after the short rest. I shook myself and sniggered at my melodramatic musings. I sipped more water and told myself to grow up. My heart was fine, and my legs weren't even that sore. But I did enjoy a few moments of satisfyingly morbid self-pity before heaving myself to my feet and plodding slowly on.

I had intended to spend a few hours exploring Atlit, and I had also wanted to visit an old British prison camp where they had interned Jews caught trying to immigrate illegally into Palestine. Most of all, I had wanted to swim three hundred meters offshore and then free-dive down to the oldest prehistoric settlement ever found on the sea floor. Ten thousand years ago, the Mediterranean was thirty meters lower than today. As the sea rose, the indented cliff became a natural rocky harbor that provided shelter for every occupier, but the community at Atlit flourished most under the Crusaders, whose Knights Templar built a castle on the rocky outcrop to protect pilgrims traveling from Acre to Jerusalem. It was the last Crusader foothold in the Holy Land, its defenders fleeing in 1291 to Cyprus. Weeks later, it was overrun by the Egyptian Mamluks and eventually destroyed.

Tempting as all this was for a history buff like myself, I was too tired, and so instead I floated in the waves, rested in the shade, ate some fruit and nuts, drank the last of my water, and started looking for a room for the night. It's a long walk around the navy base into town, and I found that in all of Atlit there wasn't a hotel or a room to rent. On a street corner in this backwater, I bought a bottle of chocolate milk and ate an ice cream, wondering where to go. Kibbutz Beit Oren, which I had intended to reach that day, was too far to walk, especially as my pulse had only just returned to normal. The climb to Beit Oren is a killer: either five miles of steep, narrow, winding roads between a cliff and a canyon, with cars whizzing by and no room to walk safely, or a shorter yet even steeper hike up the canyon itself.

I made a snap decision. I'd find a place to rest and then sleep out on the beach and continue my walk south the next morning. I was finding it hard to combine the physical effort of the journey with the intellectual effort of talking to people and investigating their stories. I felt I could handle one or the other, but not both at the same time. I would return to the area later when I had finished my trek and had more time and energy to research the story.

After idling the rest of the day away in this unremarkable community, I found a flat, sheltered spot in the sand near the empty parking lot. I rolled out my sleeping bag, zipped myself in, and instantly fell into a deep sleep.

ADAPT OR DIE

Three months passed before I finally made it back to Beit Oren. Now that I wasn't obliged to walk, I happily drove along one of Israel's most scenic roads, a winding, steep climb through thick groves of Aleppo pines, strawberry trees, and buckthorns that grow by the Palestine oaks of the Carmel woods. Beyond the scrub forest, spring brings blazing fields of purple, yellow, and white anemone, cyclamen, and orchis. On a good day, you can see wild pig, deer, and jackals. The road follows deep wadis shrouded in every shade of green. It passes stepped rock formations whose caves sheltered prehistoric man 500,000 years ago.

I took a left turn, and the road ended abruptly at the heavy kibbutz gate. I have never seen it closed, nor have I ever seen anyone in the guard post. Beit Oren is a welcoming place, perched on top of a hill so that all its streets lead up or down. It is also a simple place, a collection of modest homes whose construction evinced a common goal of living well amid nature. Children here are free to roam. You find them everywhere, playing ball, on the swings, in the pool. They run and laugh, the older ones chatting arm in arm, most of them appearing to hold a musical instrument. How things have changed, I thought—from hungry old people and bankruptcy during the mid-1980s to this scene of family bliss. I had come to find out what went right and what lessons could be learned from one of those who turned it around and who had suffered greatly for his efforts.

I found Ran Ronen on the wooden deck he had built overhanging the canyon—a splendid spot for a barbecue or for just enjoying the view. In his scuffed sandals, torn Indian cotton pants that billowed in the wind, loose shirt, and floppy hat, Ran seemed more like a hippie from Goa than a former air-force gunner and kibbutz savior; but in one revealing anecdote he explained why the traditional collectives were doomed from the start. "When I came to live in Beit Oren, they gave me a room in this house. It looked over this amazing view over the canyon all the way to the sea. Yet it had a tiny window. I asked Dov, the guy responsible for building in the sixties, why he didn't build big windows so people could enjoy the view, and he said, 'We had to save on heating.'"

"What's that got to do with it?" I asked.

Ran laughed. "That's what I said." He went on: "Dov explained that the side of the view is also the side of the canyon winds, and if we have big windows we'll have cold rooms, so we'll need more heating. And as you know, in a kibbutz nobody cares about saving electricity, because they don't pay for it, so they just turn their heater on at the beginning of winter and turn it off at the end. The community had to do something about the heating bills, so they decided to build small windows. Can you believe that? That's what happens when the community decides and not the individual."

Ran was born on Kibbutz Alumot, above the Sea of Galilee, overlooking the Jordan Valley and the Golan Heights. He lived there happily until he was ten, when his parents left, fed up with the strictures of kibbutz life. It was said that kibbutzim were paradise for dogs and children, and little Ran was devastated. He had loved the freedom and the ability to live by nature's rhythms. I sensed his longing for those earthy days when he took me from his home to view projects he had constructed recently in the nearby woods. With his friends, he had built a five-tier rock amphitheater and had rigged up a kitchen beneath the trees. He had also woven branches and twigs together to cover little clearings where they could sleep. Tomatoes, cucumbers, and mint, bay leaves, basil, and other herbs grew in his organic garden, and his trees and bushes grew pomegranates, apricots, and lemons. All were fenced off by branches and watered by recycled sewage.

When we reached the entrance to a small clearing in the trees beneath Beit Oren, Ran began to scythe a section of grass, his tall body moving in rhythm with each sweep of the arm. He told me that he was working on a new idea: a nonprofit consciousness center, where people would come to be closer to nature and to themselves. Ran wanted to change the way people looked at themselves and their environment so that, one by one, they would build a better world. "We take the best of everything—sacred songs, meditation, yoga . . . mix it all together. I want to create a community. We'll hold workshops. I hope people will come here once or twice a month. It'll be a refuge. First you fix the individual, then you fix society . . ."

Ran hadn't started out with such grand notions. As he related, he first built the amphitheater for no particular reason. "I had a deep urge to build something. I didn't really know what I wanted to do with it." Ran's transformative ideas for the future of the kibbutz movement also hadn't started from a grand notion; it was about survival. "It was insulting to live in Beit Oren," Ran said, as the pace of his scything increased. "We made money, we got nothing. I wanted to make my life better."

I breathed deeply, enjoying the woody scent of the freshly cut grass. "Okay," I said, "how about this for some cheap psychology. When your parents moved to town, you lost your lovely childhood on the kibbutz, and now you've spent the last twenty years trying to re-create that life."

Birdcalls overlapped one another, a high-pitched tweeting. He smiled. "Thank you, thank you, the shrink!"

"Is that how you feel?"

"No."

Ran explained that during the late 1980s, before he had joined Beit Oren, he had been on the fast track. Not yet thirty, he had a lovely wife and baby, their own apartment in upmarket north Tel Aviv, an executive position with an airplane charter company, two cars, a motorbike, foreign travel twice a month, and a ballooning bank account. But he wasn't happy. "It was a bad life. I worked twelve hours a day, I hardly saw my child, and my wife was pissed off. And suddenly someone said that Beit Oren was looking for new members. My wife said, 'Never, I will never live on a kibbutz.' But when we saw it, we fell in love. So we moved in. I wanted to be a farmer. No responsibility."

That's when Ran met Dodik, the new kibbutz manager. Twenty years Ran's senior, Dodik Ruttenberg was a visionary who made even Ran look blinkered. Although it was Ran and his friend Orna Dagon who eventually would enter a room and come out a week later with the plan that saved Beit Oren and most of Israel's kibbutz movement, Dodik would be the one to send them there. Like Ran, Dodik was a fighter, a former paratroop commander, a guy who would never back down. Yet their motives differed. Ran, seeking financial stability, wanted a new kibbutz life form, while Dodik sought to resurrect the old ideology and reclaim the old communal spirit, albeit in a modified way.

Back in the early seventies, Dodik believed that the community spirit of kibbutzim was essential to Israel's health. "If society is no good then the army is no good, the government, everything begins from the bottom." Yet, knowing that strict authoritarianism was killing the spirit of the kibbutzim from the inside, forcing members to leave in droves, he turned against the establishment, and they hated him for it. Dodik wanted to take decision making away from kibbutz committees and leave people responsible for their own lives, the exact opposite of the traditional kibbutz practice. A utopian by inclination, he believed that in its existing form, the kibbutz didn't work. If individuals could decide daily economic and social questions for themselves, they would naturally come together for the common good; a true community spirit would reign, not one forced upon people. Ironic, I thought, as Dodik later explained his philosophy to me: This old socialist was actually describing a free market economy. As he saw it, traditional kibbutzim had taken away choice and responsibility, wrapping the individual in a straitjacket of rules and committees. You want a different kind of cup in the dining room? The committee will vote. You want to teach math? Sorry, teach history, that's what we need. You want a big window to see the view? Sorry, we need to save on heating.

Dodik applied his theories of free choice at a series of kibbutzim. For twelve years, he tried and failed to create the perfect community in Kibbutz Gonen in Upper Galilee. He tried again on the Golan Heights in Katzrin and failed there, too. People couldn't be bothered with change; they just wanted a quiet life with their families. Still, Dodik railed against the kibbutzim and demanded more independence for kibbutz members, until one day the kibbutz establishment realized how to shut him up: Send the maverick to Siberia, send him to the worst kibbutz of all, the most hopeless case, the one they'd all given up on, the one they'd advised everybody to leave. Let him try his crazy ideas there.

"When I first arrived in Beit Oren," Dodik said, after I'd caught up with him in his home in Rosh Pina, in Upper Galilee, "there was a great view, but it had ugly houses, old people, and a shitty society. The place was beautiful, but the reality was neglected. The members didn't want to change, but they didn't have a choice." Dodik decided to take a direct approach. He told members of Beit Oren that they could see their community disintegrate, or they could agree to his changes. The simple fact was that the larger kibbutz movement wouldn't support them any longer. So it was sink or swim—not a message most members of Beit Oren wanted to hear.

Dodik's mission had been twofold—to save the kibbutz from extinction, and to rebuild the community spirit of yore. His first major task was to inject new blood. He put out the word: Beit Oren is looking for new members, strong young people with imagination and energy. Ran answered the call with his first wife, Tamar, escaping city life; Orna came with her husband, Moti, hoping to raise their children in the Garden of Eden; Imi came with her first husband, Igor, trying to save their marriage. Altogether sixty young people joined the failed community, inspired by Dodik's vision of free choice with responsibility, in a beautiful forest home.

For dark and exotic Orna, an Iraqi Jewess and a bookkeeper, Beit Oren was like a hippie commune: "Exciting, lots of hormones, affairs, love stories, all kinds of stuff, it was fun, some got hurt."

"You?" I grinned.

"Not really."

"Moti?"

"Ask him!"

For blond and beautiful Imi, an artist, it wasn't much different: "It was like an adventure, parties, lots of friends and support, easier to get around, sleep around. Many couples separated, swapped—a big mess!"

It was 1988. Each family was assigned two rooms in an old building. To use the single kibbutz phone, they bundled through the rain and cold to the dining room. They had fifty shekels a month spending money, about twelve dollars. They didn't need more. The phone was free, and so was the single kibbutz car, and so was the gas. The families ate three meals a day in the dining room, where they took turns cooking and cleaning, and they received free cigarettes and chocolate. Entrance to the two or three movies a month was free, and they used points to buy groceries in the kibbutz supermarket. Imi ran the kibbutz cultural activities as well as the club bar. They worked with the cows or the bananas or in one of the small businesses, such as the hotel or welding shop. Most of the kibbutz veterans resented the new arrivals, but they knew their backs were against the wall. With Beit Oren owing more than $6 million and unable to pay even the bank interest, it was adapt or die.

Ran soon found a role as marketing manager for the Beit Oren hotel. Despite its superb location, it had been a financial drain for decades, not making a penny in profit. Ran picked up the challenge. First he filled the empty rooms with 350 recently arrived Ethiopian Jews, most of whom, as the Israeli press enthusiastically reported, hardly knew how to use the bathroom. "We made huge money," Ran said gleefully, "a million shekels a year, paid by the Jewish Agency." After the Ethiopians came Muslim refugees from Bosnia, also a good business. Then Ran turned the hotel into a drug rehabilitation center: "That didn't last long, people were afraid of the addicts." Another good business was renting out the rooms for day use: "We're near Haifa, people need to fuck somewhere. I put an ad in the papers, but in the next committee meeting I was harshly attacked. The members were unhappy, and so was the kibbutz movement. It was a good business, but they had an ideological problem. But I didn't have an ideology. I just did what had to be done to do my job."

Dodik was impressed. He had a clear vision of his ideal kibbutz, but had always failed in its implementation. Now in Ran he saw the means to his end. In 1990, he asked Ran to manage the entire kibbutz. Ran inspected the books and was shocked to find how poorly managed the place had been. The smallest decisions had been made by committee; and as a result, incompetence, gossip, and envy ruled. More fundamentally, Ran spotted the economic contradiction that had virtually guaranteed bankruptcy: the utter lack of any incentive to earn one's keep. Kibbutzniks always complained that there were two types of members—the suckers who did all the work and the parasites who did as little as possible. Ran found there were way too many parasites, precious few suckers.

As Ran sat before me, sipping herb tea in the woods, dressed for meditation and mantras, everything about him belied the image of a tough, innovative businessman. Yet clearly Ran was a man of many parts. "Everything was mixed up," he related. "Money came in, it went out; nobody knew what anything cost. The kitchen was mixed up with the bananas, the carpentry with the chickens, the hotel with the avocados, the welding with the kindergarten. There was no separation; it was all one big pot. There were no salaries, no measurement of profit or loss. But the members thought it was wonderful. They had a job to go to in the morning, they had lunch, went to sleep in the afternoon, had a nice evening, a great life. Yet they were bankrupt, and didn't know why."

When Ran gets going he speaks a hundred miles an hour, waving his arms, his graying cropped head flopping wildly. He laughed at the absurdity of it all. This indulgent economic system was okay when sympathetic Labor governments kept forgiving kibbutz debts. But when the right wing finally won an election in 1977, the kibbutzim lost their link to power, and the banks wanted their money back.

Ran went on to evoke the challenge of making real changes, speaking so fast I could hardly understand: "Take the carpenter. It takes him three weeks to build a cupboard. His true cost is three thousand shekels. But I can buy a new cupboard for three hundred. So we had to close the carpentry. The carpenter, an old guy, said to me, 'But I've been the carpenter here for thirty years.' He didn't understand and hated me."

Ran also met great resistance from the accountants who managed the financial affairs of the United Kibbutz Movement. When he told them that he wanted to separate the kibbutz businesses, they claimed it wouldn't help. When he insisted that it would, they told him, "No, because then you'll make money and have to pay taxes."

Again Ran was incredulous. "That's all they wanted," he exclaimed to me, laughing loudly. "No taxes. It was absurd!"

As time passed, the constant battles left Ran feeling increasingly discouraged and spent. He started to doubt whether change was possible. He also was starting to question what he personally stood to gain from even trying. The very nature of the kibbutz's organization meant that he had no future, probably no pension, nothing to pass on to his children; all he would have would be the daily headache of working with people who cheated, lied, and rejected change. "Let's take one worker I know of," Ran said, refusing to name names. "He works two hours a day and disappears the rest of the time. Or there are four workers in the laundry. What do two of them do all day?"

Ran's frustration grew until one day he couldn't take it anymore. He went to see Dodik in his small apartment and told him that he'd had enough; he wanted out. Dodik asked him if instead of leaving the kibbutz he could come up with a more formal plan for change, something concrete that they could push through together. "You won't like my solutions," Ran replied.

"Try me," Dodik answered.

So Ran went home and called his good friend Orna Dagon, the book-keeper. For three hours a day, after their regular jobs, Ran paced up and down in his small room throwing out ideas, while Orna organized them in her Lotus program and contributed her own thoughts.

Their first step was to analyze the kibbutz's businesses, determining which made money and which didn't. The chicken houses and banana plantation made money, but not much, while the avocados and cotton, and the garage and the carpentry, lost lots. Even the central accounting office operated at a loss.

Next, they calculated the real living expenses of this community of close to two hundred people. Sacrosanct areas of the kibbutz came under the microscope as never before. The dining room, the swimming pool, the laundry, the kindergarten, the schools, the clinic—all were costing money the kibbutz didn't have. "Let me put it this way," Orna told me. "Of course everyone wants a doctor standing by twenty-four/seven with nurses and all the medicines updated each year. But if you pay the real cost out of your own pocket, guess what? Suddenly it's okay to have just one nurse three days a week."

Comparing costs and benefits, and also taking into account the kibbutz's traditional ideology and way of life, Ran and Orna arrived at a series of proposals, some of which were already in motion, some of which were new, all of which were now captured in a coordinated plan with a rough timetable and measurable goals. It was simple but revolutionary: Each business that lost money would be closed. Everybody would be responsible for finding his own job, and everyone would receive a salary according to market conditions. Members who had jobs outside the kibbutz would keep their earnings instead of contributing their salaries to a central fund. Later, kibbutz land would be sold or rented out to pay off community debts. The dining room would close, along with the laundry and other key services, and each household would be responsible for its own purchases, meals, and bills. Each kibbutz member would contribute about 15 percent of his gross income to a safety net that would provide a pension for the elderly and would supplement the income of those who couldn't earn enough money. Kibbutz business profits would pay for all health services and education, and they would also fund pensions, reducing the members' direct contributions. Any further profits would be divided among the members. When members died, their heirs would inherit their homes. The basic principle would be independence, within a community.

Dodik loved it, but the members had to approve the plan with a vote, and, as Ran remembered ruefully, they were not happy. For twelve months, committees fought over every aspect of the plan. Veteran members feared losing kibbutz services and their cradle-to-grave guarantees, while the wider kibbutz movement saw this upstart failure beginning to resemble something anathema: private enterprise. Angry friends and neighbors cursed Ran at meetings and ignored him in the street. "Reaction to the program was very bad, even worse than to my earlier ideas. They were afraid. They felt threatened. They hated me. They ignored me. They said I just wanted to fuck them because I was a newcomer. They said I just wanted to earn more money because I would be the manager. And of course there was a lot of ideology— 'This is not why we came here, you're from the city, how dare you tell us how to live, this is our kibbutz, you're nothing here.' I don't know how or why I carried on."

Eventually Dodik persuaded the members of Beit Oren to give the plan a chance. He told them there was no other choice; if they didn't accept it, the kibbutz would shrink again, even more people would leave, and there would be no money at all. He reminded them that the kibbutz movement had already advised them once to give up and leave, so it was better to save at least a remnant of their old lifestyle rather than see it disappear entirely. In the end, Ran's plan passed.

To avoid a conflict of interest, and to show the members he wasn't just in it for a bigger salary, Ran wound up ceding management of Beit Oren and, in the face of so much personal animosity, leaving the kibbutz entirely. Dodik stayed on to bully through the changes himself. This wasn't easy for Ran, whose marriage had collapsed, partly due to the strain. As it turned out, life for him would remain tough for years. Shimon Peres, who would become Israel's president, called the growing privatization that Ran and Dodik championed part of a degrading slide to "swinish capitalism." Leaders of the national kibbutz movement attacked Ran for destroying the concept of a kibbutz, even as they recognized that his new model could save their livelihoods and homes. The fight had become personal for Ran. He sought work in other kibbutzim; none would hire him.

Finally, Ran came to Kibbutz Gesher Haziv near the Lebanon border. Of 120 kibbutzim in the United Kibbutz Movement, Gesher Haziv was in 119th place economically, and desperate for any help it could get. "They said, 'We heard about you from many places we checked,'" Ran said, "'and Beit Oren said you were a crazy bastard!' I was very hurt. I felt like crawling into a hole. But one of them was an American, a doctor of literature or something. When she examined my plan for Beit Oren, she was amazed at what I had done. I told them I didn't want to do it again. I was ashamed. I just wanted a salary. I didn't give a shit. I didn't leave Beit Oren with pride or a thought that I had done something wonderful. Only many years later did I understand what I had done."

A PROPHET IS NEVER HONORED IN HIS OWN HOME

One of the most pleasant experiences I had while researching this book was sitting around Margalit Battadan's dining table in Kibbutz Gesher Haziv. Three octogenarian kibbutz founders were swapping hilarious memories in a small, neat room densely packed with furniture, photographs, and food. For two hours, they all shouted and laughed at the same time; it was exhausting and fascinating. Margalit prepared cakes, cookies, and drinks for the occasion and rarely stopped smiling. She beamed, saying, "The most glowing part of my life is now." When I inquired why, she answered, "Because I divorced my husband thirty years ago!"

Yishai Hariri, age eighty, a dead ringer for Walter Matthau, had been the youngest of the group that immigrated from America in 1948, and he was still considered the baby. Nachman Goldwasser, eighty-two, with a pointy gray beard and bald, Lenin-style head, kept losing his line of thought. In midsentence he would suddenly stop, screw up his eyes, and say, "Oy, my memory." He would tap his forehead, exclaim, "Ach!" then say, "*Nu!* . . . Oy, oy, oy!" pause again, and then say, "Oh yes!" and continue on a completely different topic. That was fine; nobody listened anyway.

"Remember Margalit's wedding?" someone asked. "It was the kibbutz's first." Margalit laughed and recounted how at the time they were living in tents and the only hard floor was in the chicken coop, so they all stood around in the chicken shit. "I said to my husband, 'I'm not marrying you in that silly hat.' Everyone loved him, he was the catch of the kibbutz, so he said, 'That's okay, you don't have to marry me.'" Then Margalit slammed the table so that the cups shook in their saucers. "I said, 'Get up there now!'"

For years, each bride shared the same dress. For the wedding cakes, they collected everybody's ration of sugar, except for lucky Yishai, whose wedding cake came from a ready-mix packet from America. Margalit's father sent them a professional meat slicer, but they didn't have any meat. Yet such sacrifices were taken in stride. Here, doctors, lawyers, and students became construction workers and farm laborers and felt proud and fulfilled. They lived off apricots, oranges, and tangerines from the trees and mushrooms from the fields, all of which had been planted by the Arabs of Al-Zib, whom we met in the first chapter. "We were idealists from a youth movement," Yishai said. "We wanted a complete community of equals. We came to give, not like today. Times have changed."

Just how much times had changed became clear one day in the early nineties when the kibbutz, on the verge of declaring itself bankrupt, couldn't pay its water and electricity bills. They called in an outside expert: Ran Ronen. As Margalit recalled, the whole kibbutz gathered and fell silent as Ran began to speak. His first sentence made them all very nervous. "He said, and I'll never forget it, he said, 'I wish you had the luxury of postponing an extreme change here. You must go over to privatization. I'm here to help you.' He was wonderful. It cost a fortune, but it was worth it."

Nachman interrupted: "I didn't like him, not at all."

Margalit continued, speaking over Nachman, "You know why? Natty was very traditional. It gave him an ulcer to think there wouldn't be a kibbutz anymore." There were others like him, many who recoiled at the idea that the kibbutz would be reformed out of existence, leaving people on their own. To help ease the pain, Gesher Haziv set up a fund to support those who couldn't manage under the new system. Only four families really needed help. Everything was privatized, slowly, stage by stage, over about five years. Some people did see their emotional world cave in. One man on principle even stopped reading the newspaper because the kibbutz wouldn't pay for it.

As Yishai remembered it, Ran was brilliant and extremely convincing. "He made sense, and what he said was true. When we were a kibbutz, you took three brooms home in the year, but the moment you had to pay for the broom, one was enough. Same with the sick. Half the year they were sick, then when they had to earn their salary, suddenly they were healthy. We needed change. We closed the services, the dining room, and the laundry. There had been so much waste. But one thing did bother us. Friday evening supper was the only time we all got together, and we miss that today. Togetherness slips away; it's finished."

Margalit shrugged and raised the palms of her hands in a classic gesture, the silent "So what can you do?" "We're called the new kibbutz. But you know what? Our sons are coming back. That's the best part. Thirty of our children have come back to live here with their families. How else do you measure success?"

Margalit later asked me why I was so interested in Ran. I said he was a good guy and that as much as she respected him, he had had a hard time in his own kibbutz. His neighbors had hated him. Margalit smiled. "We loved Ran. It's written in the Bible: A prophet is never honored in his own home."

THE WORLD CHANGED

Today, the greatest asset possessed by most kibbutzim is their land, which had been granted to them by the state. Whether it's swapping idle fields for 7 percent ownership of a shopping mall, as Beit Oren did, or renting land to Toys "R" Us and Office Depot, as Kibbutz Shefayim does north of Tel Aviv, income from land is the kibbutz's easy path to wealth. Many sell tracts of former farmers' fields to anybody who can afford to build villas. And like Beit Oren, many kibbutzim have agreed to give homes to the children of members, even if they didn't live on the kibbutz before. Eventually they'll be able to buy and sell these homes. All these changes have attracted investment, businesses, and young people to the previously struggling kibbutzim, and all have turned the kibbutzim again into economically sound, socially vibrant communities.

Yet none of this has come without a price. Whereas once kibbutzim provided the country's air-force pilots, special-forces fighters, and political leaders, today their numbers in special military units are barely above the national average, and nobody looks to the kibbutz movement for leadership or inspiration. The kibbutz has lost its mythic stature, standing as just another comfortable lifestyle choice among many. The early guiding concept of "from each according to his ability, to each according to his needs" has become a quaint historical slogan. A kibbutz member today could own a fancy car, work in town, vacation abroad three times a year, and, like any other Israeli, barely know his neighbor, who could be living on minimum wage. Ari ben Zwi, who joined Beit Oren in 1940 and spent many years working with the cows, was astonished when he visited another kibbutz a few years ago. "I went to the milking station. There was nobody there. Only robots! In Beit Oren we don't even have cows anymore. Too unprofitable." What ben Zwi misses most of all from the old days is the ideals he shared with his friends. "It's over," he told me outside his home after our interview, "the world we knew."

Ran, with his sultry bookkeeper friend Orna Dagon, wound up developing a healthy business managing kibbutzim. They have advised dozens on how to privatize. Ran even spends one day a week in Tel Aviv as a consultant on financial survival at the headquarters of the kibbutz movement, advising people who in the early days would have tossed him out by the scruff of his neck. Some of them are still surprised to see him sitting in on their meetings. "It's like the lion lying down among the lambs," Ran told me. "But today I'm the mainstream. Of two hundred and seventy kibbutzim, about a hundred and eighty changed." It didn't end so well for Dodik. By 1998, despite the economic and social changes, he had failed to mold the spirit of Beit Oren to his utopian vision, and so, as he had every decade or so, Dodik left to start again. When I caught up with him at his new home in Rosh Pina, I found him disillusioned with Beit Oren and the time he had spent there. "The problem was that they didn't want to do anything about their society. They were happy with their new money situation; they lived in nice homes and had plenty to eat, and that's all they wanted. They hardly knew each other. So I thought, I came to change the society, and if they don't want to change, why do I need this?"

The bullet-headed former paratroop commander was anything but bowed. Now he had a new plan for a new kind of kibbutz, and he was visiting factories and communities around Rosh Pina to sell his vision—so far unsuccessfully. "It will come," Dodik said, with a glint in his eye, "step by step. You don't lift the mountain, you do it stone by stone." As he spoke, he leaned forward, fixing me with his eyes, as if to convince me. He exuded force, even in his midsixties. Gray chest hair poked from his checkered workingman's shirt, and his rolled-up sleeves revealed a long scar on his left forearm where he had been shot in the Yom Kippur War. Not for a moment did I think this visionary would ever give up. "I think the kibbutz movement today can be the beginning of a different and better society," he said, and then, not for the first time: "I have a plan."

Instead of a local kibbutz with internal membership, Dodik explained, anybody, anywhere could join, like a virtual community. Everyone would be free and could live and work where they liked: Jews from Rosh Pina, Arabs from Tuba, anybody who cared. He smiled warmly as he spoke, seeming positively messianic. Before I met Dodik, I had been warned that he was a man of few words, dour and brusque, but here he was in full flow, transported by enthusiasm, just like Ran. "It will be a community of interests, where people help each other and look after each other, a community within a community. You pay a contribution, and you can leave when you like. We need to strengthen our society, to care for each other again."

I wished him well and took my leave. I decided to set off for Beit Oren one last time, because I wanted to run Dodik's new idea past Ran. I now thought I understood better the difference between these two original thinkers. Their basic goals were still remarkably similar, but Dodik wanted to start at the top, by changing society, whereas Ran wanted to start at the bottom, by changing the individual. Either, I thought, was a thankless task, and yet the track records of these two men were formidable.

When I reached Beit Oren's gate, at the top of the long climb, I turned a sharp right, down past the stables and the paintball course, past the café and the bicycle shop, all private enterprises owned by kibbutz members, which would have been anathema before Ran and Dodik's changes. I turned off the path and skirted a field, past Ran's organic apricot and peach trees, whose blossoms sweetened the air. I parked the car by a fence made of dry branches and walked a hundred yards, past the herb garden, to the kitchen under the tree in the woods. There I found Ran discussing with colleagues the next activities he was organizing for his consciousness center, where he hoped to make people care more about themselves, so that they would care more about the world around them. Business was taking off; Ran was receiving bookings from organizers of spiritual workshops, ethnic dancing troupes such as Biodanza from Chile, a sweat lodge that wanted to build a tepee among the trees, a small Balkan orchestra, a Klezmer ensemble, wedding parties, and Jewish-Arab friendship societies, all of whom wanted to combine their events with a closer connection to nature. Crikey, I thought, it's working!

As I watched Ran speaking rapidly, waving his arms and pointing, the others listening, waiting to get a word in, I smiled and thought, This is how Israel was built. Strong and virtuous men and women, with the power, imagination, and doggedness to chase their dream, overcome every obstacle, and build something new against all odds. Much of what the pioneers accomplished and their methods have come under criticism with the passing of time, but that doesn't diminish from the character of the individuals—the dreamers and the doers. As Ben-Gurion reputedly said, to be a pragmatist in Israel, you have to believe in miracles. Ran and Dodik had helped change the kibbutzim, I thought, and now they each wanted to do just a little more—change the world.

Miracles can take time, though, and as Ran seemed as if he could be tied up for quite a bit, I waved and walked back to my car.

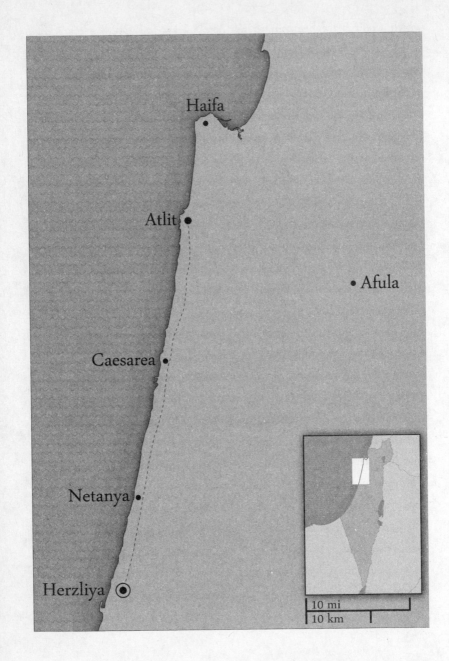

Haifa

Atlit

Afula

Caesarea

Netanya

Herzliya

10 mi
10 km

7

The Call to Arms

BEIT OREN TO HERZLIYA

Chips of carved marble lying in the sand offer the first sign that Caesarea is close; then come squared building blocks and fragments of curlicued columns half buried in the earth. An ancient wall is so overgrown it merges with the cliff. They say that in Caesarea you can dig in any direction and find an archaeological treasure. Waves lap on the pebbly beach beneath signs pointing to the Byzantine palace, the Byzantine Bathhouse, the Roman cardo and hippodrome, Herod's Palace, the Roman Theater, and the amphitheater that once held fifteen thousand people. Pontius Pilate ruled from here; the Roman officer Cornelius was baptized here; and Paul was accused here of being "a pestilent fellow" before he was dispatched to Rome for trial. Other signs point to the theme park Caesarea has partly become: The Crusader Café, the Old Port Bar, Herod's Hall ("weddings and events"), and a kosher café. The Romans killed twenty thousand Jews here in an hour, but today the Jews remain—where are the Romans? The entire coast offers a powerful lesson: Occupations come, and they go.

Day Ten of my trek. The muggy heat was finally lifting, and the huge red afternoon sun was almost touching the horizon. I picked my way carefully along the rocky beach, which had been narrowing over the past couple of miles. Now only a few yards of sand and rock separated steep, crumbling hills from the rising sea. My feet crunched on sandy pebbles that I was scanning with minute attention. I was looking for bits of broken blue glass, smoothed by seventeen hundred years of waves and current, which had fallen into the sea when the cliff collapsed beneath the Byzantine glass factory at Sidni Ali. Rough waves disturb the seabed and wash the shards ashore, where they nestle among rocks at the water's edge. I had once found a tear-shaped chunk of ancient glass as big as my thumb; a friend made it into a pendant for Hagar. Now I was so engrossed that the trembling ground and the sounds of thumping feet and grunting teenagers didn't register until the very last moment.

I sprang aside as they swept by, a bunched band of about a hundred boys and girls. They turned and whirled by me again, heading back down the beach. Some of the boys carried backpacks, probably filled with wet sand. Trundling in last place were a few heavier boys struggling to keep up. One was pulling another along, and I could hear them heaving and rasping.

Girls occupied the middle of the pack, running easily and smoothly, except for one pale, overweight girl with pigtails who looked as if she would drop dead at any moment.

I watched from a distance as the youngsters attacked a sand hill a hundred feet high, reached the top, ran down again, ran up again, then down again to the beach. There they dropped to the ground for thirty push-ups and thirty sit-ups. Stretched out on the sand, they looked like giant crabs scurrying from side to side. Dripping with sweat, they staggered to their feet and raced off along the water. After my halfhearted brush with mortality a few days earlier, I instinctively placed my hand on my chest and felt it beat, checking the rate.

I had chanced across Israel's best hope for its future defense—young people preparing to compete for entry into the nation's elite military units. Top of the ladder are the fighter pilots, followed in close order by a number of small, top-secret units that carry out the nation's toughest missions. Sayeret Matkal is the General Staff's reconnaissance unit; in their entire regular military service, soldiers in this group may carry out only one operation or even none. Their training is so lengthy, and their preparation for an operation sometimes so extensive, that it can take almost the entire three years of required duty. And then the operation can be canceled. Shayetet 13, the navy SEALs, who operate out of the secret base I passed in Atlit, are renowned for volunteering for every task that comes up, at sea or on land. Maglan, a special unit of commandos, are the multitaskers; they go deep into enemy territory to support missile attacks or kidnap top Palestinian militants at home, working alone or in groups.

Many dozens of kids apply for each spot in these units. What all those who make it share in common is at least eighteen months of excruciating training and the same psychological profile: You must be insane to want to join them. Or exceptionally motivated.

Yet these kids that I had come across represented only a small part of the total picture. Israel's defense minister, Ehud Barak, complained that the Israel Defense Forces, once the people's army, was gradually becoming an army of only half the nation, with the other half trying to evade service. Draft dodgers, he said, must face public scorn and carry "the mark of Cain." By law, at age eighteen, Israeli boys and girls must serve in the armed forces, boys for three years and girls for about two.[1] But figures had shown that in 2007, 28 percent of draft-age males and 50 percent of girls would not be drafted.

Now, as I watched these youngsters pounding away, I wondered: What's the emotional state of Israel's army? Had motivation to defend Israel dramatically declined, as Barak indicated, or were more than enough young people still eager to serve, especially in the elite units, as evidenced by the intense competition for places? What's the status among young people of an institution that had traditionally carried so much cultural weight—as a rite of passage, a national equalizer, the glue that held the state together?

These questions are of no small strategic significance. Palestinians and even many Israeli Arabs believe that they don't have to defeat the Israeli army; they just have to survive and avoid a peace agreement until Israel collapses from within. Eventually, they say, Israel will lose a war—it is the law of averages. Likewise, almost every Hamas or Al-Aqsa Martyrs' Brigades fighter I have ever met believes that their determination—born of lack of hope or any alternative to the struggle—will eventually triumph over Israel, whose people care only about how many foreign vacations they can take and how to get out of army duty. Such beliefs help prolong the conflict. But are they true?

HERE THEY CAN'T CALL ME A YID

It was an old woman called Sonya Arieli who first got me wondering about the extent to which Israeli youth really do still feel a call to duty. I had met her by chance three days earlier, sitting on a bench in Neve Yam, the first beach after Atlit. Or rather my wife, Hagar, had. She'd joined me on my walk after my little heart scare, wanting to make sure that I didn't collapse and die alone on the beach. She cheered me immensely; I realized now that walking alone for a week had been rather a strain. Hagar looked snappy beside me in her red blouse over pink, almost see-through linen pants, topped off with her red, yellow, and green straw hat. She seemed delighted to be with me, holding my hand, stopping us often to dance or bless the ocean, insisting that I sit cross-legged and meditate as the sun set. When I was searching in frustration for a fine phrase to describe the waves' gentle lapping, she immediately said, "Call it a lover's whisper." She had a friendly word for every fisherman, playful family, or stroller, and all smiled and answered in kind.

Hagar might exude friendliness and charm, but she's tougher than some of those soldiers-in-training. She was raised on Israel's third-oldest kibbutz, Ashdot Ya'akov, in the Jordan Valley. Only three days old, she was taken straight from the hospital to the communal children's home, for which she still holds a grudge against her parents. Her fondest kibbutz memories are of flying a kite in the fields and climbing onto a friend's back to spy on the boys in the showers. When Hagar was twelve, the family joined many others in leaving the kibbutz to try their luck in the city. I met Hagar when she was a nineteen-year-old army sergeant hitchhiking with her gun and beret. I, a cocky twenty-six-year-old news cameraman, skidded to a halt in my brand-new orange Mazda RX2. We never looked back.

Hagar loves to greet old people, whom she believes hunger for attention. Once, in Tel Aviv, she took the hand of an elderly stranger and chatted with him for half an hour. So when we saw an old lady sitting alone on a bench south of Atlit, Hagar said hello, and within moments we were absorbed in conversation with seventy-four-year-old Sonya, originally from Romania, owner of an inn in Nahariya where she lives with her husband, Shalom, and her 101-year-old mother.

Sonya was clever and funny, but we found her in a grumpy mood. As we learned in detail, she'd survived no fewer than thirty-two operations: heart, throat, legs, hands, and several cases of melanoma. But that wasn't what bugged her. Rather, it was the injustice of it all, the notion that misfortune had befallen her family instead of all the others she'd met at her inn. She had an unkind word for everyone. Of Fijian UN workers, she said, "They're always drunk. I had to put them to bed every night. And they're so heavy!"

Orthodox Jews: "I don't tell them what to do, why should they tell me what to do? All the time they say, 'Sei gesund, sei gesund'—be healthy—and then they stick their hands out for money. Get a job!"

Russian immigrants: "Lots of drunks, most of them aren't even Jewish!"

Georgians: "Liars and thieves. My neighbor wanted to buy my house. He threatened us and our kids. I said, 'Yossi, as long as I'm alive I'll never sell to you!'"

Gypsies: "In Romania they kicked us out and they got the Gypsies instead. It's like someone gets cancer. Serves them right! They'll take over. I hope so, anyway. Serve those Yid-haters right!"

Druze: "You try to buy a house in their village, they'll kill you! If a Jewish boy goes out with one of their girls, Oy ve voy!"

Arabs: "You can't be friends with a Muslim. Can't trust them. They'll kiss you and stab you in the back. There'll never be peace. They lie in the heart!"

With each outrageous statement, Sonya shot me a pitying smile, furrowed her eyebrows, and nodded sharply, as if to add, "Trust me!" I didn't, but I enjoyed her anyway. We had found a true gem, the uncluttered voice of the grumpy Israeli.

Sonya uncrossed her legs and leaned toward me, her voice rising, while

I kicked a ball back to a child who had been chasing it. "There have always been wars. You remember when there wasn't one? Where? When? No such thing as no war. Always was, always will be. Where isn't there a war?"

As I turned back from looking at the child, I flinched at finding Sonya's face inches from mine. "But isn't it time to make peace with the Arabs?" I asked. I hadn't wanted to go down this road; in fact, I had been trying ever harder to steer clear of this issue. But I couldn't help myself. "What if Israel loses a war one day?"

She snorted. "It can't happen. You know why? Because every Jew who can hold a weapon won't think twice. He'll fight, from small to big; we will always fight. When a Jew has a rope to his throat, he wakes up and does what he must."

Further questioning revealed that her husband had survived the Holocaust and fought in each of Israel's wars until 1973. All of her children and grandchildren were army officers. She gave me another pitying smile, as if I couldn't possibly understand. Then her smile vanished. "But what's the point? My grandson, he's a paratroop officer, and he can't get a job in Nahariya. He had to leave, while the Orthodox Jews, they don't do the army, they pray, they study. And the Arabs, they work and study. Okay, fine. Don't do the army? So, volunteer to help! In the hospitals, with poor people. Do something for the country! My boy? He can't get a job!"

So that's why Sonya was so crotchety—disappointment about her family's economic situation. "But I love Israel," she went on. "I don't want to go anywhere else. You know why? Because here they can't call me a Yid!"

I laughed. Instead she gets to call everybody else names.

PLEASURES OF MARRIED LIFE

Hagar and I walked together for three days. We slept on the beach and swam in the sea at night, letting the warm breeze dry off our bodies. It felt wonderful, like a second honeymoon. Between Atlit and Caesarea, and then south until Netanya, Israel offers a glorious stretch of coast, with small towns, kibbutzim, and a few beachside housing projects along the way. Sometimes, to gain a different vantage point, we strolled along the cliff top. Beneath pebbles, sand, and grass, we came across the mosaic floor of a ruined Roman home and the occasional ancient wine press.

We passed Dor, which the prophet Joshua mentions in the Bible when referring to the king of Dor, the king of Goyim in Gilgal.[2] When Napoleon finally abandoned the Holy Land after his defeat at Acre in 1799, his men pushed twelve thousand cannon overboard near Dor rather than surrender them to the Muslims. The weapons were quickly covered by the shifting sands, and the trove was discovered only twenty years ago when a researcher found the spot marked on an old map in a Jerusalem museum.

There are thousands of shipwrecks off Israel's coast, some dating back five thousand years. At the end of our first day's walking together, we washed off the sweat and dust by swimming out to the remains of a boat that sank in 1620.[3] Its hold was stuck in the seabed, but its wooden slats reached up into the clear water like bony fingers, schools of little fish darting through them. A nineteenth-century traveler wrote that Dor was "once a royal city, but it is a wretched place now, with hardly a single house fit for men or cattle."[4] Today, Dor has recovered and is a thriving kibbutz with one of Israel's finest camping beaches, in addition to its ancient harbor.

On our second day together, we tackled what I found to be the most beautiful stretch along the coast, Dor Habonim nature reserve, a succession of rugged coves, like canyons, at the water's edge. Water rushes in and out, spouting spray, with fish darting every which way. Hagar lost her footing and sprained her thumb while grabbing for a rock. She didn't complain, but I relieved her of our heavy backpack, which she'd been carrying for the past six hours. Fifteen minutes later, I turned to find Hagar tapping her temples with her thumbs. "It activates all the energy that is stuck in the body because of the shock of the fall," she explained. "It creates an activity in the body that wants to heal itself."

"Isn't it better to suck on your thumb?" I asked. "And what are you doing with your hands?"

Now she was holding her arms in front of her and shaking her hands violently, so that her fingers flopped around. "To say it's over. I'm releasing the poison in the body."

About three hours later, our bodies itchy from the sea salt after our frequent bathing to relieve the heat, we reached Jisr al-Zarqa, the only Arab township left on Israel's entire coast, and by far the poorest place on the coast. From the sea, Jisr al-Zarqa looks alluring, an oriental contrast to the manicured Jewish settlements. Water laps onto the beach and channels gently toward the town in a winding stream lined with green bushes on which birds flutter. The meandering flow points toward a white minaret that rises above a nearby dome, and there is a busy little fishermen's port with colorful boats and men working on nets. The breeze brings an appetizing aroma of fresh-brewed coffee.

The place seems perfect for tourism, yet there has always been resistance, especially from the town's southern neighbor, Caesarea, located on the other side of an artificial wall of earth and sand. The juxtaposition of these two towns is nothing short of damning. The poorest coastal community smacks up against probably the wealthiest, a private community established by the Rothschilds in 1948. Jisr al-Zarqa's roads are unpaved and dirty, and the houses are broken and shabby, while Caesarea is a model of suburban planning: wide, tree-lined streets, overflowing stands of bougainvillea and jacaranda, large villas with swimming pools and palm trees, and Israel's only full-size golf course. Caesarea's residents include former Russian oligarchs, Israeli business tycoons, former presidents and prime ministers. Their routine complaint about Jisr al-Zarqa is the noise of the Muslim call to prayer five times a day and the loud music that wafts over during frequent Arab wedding celebrations.

The beloved Rothschilds founded modern Caesarea, but the ancient town, which once rivaled Jerusalem, owes its status to Herod, the Roman-appointed king of the Jews. Herod was the evil genius of Jewish history, a reluctant convert, a brilliant statesman and tactician, and a Roman tool. Yet he left a unique mark on the landscape by rebuilding the Second Temple in Jerusalem, constructing his summer palace in Herodian and turning Caesarea into one of the great towns of his age. Caesarea remained the Roman capital in Palestine for 250 years. This is where Peter baptized the Roman centurion Cornelius, where Paul was imprisoned, and where Pontius Pilate governed while Jesus preached. It was the place from which Pilate set out for the Passover festival in which he sentenced Jesus to be crucified.

Hagar and I strolled along the bumpy cobblestones, admiring marble columns and headless statues. We also passed a great deal of tourist kitsch, including the Herod's Hall banqueting center, the Crusader Café, and a multimedia Time-Trek display. We hauled ourselves around metal barriers to climb the steep stone steps of Caesarea's amphitheater, which had not yet been opened for the day. Once I saw the Bolshoi Ballet perform *Giselle* here, but it is also where Titus, the son of the Roman general Vespasian, decided to celebrate his brother's birthday by forcing 2,500 Jews to fight wild beasts.[5] That was mild compared to another culling during the same period. In AD 66, Flavius Josephus wrote: "In one hour over 20,000 were massacred, and Caesarea was emptied of Jews."[6] The word often used to describe relations between Jews and non-Jews at the time is "acrimonious," which seems an understatement.

UNIFORM MAKETH THE MAN

As we passed through the dusty remains of the Roman horse track, the hippodrome, and continued down the coast, I reflected on what Rome's destruction of the Jewish presence in Palestine, and the two-thousand-year Diaspora, has meant for Israelis today. I thought of Sonya Arieli, who fled from Romania to Israel, and who helped build the country, thus closing the circle. Her hard life had a profound compensation for the Wandering Jew— "Here they can't call me a Yid!" She was sure that anytime Israel faced a real danger, no able-bodied Jew would think twice about fighting. It is this conviction that buttresses little Israel today—but again, how true is it?

Months later, I would visit an acquaintance to inquire about young people and changes in perception of the army. Reuven Gal is a former paratroop officer, chief army psychologist, and member of the National Security Council. Today, he runs a military research institute in Zikhron Ya'akov, near Haifa. When I mentioned Ehud Barak's criticism of the Israeli public's attitude toward service, Gal immediately accused Barak of both getting it wrong and making Israel's strategic situation worse. Gal said Barak had given gratuitous comfort to the enemy when he gave the impression that half of Israel was evading army service. The truth, Gal said, is that nine out of ten eighteen-year-olds who don't serve are Arabs who aren't allowed to serve, Orthodox Jewish boys who aren't required to serve, and religious girls who get an exemption. Of the remaining 10 percent who don't serve, half are genuinely unsuitable for medical or other reasons, such as a criminal record, while others, such as promising sportsmen or musicians, get special deals. Those who outright evade service comprise less than 2 percent of eighteen-year-olds, a figure that has hardly budged for forty years. So in Gal's view, it's wrong to say that motivation is declining. It's hardly changed. What has changed is the higher proportion of Arabs and Orthodox Jews in society, thanks to their higher birthrates.[7]

Gal admitted, however, that the number of soldiers who drop out during their service has grown considerably: Of conscripted male soldiers, 15 percent drop out before the end of their three years.

Well before I spoke with Gal, I had begun my research into the issue of young people's motivation by speaking with a person intimately qualified to know: Yuval Eilan, the trainer of the kids who nearly ran me over on the beach. Yuval has been putting kids through the ringer for twenty-three years. He runs an army-preparation course in Herzliya that toughens kids up physically and prepares them mentally to realize their dreams of joining the toughest combat units.

I met with Yuval in his home base of several drab, hangarlike rooms located within a fenced-off compound. In the yard, poles and barriers were set up as an obstacle course. Boys and girls leaned on them, changing from their school clothes into shorts and T-shirts and doing knee bends and push-ups, as others stood by chatting. Yuval told me that I had just missed the annual commemoration ceremony for graduates of his academy. Of five thousand graduates in twenty-three years, twenty-six had been killed. "In combat?" I asked. After all, many had gone into special units, almost all into combat divisions. But it turned out only five had died in action. The others all died in army training or in accidents off base.

Yuval kindly allowed me to sit in on a lecture. He stood in front of the blackboard like a regular teacher, although with his powerful build this forty-year-old looked more like a boxer. He wore a white-and-blue baseball cap with the emblem "Champion," with a tuft of hair sticking out the back. Sixty boys and girls sat transfixed, a degree of dedication most teachers could only dream of. Many of the boys had zits, and some wore braces. Their hairstyles varied; some wore it long, some had cropped it short, some had shaved it all off. There were beards and a few tattoos. All these kids had bright eyes and seemed eager to embrace life's challenges. I wondered how many would be dead in a few years. It's a thought you seldom have anywhere else in the world.

Later, as the boys and girls stretched and warmed up before a twelve-mile run, I asked Yuval what motivated the kids to work so hard, putting in five hundred extra hours a year after school. His answer surprised me somewhat. Mostly, he said, it isn't about the country, but about status. "The country's important, sure. But most of the kids want to succeed in life. In society, a special unit means you're a special man. Also, it's a way of being macho. Skinny little boys become accepted as men if they pass the test and get into a special unit. People look at them differently."

Yuval further noted that if you ask the kids directly why they want to be in a special unit, they are unable to answer. Sometimes he asks them, "How many of you would join a special unit if you had to wear a simple unit uniform, if nobody knows you're doing anything special? How many would want that?" According to Yuval, they get embarrassed and don't respond. Thus, he concludes that it's mostly about status.

Yuval explained that the true source of motivation comes from the parents and the love for country they impart by taking their children on trips into the desert or the mountains, listening to Israeli music, attending religious ceremonies, and talking about their own army experiences. "The kids themselves," he said, "it's amazing. They don't see anything, they don't listen to the news, they have no idea what's happening, they don't know history, the '67 war, the '73 war, nothing." But now, he said, the parents themselves are changing. They are questioning whether the special units are too risky. And while twenty years earlier many of the local boys wanted to become elite fighters, today their parents are telling them to go into noncombat areas such as computers or intelligence. "They're saying, use your head, don't fight. No sacrifices, less dangerous. It's changing."

"But why is it changing?" I asked.

Yuval shrugged, with a sad, knowing smile. "They got tired. It's all been going on too long."

A growing number of parents deliver a message, indirectly, to their kids that army service is not as important as it was, that they should do what's required of them and get on with their life. Israel is no longer seen as a country fighting for its survival. It has survived. So sacrificing oneself for the country seems less critical. "Now it's about, 'What kind of life will I lead? What can the army do for me?' People have changed. The most motivated are the religious, the immigrants, kids from the development towns. They see the army as a way to make their mark."

THE NAVY SEAL

Although I believed Yuval's argument that army youths today were mainly trying to get ahead, I wanted to hear from some of the young men myself. I knew from my own circle of friends how traumatic army service can be for most people. In a volunteer army, like the American or British, soldiers are intuitively more prepared for battle, or they wouldn't volunteer in the first place. But when everybody is conscripted, obliged to answer the call to arms, anybody with a reasonable level of health can find himself on the front line, regardless of mental aptitude. Three months of basic training is supposed to toughen up the body of the most coddled mommy's boy, but it doesn't always prepare them emotionally for what they will face. While Israeli combat soldiers may achieve high status, a high number are also screwed up.

I chatted with one boy in Yuval's course, and we agreed to meet the next day at his home in Ramat Hasharon, an upscale little town ten miles from Tel Aviv. Ofir Minsk didn't have much time: The next day, he was taking the last of his high school exams, on civic responsibility. His books and papers covered the whole kitchen table, the television was on ("just for the music"), and his baby-faced younger brother smiled sweetly and turned the volume down. Ofir was of medium height but muscled, with a confident, clear-eyed gaze. Before he started with Yuval, he hadn't been a skinny little boy who had wanted to become a man. He'd been a fat little boy. "I weighed two hundred pounds and lacked confidence. I just went with the flow. Now I've changed a hundred and eighty degrees. I was with Yuval for a year, and I'm a different person. I'd never run a mile before or done push-ups. Now I weigh a hundred and seventy pounds, and it's muscle. I'm being conscripted in two months."

"Do you know what you're going to do yet?" I asked.

"Shayetet Thirteen," he answered proudly. So this former fatso was going to be a navy SEAL.

"Good for you," I said, "congratulations. But why join Shayetet?"

Ofir explained that he was a Boy Scout leader. His father, a doctor, had once been a paratrooper and had continued in the reserves in an elite rescue unit known as 669, Yuval's unit. Ofir's mother was an architect. His grandparents were Holocaust survivors from Romania. It was a classic Israeli pedigree, as classic as his reasons for wanting to serve in an elite unit: "I really like this country. It is very small and we have many bigger enemies. We need to protect it. If I don't do it, who will? It's just clear to me that I want to do what I need to do, more than I need to do, even, and be an officer. I don't know why. I want to improve myself and improve others. I want to keep the chain going. It comes from the Scouts. From Dad. I don't know why. I feel like a leader."

Ofir had hardly thought about the army before he went on a Scout trip to visit Yuval's training course. Then he got interested. He researched the different army units on Wikipedia, googled them on the Internet. "It turned me on," he said, and as he gestured I noticed how easily his biceps flexed. "It's a great feeling to know that what I'm doing really counts, to protect the people you love. Some people wanted to join a special unit. Others just wanted to lose weight. I did both!"

To pursue an officer's track, Ofir planned to spend five to six years in the military. Observing that this was a pretty large chunk of time, I asked him what he planned to do afterward. His answer hewed closely to Yuval's interpretation: "I'm not worried. Being an officer in Shayetet will only help me later. It helps to be a combat officer in Israel. The whole country will be open to me. I want to be something in national security, maybe start as a security guard with El Al, then join the Shin Bet or Mossad maybe. But who knows? Maybe I'll be a biologist."

I apologized for taking up valuable cramming time and turned off my recorder. As I got up to leave, I thought of a final question: How about the kids who get out of army service?

"I don't say I hate them," Ofir instantly replied. He paused, giving me enough time to snap the recorder back on. "Maybe they have their reasons, but I think they should lose some rights as citizens. Because they don't do their duty as every citizen does. The country gives you schooling, a home, supplies, and you should give something back, at least three years. Not everyone needs to be combat; each according to his ability—if you're good at computers go to intelligence. Help the country, that's the first thing."

YOU HAVE NO CHOICE

Hmmm, help the country. What does that really mean to a young soldier today? Israeli soldiers are admired abroad as highly skilled, highly motivated fighters, and they are also reviled as bullies and Nazi-like murderers. Yet the fact is that most combat soldiers spend at least half their service in a mundane and difficult role, as superpolicemen overseeing the Palestinians. Is that what they're so motivated to do? Can such a motivation last on a national scale? Will it ultimately sap the strength to fight in a true war of survival? I wanted to find out, so I asked my son to gather together a few friends, enlisted soldiers, whom some around the world call war criminals.

Because Israel is so small, it is common for even combat fighters to come home for the weekend. One summer afternoon shortly after my visit with Ofir, four kids who had known one another since kindergarten gathered around my kitchen table, picking at grapes, strawberries, and nuts.

There was Alon, whom I had known since he was four or five years old. It was bizarre to see him as a fighter; when you think of the fearsome Israeli soldier, you don't think of the little boy you fished out of the pool because he couldn't swim, or whose little black dog barked too loudly at night. Now he was a veteran army medic in a combat search-and-rescue unit. Opposite him sat Daniel, approaching the end of one of the army's longest and toughest training courses in a supersecret combat unit. To his left sat Guy, a paratrooper who had seen almost constant service in the West Bank. And at the head of the table was Ofer, a slim, swarthy boy in intelligence (nobody asked for details, and none were offered). They were all twenty years old. At first they talked quietly and softly, defensive before the elderly foreign reporter who posed the questions, but soon they loosened up, laughing with one another and treating me more like their friend's dad. They were talking about the West Bank and how they treated the Arabs. I wondered whether fear or hatred of the Arabs was what made some serve so keenly.

"Tell me," I asked the group, mindful that roughly 20 percent of Israel's population were Arabs. "Before you joined the army, did you ever actually meet any Arabs?"

All four started talking at once. Their rapid-fire Hebrew was laced with slang and cusswords. Clearly, I had touched a nerve.

"You know," one of them said, "at work and stuff, nothing really . . ."

"You had Abu Snena . . ." another pointed out.

"Yes, there is an Arab school and we chatted with them all year long by e-mail, and one time we went to visit them . . ."

"No," one broke in, "there's not much dialogue. There's no connection."

And then the first: "The cleaner at school is usually Arab."

The conversation went on, each talking more quickly and more animatedly than the last. Somehow they were all able to talk at the same time, listen to the others, and respond appropriately, but I was quite lost. I went to my home office and returned with my Masai talking stick, which a chief in Kenya's Masai Mara once gave me. The Masai sit under a tree, and only the man holding the colorfully beaded stick is allowed to talk. I explained this arrangement and gave the stick to Ofer. It was immediately ignored.

"We don't have a reason to connect to them, to be in touch with them."

"Before we even know Arabs we're saying that the Arabs are sons of bitches, they're shit, they're thieves, et cetera. Now, if you grow up with Arabs, for sure you won't think they're sons of bitches, but you'll think they're people. When I'm at the checkpoint, when I speak to Arabs, I come with the attitude that they're people . . ."

"Its not the same at the checkpoint . . ."

"It's the same!"

"It's not the same. An Arab can come to you, a great guy, not a Jew hater. You chat, and he'll go tell his friend, 'Listen, this checkpoint is not serious, they're *hafif*, not doing their job properly, and he goes this way, and the other one goes the other way, and at the end, brother, after two days you get a car bomb there. So you're not allowed to take it easy at checkpoints, even if the princess of England comes."

"Sure, there are things you better not do, but okay, why do so many Arabs hate us? Because we're making their lives hell at the checkpoints . . ."

"You can never know. When eleven-year-old girls come to you with explosive belts, I believe . . ."

"It's a problem . . ."

"You have no choice. You can't take the risk of not checking her because she looks okay to you . . ."

"No, God forbid not to check, I'm checking everyone at the checkpoint.

I'm talking about what's happening at the checkpoint in general, these are things that . . . You were at checkpoints, right? You know how it works there. You take somebody aside . . ."

"I didn't abuse them too much. There were Arabs whom I left with their underwear, they looked . . ."

"But I'm talking about people who're looking at it from the side, like Martin. They say, 'How can you judge based just on what he looks like?' You can say, 'This is the reality,' but you can also say, 'Listen, the reality shouldn't be like that.'"

I offered the talking stick again but nobody took it.

"At the beginning you feel sorry, and after a while, like three weeks, four weeks, you're getting into a routine, so you just do it without thinking."

"Do you think whether it's the right thing to be there?"

"It doesn't really matter what you think. We had a soldier, a British soldier, he was twenty-five years old, he came here as a volunteer, and he thought it was wrong what we're doing to the Arabs, he was totally against it, but it doesn't matter, if someone says you have to do it, so you got to do it. You know, it's an army."

"You don't have your own mind in the army, let's say that, it's not your mind thinking."

"You have no choice . . ."

"We had a bomb explode by us. . . . You should have seen it . . ."

"I believe that a soldier's finger is worth more than the whole of Gaza, that's what I believe in, that the security of one of our soldiers is worth more than the lives of all of them."

"No problem, I agree with you, but do you agree that the world sees it and thinks that it's not right?"

"But the world doesn't live what we live."

"Yeah, his cousin in Holland, he's twenty-two, he knows nothing about these things."

"Okay, how do you want him to know?"

"I don't want him to know, but I don't want him to criticize if he doesn't know."

"Nobody wants to go to the army."

"I would also prefer that we'll be okay with everyone, and that there will be no wars for three thousand years."

This last point was greeted with mutters of agreement. Nobody disputed that, nor did they believe it would come to pass. The boys offered affirmative grunts that basically meant "Keep dreamin', baby." It was the kind of hopeless final thought thrown out by someone who knows in his lifetime he'll fight at least a war or two.

It was painful to see how quickly these young men have to grow up, and it starts way before the army. I remembered taking a carload of eleven-year-old friends of my son to a soccer match. They were chatting gaily during the twenty-minute journey, but it was all about bombs—what kind there are, how terrorists conceal them, in a radio or buried in a loaf of bread, how to spot one, how many pounds of explosives do what kind of damage, the difference between an explosion in an open street or inside a mall. One remembered a television report he had seen that showed a terrorist's head lying in the road and explained that the bomb always blew off the bomber's head because it exploded as he carried it on his chest, so if you see a severed head it's usually the bomber's, although not always—one bomber grabbed a girl, and her head was blown off too.

Growing up in London, I used to go to soccer matches at that age, but I don't remember what we used to talk about—probably a television program, or maybe Miss Gibson, the young schoolteacher who taught biology and the solar system. We all used to giggle and ask her to show us Uranus. Different place, different times.

Then again, what's it like to be an eleven-year-old Arab growing up in Gaza?

NERD FOR A DAY

I was probing deeper into the minds of these young soldiers, and I was finding their mental world to be a rather confused place. My son's friends were forced to relate to all Arabs, even eleven-year-old girls, as potential killers, while knowing that the vast majority of them were not. And then they returned home on furlough, to find their friends frolicking on the beach. Who wouldn't be confused? I wanted to take the boys aside one by one to delve a little further. First I spoke to Alon.[8] We were sitting around the pool after the other boys had left. It was dark now, and with his friends gone I found him speaking more frankly. What he said surprised me and added quite a bit to the picture Yuval had given me.

The truth was that after eighteen months as a medic, with the same length of time looming ahead of him, Alon thought he'd done enough to help the country. He wanted out so that he could help himself and get on with his life. He hoped to begin studying business management as soon as possible. He had already started a real estate company with a friend, who hadn't joined the army at all, and they were looking for business opportunities together. "All my army service, I knew I wanted to leave early. My head was never in the army. I always told my friends that I don't really need this, an eighteen-year-old isn't supposed to do this. They take you straight out of one structure, school, and put you right into another one, the army. It isn't right. You don't have time to think."

I asked him whether his desire to leave came as a shock to his friends in the unit. After all, they had been together for a year and a half, had fought in Gaza together, and come out with just a few scratches. Alon's own head had smashed into the metal wall of his armored personnel carrier when it crashed into another vehicle at night. His helmet cracked, but it saved him.

Alon shifted uncomfortably at my question, and I knew that it must be doubly hard to feel that he was deserting his mates. "Well, they said, 'So why are you here in the first place?' I said, 'I dunno, my father, I guess.' My dad was proud; he could tell his friends he has a son in a combat unit. Whenever he saw me, he gave me two hundred shekels! But nobody would be surprised if I left the army. Nobody would think it's a shame."

Alon revealed that he had already begun his journey home by pretending to be sick. His mother had given him a niacin pill, which causes as a side effect a temporary rash. With red blotches all over his body and face, he had visited the army doctor, complaining of nausea and headaches. The doctor took one look at him and sent him home to rest for three days. Before returning for another checkup, Alon took another pill. The rash reappeared, and he was immediately sent home again. "It worked like a charm," he said, smiling. He had seen a social worker and was now waiting for an appointment with an army psychiatrist, one of several he'd need to fool on his premature journey back to civvy street.

I asked Alon how he planned to persuade the psychiatrist to release him from the army. He cracked a boyish smile that belied the deceit he was planning. "I have a game plan. I'll start off the same as with the *kaban*, the social worker. With the *kaban*, I crumpled up my uniform so that I looked scruffy. I hitched my pants up high. Went in like a nebbish, a nerd." That couldn't have been easy; Alon is handsome, well built, and outgoing. He went on, "I carried a book, elves and hobbits or something, and I never looked him in the eyes. Eyes on the floor, you know, no confidence." He leaned forward, demonstrating, looking miserable and lost.

"You should be an actor," I said.

Alon raised his eyebrows in acknowledgment, looking even more boyish. "The *kaban* asked right away, 'Why are you here?' I felt bad about saying, 'I want to get out of the army,' so I waited a bit, worked myself up, and burst into tears. I said 'I can't be here, within the system, it's hard for me.' Then I said, 'I can't talk about it.' I held my head in my hands. I said I suffered depression because of my mother's sickness, and my grandfather had a stroke.

I cried, quite loudly. Actually, I always do that when I talk about my family. My family's much better now, but I just behaved as if it was all still going on. I said there was nobody else to look after them and I felt bad, depressed. I said I'm scared to die. I didn't mention suicide. That used to be good, but everybody does it now, so they get suspicious. He asked if I have friends and I said, 'Yes, one.' I only smiled when he asked about the book, you know, to show I'm lonely. I said I never had a girlfriend. When he asked why, I said I didn't know. You know that group in school, the nerds? I put myself into that group. Nerd for a day! If he asked me whom I loved the most, I was going to say my dog. But he didn't ask. My eyes were red when I left the *kaban*, but really red. I felt, whoa, damn, my life really is like that! I really almost was depressed! He wrote that I'm medium depressed, so that's a start. I gotta see the psychiatrist in two weeks."

A little over two weeks later, I called Alon to learn what had happened at the army psychiatrist, and he said he was practically in shock and would come right over to tell me. "I couldn't believe it," Alon said when he arrived. "I stuck to my plan. When I got up in the morning, I had butterflies in my stomach. But I knew I was doing the right thing, I just had to get through the day." He was speaking quickly, excitement garbling his words, and I had to ask him to slow down. I knew he'd lost all motivation to serve, and I wanted to understand exactly how hard or easy it was to get out of the army. It was common knowledge that the army didn't really need all the conscripts; they were called up mostly to keep up the appearance that everybody shared an equal burden, which everybody knows is patently false. Combat fighters are in the minority, yet they do the lion's share of time in the reserves.

Frankly, Alon's case for dropping out didn't seem that strong to me. I thought the army would tell him that if he didn't want to be in a combat unit, or be a medic, there were plenty of other ways he could while away another eighteen months. And if he was so needed at home, they could give him a job that would enable him to go home every night.

Alon told me that he'd arrived at the psychiatrist's and after waiting a bit had been called in. It was a small room, and the shrink was a big guy, a Russian. Alon had pushed his shirt into his bag for a day to wrinkle it all up, and he'd shaved his stubble to make himself look like a good little boy. The psychiatrist began by asking him why he was there. Alon couldn't speak, so he slumped forward and held his head in his hands and looked at the floor. "He said, 'What's your problem, you got problems at home?' So then I started crying. He said, 'Do you want pills to calm down?' and I kinda shouted at him, 'What, you think pills will solve my family problems?'"

Alon laughed in recounting this, making it clear that he hadn't really been angry but had just been acting. "He asked, 'Do you want to continue in the army?' I shook my head, no. He says, 'What's your mother's phone number?' I didn't expect that. So he sends me outside for a minute and calls. I'm waiting, and I don't know what's up. Then he calls me back in and says, just like that, 'Okay, I'm letting you go.' I say, 'What do you mean, letting me go?' He says, 'I'm letting you go out of the army.' Then I broke character. I was too surprised. I looked right at him, in the eyes for the first time, no stuttering or mumbling, and I said, 'That's it?' He said, 'Yeah, that's it.'"

Alon had spent only three minutes in his first meeting with the army psychiatrist, and the psychiatrist had asked Alon's mother only one question: Do you want your son to leave the army? She had answered affirmatively, and their conversation was over.

An hour later, Alon appeared before a medical committee that also asked one question: Do you want to leave the army? Again Alon answered that he did, and that was it. "I was in shock," he said, "it was so quick." He called a few friends, and reactions were mixed. "My ex-girlfriend was devastated, disappointed in me, happy for me, but totally against what I did. Some guys in my unit said congrats, I'd do the same but my parents wouldn't let me. You know, it's hard to be in the army, but it's harder to go against the flow, say no and get out of it."

I JUST LOVE THE COUNTRY

I was as shocked as Alon at how easy it was for him to evade service, for I knew plenty of soldiers who had failed to persuade the psychiatrist. Just the day earlier, a friend had told me how miserable his son was in the army. He had been a combat soldier for two years, and then suddenly, abruptly, felt he couldn't continue. But when the psychiatrist asked him why, he just said he didn't like it anymore. "He doesn't know how to lie!" my friend complained bitterly, and his son was told to report back to his unit as a cook. Now he was in jail for a month for refusing to go. Alon, meanwhile, was chilling out on the beach.

"How do you feel about Alon getting out?" I asked Daniel Shaki, the tough-looking lad with tightly cropped light brown hair who had sat opposite Alon at my kitchen table. Daniel had come over for a swim in the pool on one of his rare army furloughs. Like Alon, he had been in the army for eighteen months, but his story was different. While Alon felt he'd done enough, Daniel felt he hadn't even started. All he had done for a year and a half was train. He'd been recruited to Maglan, the special commando unit. Physically he looked the part, yet he also seemed painfully young. I could see he was torn between loyalty to friends in his unit, who were ready to sacrifice their lives, and to childhood friends such as Alon, whose sense of serving the country was, shall we say, more flexible.

"Look, do I like people leaving the army? No. It's hard for me. I come back on the weekend, my back is killing me, my legs ache, all I want to do is sleep, and all my friends are calling, saying, 'Let's go out, there's a party.' They're on the beach, girls, lots of fun. But you know, I made my choices. I don't mind about Alon. It's his life."

I felt that Daniel really meant it. Despite all his physical sacrifice, he understood well the larger context. "Look, my cousin in Holland is about my age, soon he'll have his first degree, but us, we live this reality, with enemies all around us. We have to give so that we can live here in peace. At age eighteen, if that's what the country asks of me, it seems fair to me."

A few weeks later, Daniel dropped by again. He was totally psyched. Finally he'd finished his course. After a weeklong mission, hiking fifteen hours a night, carrying ninety pounds of gear, four men carrying a fifth on a stretcher, one hour's sleep a day, they had finally reached the top of a hill in the Negev Desert. There, as they struggled up, almost crying with exhaustion and pain, all the veteran fighters from the unit ran down and helped them to the top, supporting them, carrying them. "It was so moving," Daniel said, his eyes gleaming. "There was a big red sunset. Everyone was cheering and shouting. We had champagne, cigars, music. They called our names, and I was the last because of the alphabet, and then the commander pinned the badge on my chest. What a moment. It's one of the toughest courses in the army. So now I can piss in a bottle, crap in a bag, and sleep in a tree for a month. For Israel!"

"Wonderful," I said, shaking his hand. "But I still don't get it. Why? What's the difference? You grew up together, Alon wants out, you want in. You both have a foreign mother who doesn't really care about the army, fathers who didn't particularly push you, although both preferred you do combat, so why does Alon want out so badly and you want in so badly? What motivates you?"

This big, strong, elite warrior looked at me, smiled, and shrugged. "I don't know. I just love the country. When I see all the people on the beach, I just feel warm and love them. It grows on you in the training. I walked six thousand miles in the course. We carry up to seventy percent of our body weight. It was freezing at night, boiling in the day, guys dropped out all the time. We went up one hill, and I was in agony, I was crying. Seven months later, and I'm still having physical therapy for the damage I did to my knee. But I knew I would never drop out. I had to finish it. It's inside me. I don't know why. Now I'm excited. I'm ready. I can't say it'll be fun, but we're trained for this."

What exactly he'd been trained for, he wouldn't say. It's secret.

Not entirely, though. A simple Google search on Maglan reveals a small unit that stresses camouflage and can operate secretly all over the Middle East. The unit carries out shoulder-fired missile attacks on enemy targets and lights them up with lasers to guide airborne bombing runs. Counterterrorist operations at home include, among many unpleasant tasks, the ultimate one: assassination.

IT ISN'T ABOUT A NOBLE DEATH

Alon had said that the hardest thing was to go against the flow and leave the army, but actually, the hardest of all may be to go against the flow and stay in the army anyway—to put your life on the line for something you're not really sure about, to fight not out of motivation but obligation.

That's how it was put to me by another soldier, Matan Shimon, the son of a close friend in Herzliya. Matan knows whereof he talks. He started out in Daniel Shaki's fearsome unit, Maglan, and is now a twenty-nine-year-old staff sergeant in the paratroopers' reconnaissance battalion, part of Israel's half-million-strong reserve army. Matan is a machine gunner who totes the Negev, an Israeli-made weapon that fires a thousand rounds a minute. "When you ask about motivation, you're talking from a different textbook," he said. "That's past. All I do is carry, walk, shoot . . ."

Matan sniffed at the great Zionist heroes such as Herzl and Nordau. He dismissed Yosef Trumpeldor, the Hebrew warrior who died on the battlefield after exhorting his comrades, with his legendary last breath: "Never mind, it is good to die for our country." This mythic message is drilled into all Israeli schoolchildren, although Yuval Eilan, the youth trainer, said Trumpeldor's last words were probably in his native Russian and more along the lines of "Oh shit!" And the historic battle of Tel Hai, where he was finally killed in 1920, according to Yuval, was more of a minor skirmish involving a dozen fighters: "It was like a fight with local bandits and others—and now it's in our mythology."

Matan's take on soldiering is just as prosaic: "Slogging though south Lebanon, you don't think of Trumpeldor and the country. You're scared, the camo paint itches the face, and you need to take a dump."

Bringing cold beers from the fridge in his small Tel Aviv apartment, Matan, a lawyer of medium size and build, struck me as every bit the reluctant warrior. There's nothing macho about him; he's sensitive, clever, and soon he appears nervous, running his hands through his hair, frequently clearing his throat. I couldn't see Matan with a blackened face, carrying a heavy machine gun and an eighty-pound backpack. He sat by the open window, overlooking the sea just a block away, drinking beer from the bottle and blowing cigarette smoke outside to avoid my face. Loud opera wafted in from a neighbor's stereo. It was peaceful and pleasant, which made Matan's subsequent outburst slightly shocking. He was rejected from Maglan[9] after eight months' training, and I had asked him why. His response: "I felt I was being abused. The sergeant was a fucked-up guy who saw his best friend kill himself in the army, and the officer was a virgin religious officer who doesn't know shit from brains, a stupid fuck who obviously didn't like me because I was against everything they stand for, and they had the power and I didn't."

Whoa, I thought. What happened to the calm, gentle guy?

Matan also grew uncomfortable when I asked him to describe what happened the day his unit was ambushed. It was the most publicized fiasco of Israel's 2006 assault on Hezbollah in south Lebanon. "The whole mission was dumb," Matan said. "The orders were stupid."

A large force of soldiers, their faces blackened, walked across the border at night in two long lines. But they didn't carry the proper equipment; they had the wrong flak jackets, Matan's helmet was too big, they had to buy their own food, and they drew water from wells in Lebanese villages, which luckily Hezbollah hadn't thought of poisoning. The grenade launcher lacked grenades. Worst of all, they set off much too late and walked much too slowly. Some of the guys were fat and slow, Matan said, plucked too abruptly from civilian life. Instead of arriving in the dark and hiding, they arrived around nine in the morning in bright daylight. "So we were spotted, obviously," Matan said, pausing to swallow.

He ran his hands through his light brown hair. Three years were not enough to remove the trauma. He sat cross-legged, like a Buddha, on the chair. "Instead of spreading out in the fields and hills, we were told to crowd into two houses. That's what we do in the West Bank, but here in the open, it's the wrong thing to do. What a mistake!"

About 120 soldiers crammed into the bigger house, with all their gear, and another 40, including Matan, who couldn't get in, bedded down in the next house. "That saved us," he said quietly. "We were sleeping, dozing, lying across each other, waiting. We heard the noise, the planes, bombs, explosions, shooting, yelling. It was getting closer all the time. And then, around noon, well, we didn't really hear or feel anything, just a bigger, closer bang. Then we heard it on the radio: Two, maybe three missiles hit the other house. We had nine dead and twenty-nine wounded. Basically, everyone said, 'Let's get the fuck out of here. It's becoming crazy.' We left the house and spread out in the bushes and fields, like we should have in the first place. Ammunition was exploding in the fires. It took four or five hours to get the wounded away, much too long. We stayed there four days; people were looking for body parts."

Matan didn't have the words, much less the inclination, to describe what he'd seen or how he'd felt. "Look, it took me a year to deal with this and even now I try to keep it far away, not to get traumatized." He went on: "What was it like? I don't know, scary, shitty. I feel awkward because I can't explain it well. For me, bottom line, I didn't get hurt, they did. I had a lot of friends who got killed and wounded. I was lucky. That's all, no big words or ideas. I was also lucky not to get sent in to clean up the body parts. It's sad, scary, frustrating, basically sad and scary, I dunno . . ."

He took a long breath and gave one of the deepest sighs I've ever heard. "I dunno. Some people can describe it better. I dunno."

After sitting in silence, I asked him what had happened when he'd returned home. He answered sharply that he had to take his university exams in law and government. Not surprisingly, he failed miserably. "It must be hard to balance war with a legal career, or any career for that matter," I commiserated. "But you're twenty-nine, so probably you'll fight another war one day."

"You think so?" Matan said. "I hope not."

"You can always leave . . ."

"Yes, but I think I'll just plan on inertia. You know, it isn't hard to get out of reserve duty. But when you get *tsav shmone*, the call-up to war, that's it. By then you can't leave. You'd be the ultimate pussy. We're really good friends, my unit, and that's part of it. It isn't about a noble death, dying for my country. No. I don't know anybody who thinks like that. But if we want to live in this country, and maybe have to die for the flag, well, I don't have any real opportunity to live anywhere else."

After his three years of regular service, Matan followed the time-honored postarmy trail to India, where, like many other Israeli ex-soldiers, he got into drugs to recover. A few fall into a deeper pit, but most return home and get on with their lives. When I asked him whether he would fight again, he said that he and all his fellow reservists feel the same. "It's hard, but someone has to do it, to take care of the country, and that's it. It's part of our life here."

By chance, I'd caught Matan just as he was preparing for a month of reserve duty, set to begin three days later. He will do up to thirty days a year until his midforties, or as long as it takes if there's a war. He was pragmatic. His kit list included a small television set, a poker set, backgammon, cigarette cartons, music, books, coffee, and a pillow. He wasn't upset at losing another month of his life. On the contrary, he was delighted to spend four weeks with his army mates, happy also to miss a month of his legal internship. I ran by him the Palestinians' fervent hope—or, maybe, their crutch—that Israelis like Matan ultimately couldn't hack it, that they didn't have the staying power of the Arabs.

"Huh," he said, "it just isn't true. Demographically, maybe they can beat us one day. But to fight? Sure, they have more rage than me. And you know what? In the territories, when we're patrolling, roadblocks, the rest, I don't hate anyone. I feel shitty about the stuff that we do. We may not have the same determination as their fanatics. It's true that people here may be less willing to die for our cause, but when we go to fight, nobody thinks he's going to die. It's an obligation. As I said before, we accept this, it's just part of our life."

A PEOPLE'S ARMY AFTER ALL

On the whole, my son's friends, with some notable exceptions, seemed to bear out the idea of waning enthusiasm for the military. They, too, were going through the motions, with varying degrees of conviction. Yet enthusiastic or not, all the boys said the same thing: This is their country, and they don't have anywhere else to go. So while the call to arms, once a glorious opportunity to serve the nation, has for most become less venerated, it still constitutes a vital imperative. Even if they do like their foreign vacations, most Israeli youth feel they have no other choice but to fight. In this respect, they are just like the kids on the Palestinian side.

Of course, still another decisive factor for any soldier is the confidence he or she feels that society supports them. This brings me back to my wife, Hagar. After the Lebanon war, Matan and his buddies wanted a fun day for everybody in their unit, with families, at a hotel somewhere on the beach— lunch and dinner by the pool, massage in the spa, that kind of thing. It would be a way of winding down from the disaster that hit them in that house near the village of Debel in south Lebanon. These young veterans couldn't afford it, so they asked for help. The word got around, and somebody volunteered to raise the money. Matan reminded me: It was Hagar. She persuaded the manager of the Sharon Hotel in Herzliya to open his doors to the unit for free, while her friends chipped in for the food and drinks. I'd forgotten. It's just like her, though.

It wasn't the first time she'd helped out. Early in the war, as I was cruising the border with my television team, I chanced upon a friend in the hills just inside Israel. Tamir Salomon, a sergeant in a jeep reconnaissance unit and my son's surfing buddy, was frustrated. "What, no waves?" I said. No. His team was raring to go to war, their jeeps lined up along the road, but they didn't have any flak jackets—still another army screwup. They were about to go in without them, even though they knew it was foolish. I mentioned this in passing to Hagar when I called her that evening. She immediately called Tamir and said, "Wait. Come to my house tomorrow morning, I'll have the flak jackets. How many do you need?"

The next morning, about fifteen hours later, Tamir and a fellow soldier turned up in their army jeep, and by that time Hagar and friends had raised the money, bought the flak jackets, and had them delivered overnight. She handed Tamir twenty-five, at a thousand dollars each, as well as webbing. After the war, the unit gave her a plaque in recognition of her aid in a time of need.

Hagar was far from alone; during the Lebanon war, many civilians stepped in to help the undersupplied troops, who after all were their own children and spouses and friends. Civilians became so involved that the army later complained about interference in the work of the armed forces. On the whole, though, such devotion may comprise Israel's true and enduring strength, the best argument of all to continue conscription. Because everybody is supposed to serve, and because everybody has friends and relatives who are serving, the general population does truly care about its soldiers, and this keeps morale strong—or at least, stronger than it would otherwise be.

I saw how deep the feeling goes—and how tortured and complex the underlying emotions are—in a report of a memorial ceremony on Mount Adir, on the northern border, overlooking Lebanon. Three years after the war with Hezbollah, a grieving knot of families and friends cried together, held hands, and prayed. They all knew that Hezbollah had rearmed and regrouped, and that the Israeli army considered another round of fighting inevitable. One day their men would march across the border again to answer Israel's latest call to arms. As they hugged and searched for words to relieve the pain of losing their loved ones, one mother, Danielle Dan, whose son, Elad, was killed in the battle for Bint Jbeil, spoke for them all. "Every single day is a hard and painful one," she whispered. "Personally, I have never found comfort at these ceremonies. If we put less energy into commemoration and more into peace instead, maybe we would not be here today."

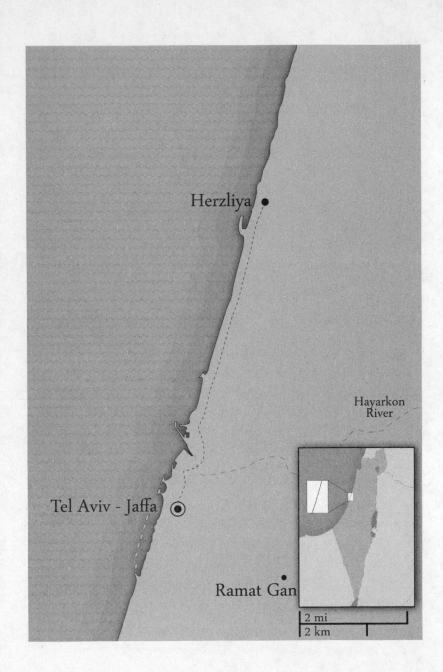

Herzliya

Hayarkon
River

Tel Aviv - Jaffa

Ramat Gan

2 mi
2 km

8

The Off-White City

Just as a man tells me no sharks live in the Mediterranean, a fisherman passes on a horse and cart ferrying two large leopard sharks. I smile: Everything about Tel Aviv is a surprise. This jumbled noisy mess of postmodern skyscrapers and Bauhaus homes, boulevards and beaches, markets and museums, has grown organically from a few red-roofed homes dotted about the sand dunes a hundred years ago. It has eclipsed its neighbor, five-thousand-year-old Arab Jaffa. It's as if a European city was plucked from one side of the Mediterranean and set down on the other, complete with cappuccini and chocolate croissants. The people are surprising too. Men with gray ponytails glide silently by on electric two-wheelers while panting girls in tiny shorts bicycle through the stoplights. A police chief watches, smiling, as an irate motorist abuses and curses a policewoman who is issuing him a parking ticket. A man threatens to throw a chair through a café's plate-glass window because the owner won't give his pregnant wife a glass of water. Yet when a woman spills her bag of groceries, three men spring up to help. Go figure.

I once knew Tel Aviv well. I lived there from 1973 to 1975, as a young news agency cameraman. I had arrived the week before the October war to find a fun-loving, confident city still enjoying the calm that came with twenty-six years of military superiority. Then on October 6, 1973, Syria and Egypt invaded, surprising Israel and destroying its myth of invincibility. As men of all ages threw on their uniforms, grabbed their guns, and hitchhiked to war, I watched Tel Aviv transform in hours from a hedonistic playground to a silent, fearful place with blackout curtains and sirens. Three weeks later, after the battered army had fought back to turn probable defeat into overwhelming victory, the city still didn't return to revelry. It would take years to mourn the dead.

When I returned to Tel Aviv in the early eighties, it was partying with a vengeance. Young Israelis now behaved as if there was no tomorrow because, as many have pointed out, they really didn't know if there would be a tomorrow. The city surpassed Beirut as the pleasure capital of the eastern Mediterranean, anointing itself the "city that never sleeps." All this happened, unfortunately, without me. I became an infrequent visitor to Tel Aviv's fleshpots. Rather, I spent my time in affluent green suburbs where I raised children, worked like a dog, and generally acted in an age-appropriate manner.

Even after Tel Aviv's old city received international recognition for its architecture, I paid little attention, dismissing the city as an ugly, shabby place on a beautiful beach. Now that I was on my trek along the coast, though, I looked forward to rediscovering Israel's secular capital. I was especially keen, for strictly scholarly reasons, to venture into the bars and clubs of south Tel Aviv. With thoughts of my own youthful adventures firmly in mind, I wanted to study how these establishments earned their sleazy rap. In particular, I wanted to answer a question that busies the minds of 87.6 percent of late-middle-aged men: Do young people really have sex with drunken strangers in the bathroom?

DON'T MESS WITH FELIX

I reached Tel Aviv on Day Eleven of my trek. The night before, I had enjoyed a blissful sleep in my own bed in my hometown of Herzliya Pituach. It was a welcome layover after nights spent in strange rooms and in the great outdoors. At 5:30 in the morning, I kissed Hagar good-bye and hurried past the ugly new Herzliya Marina, which blocks the view south. I let out a sigh as the wide, sandy beach opened up with a view all the way to Tel Aviv and Jaffa.

A few other early birds were already playing beach soccer, while two straining men pushed a Jet Ski through the sand into the only part of the waterfront reserved for their noisy and smelly sport. Then came the green tarpaulin that divides the beach into separate areas for Orthodox Jewish men and women. I walked more easily than I had in recent days, as the load I carried was lighter. At home I had dumped all my smelly clothes, replacing them in my backpack with what I imagined to be suitably cool party apparel. I also left behind my tent, dried fruit, and heavy bottles of water. From here to Gaza, much of the coast was built up. I planned to pick up the pace of my walk, sleep in cheap hotels, and eat and drink in beach cafés.

Dawn was arriving and all was peaceful until I approached a line of rocks just past another concrete eyesore, the Sea and Sun apartment complex. A lone fisherman on the beach was gesticulating, and from a distance I could hear a faint, angry voice. As I approached, I saw that the fisherman was shouting abuse at a swimmer who was draping fishing nets between the rocks. A stocky, bronzed sixty-year-old, the fisherman had a crab tattoo on his shoulder and a deep, powerful voice that boomed across the beach, drowning out the waves. The swimmer gave him the finger and dove down. I stood by the fisherman and commented how strange it seemed that in such a peaceful place the only two people present would find something to fight about. His response: *"Ze baya shelcha?"* Which is, more or less: What's it got to do with you? Clearly I was approaching the big city. I wished him a good day and strolled on.

For all its reputation as party central, Tel Aviv still has elements of the gruff frontier town it once was. The city was founded in 1909, when sixty-six Jewish families decided to escape the ghettolike walls and crowded, stinky streets of ancient Jaffa and build a European-style suburb in the sand dunes. They began by purchasing twelve acres of empty land from the Bedouin. An iconic, blurred photo shows these mavericks on the beach casting lots, reputed to be gray and white seashells, to see which family would get which bit of land. Long camel trains soon delivered tons of sand to the builders, who laid out the new homes in neat rows. Jaffa's Arabs gazed in consternation at women frolicking in the sea in shorts and blouses, as well as at the new cafés where growing numbers of European immigrants ordered *Apfelstrudel mit Sahne* and chatted in German and Russian.

Today, 400,000 live in Tel Aviv proper, while three million—almost half of Israel's population—live in the greater Tel Aviv conurbation of Gush Dan. Waves of Jews fleeing Russia in the early 1900s, Poland in the twenties, Germany in the thirties, almost everywhere in Europe in the forties and fifties, and Ethiopia and the former Soviet republics in the eighties and nineties contributed to the exploding population. In a place that grew so rapidly, if you were lucky, or a builder, your boat rose with the tide.

One of my favorite Tel Aviv old-timers was introduced to me years ago with the warning "Don't mess with Felix!" He was a tough man indeed, short and wiry with a quick, crooked smile. As I was told, he reputedly had a lot to smile about. In his youth, Felix had killed a man and served fifteen years for murder. Upon his release in the fifties, the prison service had arranged for him to sell watermelons on Tel Aviv's outskirts. Like any Israeli at the time, he established facts on the ground by roping off his little area, then extending it, and finally fencing off a couple of acres on which he planted vegetables and trees. Nobody cared at the time because the land in question was a remote, desolate area by a small road, and anyway, nobody messed with Felix. The city spread, and today Felix's plot of land is in the middle of a large shopping center. Felix dumped the watermelons and now rents his plot to Toys "R" Us, the cell phone company Orange, and Shilav, a chain of nursery stores, for a reputed fifty thousand dollars a month.

Khalouf Battito, a friend of a friend, has a similar rags-to-riches story. When Jews after 1948 were given the homes of defeated Arabs in the village of Sheikh Munis, near where I was now walking, Battito, a Moroccan Jew, received a stone building belonging to the Arab cemetery. In the middle of his living room stood a long marble slab on which funeral attendants had washed the corpses, and for a time the Battito family used it as their dining table. This soon became too macabre, and so Khalouf moved into an old bus on the cliff overlooking the sea, leaving his wife and kids in the Arab house. He brought four big dogs for protection. Over the years, his cliff-top home, with its superb sea view, and the surrounding land that he had colonized, became prime property. To get him to leave, the municipality, which wanted to return the land to the public, reputedly had to pay him several hundred thousand dollars. Then his home with the funeral slab became highly coveted because the Arab village land had become part of the grounds of the new Tel Aviv University. Khalouf received another couple of hundred thousand to move the family. He built a villa in an obscure neighborhood called Tel Baruch that, with his luck, soon became one of the region's most expensive. Today, his friends say, his house is worth millions and he lives like a king.

ENCOUNTER OF AN INTIMATE KIND

Still, I was not going to Tel Aviv to investigate real estate—at least not primarily. I was going to rediscover my youth, and as it turned out, it didn't take long. Continuing south past Tel Baruch (the place where I landed in the arms of hookers after my night lost at sea), I fell in step beside a very attractive, fortyish woman out for an early stroll. One of the charms of Israel, which can also be a curse, is the intimate turn that conversation rapidly takes with strangers. It is considered reasonable to meet somebody in an elevator and by the time you reach the sixth floor to have divulged what you do for a living, how much you earn, and depending on your answers, whether you want a *shidduch*, a date with a view to marriage.

Lora, an Englishwoman who came to Israel as a child, must have been in a time of transition, because she soon fell to musing on intimate matters.

After we agreed, as two Brits would, that it was a nice morning and that soon the day would become unbearably hot, and after we had swapped family details, she said that she had recently separated. "I no longer need someone to have children with, so what else do I need a man for?" she asked.

I did a double take and looked at her sideways. Lora was closer to the sea, and the early morning sun from the eastern hills bathed her face in a pinkish glow, softening it as she smiled. She had brown hair and full lips, and she wore a loose, low-cut blouse and long crepe skirt; she could have been strolling in a Cotswolds village. Behind her, the gentle waters rippled on the sand, murmuring, as Hagar had said, like a lover's whisper. "To do the dishes?" I suggested.

She went on, oblivious: "I have a house, security, the children are almost grown up. I don't need financial help, I don't need a man. So why worry?"

"Sex?" I wondered helpfully.

Lora looked at me quizzically. She was barefoot and walked in water up to her ankles. "But do I need one man or can I have a few? I'm surveying what I need in a relationship at this age, and it's so different from what it was. I'm looking for a man who is totally content and wants a relationship that is not the main thing in his life."

I liked her way of thinking. "Or several relationships?"

"I'm like a sheep," Lora said, ignoring me. "I have this automatic behavior, which is to find a mate, be in a relationship, have a man next to me. That's what society says I need, and I wonder, am I okay?" I took off my own sandals and joined her in the water, kicking idly at the waves. "Will anyone ever love me again?" she continued. "Will I grow old alone? But I like the way I am now. I'm alone, reading, writing, creating, dancing. It's what I want. I feel stimulated and fulfilled." She turned to me. "Do you know what I mean?"

I nodded. "I think so. Maybe it would be nice to meet someone who is in his own relationship, who is content and happy but has similar needs." I paused, groping. "Maybe someone a little bit . . . older? Somebody who also believes that maturity means that exclusivity is not necessarily mandatory or exclusively necessary." What?

"Exactly."

Encouraged, though confused, I ventured, "Your default position is to find a regular partner, but that's not actually what you want. You're happy enough as you are, but there are little things you have to plug in to, parts of a relationship occasionally—like sex."

She stroked her hair thoughtfully as she walked. "Yes, not full-time and not with only one person. The trouble is that I can't imagine myself having an intimate relationship with a few men. It's a fantasy, but I've never ever done it in reality. It's attractive, but it feels like it's hard to imagine." She stopped for a moment to look out to sea, stroking the sand with her bare foot, and then we walked on. "I do put my heart and soul into deep relationships, and it's hard to know whether it's just because of society that I feel I can't have several guys at the same time or whether I am frightened of . . ." She smiled sweetly and shrugged, as if unable to explain. "Oh well, I don't have an answer."

We were approaching some wooden steps that led from the beach to a grassy knoll and a parking lot. "Well, nice to meet you," she said, putting out her hand.

I took it between both of mine and held it a little too long. "You know, for somebody whom I just met for five minutes on the beach, it's been very interesting to talk to you."

She threw her head back in a raucous laugh, and as I was now closer to the sea, the sun framed her soft hair with a line of light. What a cute mouth. "And your telephone number is?" I asked.

She laughed again. "At seven o'clock in the morning? I don't know if I'll give it to you. Maybe you'll give me yours?"

I quickly did, using her back to write out the little note. When I gave her the paper she turned away a little too sharply and I watched her depart. It had been a nice meeting.

I wonder if she'll call, I thought, ambling alone toward Tel Aviv. If she does, will Hagar pick up the phone? What disaster would ensue? Probably none. Shortly after I met Hagar, and before we became serious, she drove through northern Israel and picked up a young hitchhiker called Irit from Tel Aviv. It didn't take them long to discover that they were both in a relationship with the same man—me. But we're all still friends.

THE MUSEUM AND THE MOSQUE

It served me right: With all this juvenile reminiscing, I missed a left turn I had intended to make. I continued down the coast until I reached the fenced-off dead end of Sde Dov, north Tel Aviv's small civilian airfield. Doubling back the entire length of the runway, I walked along the street past the airport and the power station to a renovated port that now serves as a busy and chic safe haven for party folk. Passing through its guarded gates, I made my way among the large warehouses-turned-nightclubs and simple sheds that have been transformed into trendy restaurants. I strolled along seaside boardwalks that have a South Street Sea Port, New York, feel. After a few minutes, I decided not to stay. I wanted a late breakfast, but not in an imitation brasserie or trattoria. I'd head to a good, old-fashioned dive I knew called Banana Beach, on Tel Aviv's main seafront.

This is Tel Aviv as it once was: wobbly tables, wonky chairs, and dismal service, all on a floor of wooden planks and sand. At the next table sat a bronzed and wrinkled older man with long gray hair pulled tight in a ponytail, bare-chested in denim shorts and flip-flops. He gazed blankly at the sea. Next to him, two women in straw hats leaned forward and talked at the same time while sharing pages of a newspaper. Another woman with a long cigarette called for a *café botz*, or mud coffee, thick and black. She called four times, sighing impatiently. Cars hooted on the beach road behind, while on the sand in front young people arranged their towels for the day. Pairs of old men in baggy underpants bashed a small, hard black ball playing *matkot*, an Israeli version of paddleball, while strollers ducked and weaved to avoid getting brained. A man walked by shouting, *"Artic, Artic"*—popsicles named after the Arctic. Within the narrow compass of my view, it could have been Tel Aviv, circa 1950.

After I finished my freshly squeezed lemon juice, omelette, finely diced tomato-and-cucumber salad, and mint tea, I decided to stop off at another place frozen in time, the museum of the IZL, the Irgun fighters who died attacking Jaffa in 1948. The battle of Jaffa led to Tel Aviv's conquering of the Arab town, which under the 1947 UN partition plan was to be part of the newly created Palestine. Tel Aviv's victory allowed the city to extend its sprawl farther down the coast. Soon the city was renamed Tel Aviv–Jaffa. I had never found time to visit the museum before.

An old Arab stone building with a boxlike glass addition, the museum stands alone on the rocks close to Jaffa's harbor, a few dozen yards from the sea. The museum's collection of warrior artifacts was interesting enough, but the true treasure there, I soon discovered, is the guide, eighty-four-year-old Yoske Nachmias; he had personally carried out many of the deeds celebrated in the museum. I had wanted to meet him after coming across his name during my research into Acre. He was among the only group ever to escape from the centuries-old fortress-prison. In May 1947, Irgun fighters smuggled explosives to the prisoners, and then, disguised as British soldiers with their "short back and sides" haircuts, blew open one of the fortress walls, freeing twenty-seven Jewish inmates. Nine of the Irgun died fighting the British guards.

As I strolled about the museum, I found a photograph of a young Yoske as a bright-eyed teenager in British army uniform. There was still something of the shiny eyes in the old man I met, with his tufts of gray hair adorning an otherwise-tanned, bald head. Yoske's office wall was dominated by a large poster of Menachem Begin, the Irgun's leader and future prime minister, who had ordered the prison break. Each time Yoske mentioned Begin, he leaned back, half twisted his torso, and pointed respectfully at the poster as if for the first time. Then he showed me his own wanted poster from 1938 and said, "Do you recognize me?"

These preliminaries out of the way, I clicked on my recorder, and Yoske immediately launched unprompted into his pitch: "My name Yoske Nachmias, sixth-generation Jerusalem, ten brothers and sisters, two in the

Palmach and three in the Irgun, Begin our leader. We have to fight because the war will end soon, the big powers will divide the world. They won't know we exist. If we fight, they will know we exist." It was the neatest justification I had heard for terrorism, and it was all conveyed in the present and future tense.

Yoske had forged his birth certificate and joined the British army at age fourteen, fighting in Syria, Lebanon, and Egypt until he was wounded in Cyprus in 1944. His true loyalty lay with the Jewish underground, which he had joined even before his teens. After Hitler's defeat, when the Jews in Palestine turned against the British, young Yoske proved invaluable. The Irgun had two language units, black and white—black for Arabic speakers and white for English speakers. "I could pass for both," Yoske recalls.

In 1938, at the age of ten, Yoske waded through chest-high seas at night, carrying Jewish babies to shore in Tel Aviv, defying the British immigration limits. Ten years later, he was on the Irgun weapons ship S.S. *Altalena* when it was destroyed on Ben-Gurion's orders just off Tel Aviv's beach. A famous photo shows smoke pouring from the ship as people in shorts on bicycles watch from the shore. In between these historical events, Yoske helped capture a British ammunition train carrying twenty thousand three-inch mortar shells, a feat that proved decisive in the fight with the Arabs; he helped kidnap five British Army officers; and of course, he did what had never been done before, escaped from Acre's prison. But his biggest battle was for Tel Aviv's neighbor, Jaffa. It was one of the bitterest fights in Israel's 1948 War of Independence, which the Arabs call the Nakba.

Yoske's job was to suppress murderous sniper fire coming from the tall minaret of the Hassan Bek Mosque, the closest to Tel Aviv, and to pin down the Arab fighters inside. "My unit kept firing rifles and small arms at the mosque for three days," Yoske told me. Clearly he had told this story thousands of times, but he talked and waved his arms as if it were happening now. Behind him, through the window, colorful sails of the wave-skiers floated by in the strong breeze. "We succeeded; they didn't come out. We put explosives by the walls to blow it up, but Begin said, 'It's a holy place, don't destroy it.'" Sixty years later, Yoske still seemed disappointed as he sighed, leaned back, and pointed again at the image of his leader. "They destroyed four synagogues in that area, but Begin said: 'Respect their holy places.'"

Today the Hassan Bek Mosque has been subsumed by Tel Aviv. Located on the beach side of a parking lot by the crowded Carmel vegetable market, the mosque's tall minaret and prayer hall comprise an exotic Muslim outpost among hotels and surf shops. The surrounding Arab homes of the Manshiye neighborhood were razed in the years following the 1948 war, and today the gargantuan Dan Panorama and David Intercontinental hotels loom over the mosque. As Yoske recounted, Arabs ignored Hassan Bek for many years; the Turkish governor who built the mosque in 1916 was notorious for his drinking and womanizing, and so local Muslims had always regarded it as unclean. But during the first Palestinian uprising, in the late eighties, Arabs from Jaffa did an about-face, turning Hassan Bek into a resistance symbol; now dozens of Arabs pray there daily. "It's very quiet at Hassan Bek," Nachmias said. "Jews respect the Muslim holy place, we all get on very well today. That's the message of the mosque."

I wondered what the Muslims thought about that; it is easier for the conquerors to appreciate the status quo than the conquered. I decided to find out. But I left town earlier than expected. That evening, joining the throng of young people on Rothschild Boulevard, I found that after my days of quiet, meditative strolling along the beach, I couldn't take the traffic noise and bustle of the crowded streets. So despite my eagerness to explore the seedier side of town, I decided to go to bed early and leave at dawn; I'd come back later when I was in the mood. The years had taken their toll after all.

Thus it was that almost a year passed before I found myself sitting opposite Nawar Daka, the bearded, broad-shouldered young imam who led prayers five times a day in Hassan Bek. Nawar had just returned from the hajj, the pilgrimage to Mecca, and at first he had a different take than Yoske. "At night after their parties, the Jews piss against the walls of the mosque. It is disgusting; it stinks. They bring bottles of beer, and their women are naked, but my job is to let Muslims know that the Jews get drunk and do not mean any harm against Islam. I smooth things over, that is my job." These were harsh words, I thought, but he didn't appear angry, and as we talked he asked his Jewish assistant to make tea. We were sitting not in the mosque but in his business offices nearby.

Nawar supplements his income as a Muslim holy man by running a construction materials business. He is also studying for an MA in Sharia, Islamic law, at the American Open University. Since his home is located on Jaffa's southern edge, an area that borders the Jewish community of Bat Yam, most of his neighbors are Jewish. "We do have excellent relationships with the Jews," he said. "They are my friends and colleagues. I never had a problem; we respect each other. But Hassan Bek? I see it differently from that Jewish man. It is true that the mosque's very existence shows that Jews and Arabs respect each other. That is one message. But for us there is a different, stronger message." Twisting as Yoske had when he'd pointed to Begin, Nawar gestured over his shoulder to a map of Jaffa in the old days, before Tel Aviv. "For us, Hassan Bek shows that this land belongs to us, that this is all Palestinian land. It shows our identity, that Arabs lived here long before anybody else, that once there were many mosques."

As Nawar proudly noted, his family was Jaffa's largest, their roots in the city stretching back as far as anybody could remember. I asked whether any of them had fought the Irgun in Hassan Bek. Nawar's lips tightened. "Jews always ask me this, and I say, 'If you go *pssss* to a cat, it will run away. But if the cat has kittens, she will stay and fight.' I believe a Jew will do the same thing; he will defend his home and fight and kill till the end, and this is what happened. History shows what happened. All we have now is the mosque, but it proves this is our land."[1]

After our talk, I sat in a beach bar between Hassan Bek and the museum, watching Arab women in long black dresses and covered hair pass Jewish girls in shorts and T-shirts. I liked the cultural mix. Difficult issues divide these two native peoples, yet day by day they get on fine. Still, I wondered: What is the true lesson of the museum and the mosque? Are they respected relics of a violent past or, more menacingly, symbols of time-out in a battle yet to be resumed?

I paid for my coffee and left, my thoughts returning to more immediate, and pleasant, concerns. Almost a year after my walk, I had now reached the stage of my field research that I most eagerly anticipated—reconnecting, however vicariously, to my wilder, younger self. While I didn't approve of young people emptying their bladders against the walls of the mosque, I did look forward to my plan to wander among them, for an evening or two, to see how Tel Aviv's attractive and lewd nightlife had earned its worldwide reputation.

A TASTE OF NIGHT LIFE

There was only one problem: The average age of the tens of thousands of crazed weekend revelers is about twenty-three, and I am a rather worse-for-wear sixty-two. I would have to be selected by doormen to get into the clubs. The more I thought about it, the more I realized that my proposed investigation held every prospect of being deeply humiliating. Moreover, I didn't know anyone who frequented the dens of iniquity to which I aspired. But I did know someone whom I thought could help.

Barbara[2] is a standout character by any definition. She's an American Jew whose despairing parents sent her to Israel at the age of sixteen to save her from the Roman Catholic she was dating. Unhappily for them, she then ran off with an Arab poet. After bouncing back and forth for a time between Boston and Tel Aviv, she moved to Israel. For the past twenty-five years, she has combined academic research and lecturing with belly dancing, which she claims is a great way to understand Middle Eastern culture, her specialty. She lived ten days in a harem in Abu Dhabi, strictly as a dancer, and she performs frequently in weddings and private events in Cairo, the Persian Gulf, and throughout Israel, while teaching at a prestigious Tel Aviv dance studio.

Barbara overflows with optimism and energy, fueled partly by a foul daily dose of wheatgrass. When her hair fell out during chemotherapy, her response to the painful treatment was "I had a wonderful time—I met such lovely doctors and nurses!" When her hip was replaced: "I had the best doctors! They couldn't believe how quickly I was back dancing!" After a terrorist bomb blast on Dizengoff blew her off her bicycle in 1994, grazing her arms, legs, and face in the fall, she kept her teaching appointment, saying, "I have a responsibility, you know!" So when I explained that I felt way too old to be rejected from a nightclub line by a bouncer more than half my age, she answered, "Oh, what nonsense! Leave it to me!"

That is how I soon found myself awed by dozens of hot chicks in Minerva, a loud bar at 98 Allenby Street. Scarcely had I arrived when Hagit, Barbara's neighbor, a beautiful young girl with short black hair, pulled me so close our cheeks touched. Oh, have I come to the right place! I thought. Hagit shouted into my ear, over the music, "You do know this is a gay bar?"

No, I didn't, actually, but it explained a few things, such as why I was the only man there. I found it oddly reassuring. Nothing was expected of me.

"Freedom, freedom . . ." rang around the bar, and a couple of girls danced to the music in their short black dresses, throwing out their arms, revealing more and more of their thighs. The girls sat mostly in pairs around the bar or in darker alcoves, a few kissing or embracing, while others moved by, exchanged a few words, and sat down with friends. One girl slowly massaged the shoulders of a friend sitting at the bar. The atmosphere was reserved and pleasant, although Hagit assured me that later the place would grow so crowded you couldn't move, with everybody dancing and laughing.

Hagit had joined me briefly for a drink, and with a little prodding I got her to describe life on Merom Golan, her kibbutz in the Golan Heights. "It was too weird being gay on the kibbutz," she said, sipping what seemed to be a large glass of whiskey. "People have closed minds, my mom took it badly, my dad was okay, and my friends were fine, too. But here in Tel Aviv, well, it's like home, especially the bar." She had been a regular here for three years before getting a job as a shift manager. "A few gay men drop by, and a few older, single men who we usually have to ask to leave. Their staring makes us uncomfortable."

That got my attention. I had been nursing a beer for twenty minutes, and now I ostentatiously wrote notes, trying to convey that I wasn't staring like a dirty old man so much as a dirty old writer. I realized that it was probably time to go, so I said good-bye. I did like the place, though. It seemed cozy and safe.

Walking farther up Allenby Street, I reached the corner of Rothschild Boulevard and stopped at Iceberg, which has the world's best ice cream. I ate my favorite, pistachio halva with hardened strands of chocolate. It was Thursday at midnight, and Rothschild was a mob scene. There was a line at Iceberg and next door at Arcaffe, a chintzy café chain, while over the road at the bar beneath the yoga center people crowded the steps and spilled onto the sidewalk. Strollers streamed up and down among the trees, people on electric scooters dodging past them. Dogs on leashes forced the scooters to suddenly brake; couples on wooden benches watched while sipping drinks. Taxis continually disgorged girls in high heels and boys in shorts. Kiosks on corners served cold drinks and coffee, and a sea breeze helped lighten the sultry air. The only discordant note was struck by shadowy bats that swooped between the mulberry trees, gorging on their berries.

I walked beneath the trees to a recently opened bar Barbara had recommended, at 64 Rothschild. Vaad Habayit (its name, oddly, means House Committee) was partly owned by another of Barbara's friends, David. Before becoming a bar, it had been a famous Chinese restaurant downstairs, and upstairs a Hasidic food kitchen for the poor. Now loud music boomed through the windows, while at the door an alluring girl of Yemenite origin named Maayan sat guard. She had olive skin and wore her hair in curly braids. Her miniskirt rode to the top of her thighs and her bare crossed legs held the crowd at bay as effectively as the crossed brawny arms of the toughest doorman. She would let only a few people enter as others left, and five minutes later, when I had finally edged my way to the bar, I understood why.

The place was so packed that you couldn't even lower your arm; everybody's drink-holding hand was frozen at his or her mouth, like a toy figurine's. All shared the same muggy air, save for a few tall men who breathed more easily. Elbows, shoulders, and bags poked me from all sides and heights. Babies could be conceived here and nobody would know. There appeared to be several bars and a snooker table, but access was inconceivable. I asked for a beer that never came. After ten minutes, I shuffled to the exit, my shirt dripping with sweat. Everybody else was laughing and shouting, some were singing to the music, others raised brandy glasses in a joyous toast, and a boy and a girl eyed each other across the room. The city's youth seemed to be buzzing around and getting nowhere, like a swarm of midges on a hot summer night.

"Thanks," I said to Maayan, "that was nice."

"Good," she replied, and let the next person in.

I stood among the trees, stifling a yawn. It was now 1:30 in the morning, and the boulevard was busier than a street market at noon. I had heard that the scene would be just as frenetic in the clubs of south Tel Aviv, where a younger, out-of-town clientele hangs out, and in the renovated port in north Tel Aviv, where patrons are older. All the beach cafés and bars would be crowded, as would the promenade. In addition, Tel Aviv has dozens of small corners and neighborhoods frequented by locals. So where to go?

I waited at a stoplight on the corner of Nahmani Street. Suddenly I heard a sharp, fluttering sound, like a shaken towel. A shadow flashed by me, and something brushed against my mouth. I jerked my head back in disgust: I thought it was a bug. Then I felt a plop of sludge in the corner of my mouth. My hand shot up to clear it out as I spat, coughed, and spat again, wiping my lips. It was a gritty, slimy thing. Worst of all, it was warm.

I noticed more fluttering, higher this time, and the dark wings of flying rodents flashed between the trees. "Fuck!" I shouted. *"UUUrrrggghh!"* I spun around, spitting. "A bat shit in my mouth! There's goo on my shirt!" I pulled and tore at my mouth and spat some more. Then I cleared my throat and spat again into the gutter, wiping my mouth with my hand. It had to be a bad omen!

From a wooden bench nearby, I heard fits of laughter. Two girls were in hysterics, slapping each other. They couldn't stop sniggering and laughing, and then I laughed too. *"Uurrgghh,"* I spluttered again. "I can't believe that!"

"It's good luck," one of the girls said.

"Yes," the other one agreed. "Tonight you'll get lucky."

Well, not quite. What I did do was eat a lemon sorbet at Iceberg, hoping to lose the taste of the bat shit. Then I went home and fell into bed.

THE ATTACK ON NAHMANI STREET

I had left the Minerva bar thinking it a warm and welcoming place for gays, and indeed Tel Aviv is renowned for its easy acceptance. Every year, as many straight people as gays turn out to support the Gay Pride parade.

Gay tourism is a quickly growing niche, encouraged by some parts of the government that believe this helps portray Israel as liberal and tolerant. But during early August 2009, when I was cautiously tasting Tel Aviv's nightlife, a terrible thing happened. Just off Rothschild, on Nahmani, a few houses from where the bat shat in my mouth, a gunman in a black hood barged into the basement of a private house that served as a safe haven for teenage gays as well as for boys and girls who had not yet declared their sexual orientation. The gunman sprayed the teenagers with a semiautomatic weapon, killing two and wounding a dozen more.

Crowds quickly gathered outside, lighting candles and leaving flowers. The next night, the streets were as crowded as always. Spokesmen for the gay community asserted that they would not allow a lunatic to intimidate them. I had asked Barbara if she wanted to come to a nightclub with me and yet another of her friends, a twenty-four-year-old dancer. She answered with this e-mail: "Friday might work. By the way, I met with a friend whose daughter was shot at Nahmani last Saturday. She's sixteen and came out of the closet about six months ago. She was very lucky, since the bullet ended up in a part of her body that had layers of fat. I ran into them at the hospital where she was undergoing treatment for trauma. Ciao Barbara."

Initially Barbara's blithe, bare-bones tone caught me by surprise, but then I realized how appropriate it actually was. Since its birth, Israel has fought a war a decade. Tel Aviv has been hit by Iraqi scuds and suicide bombers, and Hezbollah and Hamas both warn that during the next war they could shell the city. Iran threatens to wipe the country off the map. People here have learned to accept danger and go on with life without missing a beat; if not, they like to say, the terrorists win.

Barbara herself has had four near misses. She was blown off her bike by a bomb, as described earlier; she was a minute away from withdrawing money at an ATM on Dizengoff when a suicide bomber blew himself up next to it, killing twelve; she was walking her dog across the road when a suicide bomber killed himself and wounded thirty near Café Bialik on Allenby. (Her dog shook and howled for days.) And when a bomb killed eight students in the cafeteria of the Hebrew University in Jerusalem, she was reading nearby in the library. During the first Gulf War, when the alarm sounded, she sometimes sheltered in her friend's sealed room; other times she just stayed in bed. Yet she loves the place.

In the days that followed the killings on Nahmani Street, neither the lack of a suspect nor the threat that the murderer could strike again succeeded in slowing things down. Gay bars uniformly defied police instructions that they should close. About twenty thousand people gathered in Rabin Square in support of the gay community. Politicians and artists spoke while Israel's president called for tolerance. "The bullets that hit the gay community at the beginning of the week struck us all as people, as Jews, as Israelis . . . criminals will not set our agenda," President Shimon Peres insisted from the podium. "The Creator of the world did not endow anyone with the power to murder his peer." Later, demonstrators waving the flag of Israel and the rainbow flag of Gay Pride flooded the bars and clubs—yet another reminder that young Israelis can't know what the morrow holds, and so make sure to party while they can.

THE WORST OF THE WORST?

I never did hook up with Barbara's friend who knew all the nightclubs, so I decided to go it alone. My destination the next weekend: Haoman 17, a notorious discotheque off Salame Street in the city's southern area. Of the roughly 140 discos in the Tel Aviv area, I chose this one because the head of the Tel Aviv police, Superintendent Itzhak Gatenyo, said it was the biggest and the worst. "We always station officers outside, and sometimes plain-clothes officers inside. I've had to close the place down several times. They sell drugs there, they get drunk, violent. Mothers don't want to know what their daughters get up to." A former army paratrooper and murder investigator, Gatenyo had the burly, hairy forearms that seem mandatory for his job. He also had a season's subscription to Gesher, Tel Aviv's Hebrew- and Russian-language theater troupe. He enjoys Russian culture and appreciates what the Russian immigrants have brought to Israel, but he also appreciates all too well the mischief they get into.

I met Gatenyo in his office on the fourth floor of Tel Aviv's new police headquarters in south Tel Aviv. Two photos on the wall sum up this man of many parts: One shows a military helicopter crashing in flames into a car; the other shows Gatenyo with the pope. But it's the influence of the Russians on Israeli society that interests him now. "When I was a young officer, the Russian immigrants surprised us. Suddenly they came, and they're drinking in the morning, the afternoon, on the streets. So we said, we must infiltrate them, so we know what to expect." As he spoke, he spread his arms in a supplicating manner, as if asking for understanding. He stressed that most of the new immigrants were good, honest citizens. But too many of them brought bad habits. "Their drinking changed our society. Israelis don't know how to drink. We're in the Middle East, it's a hot country, Arabs, Africans, suddenly everyone's drinking. All this in a small, crowded place. So there's violence. I wouldn't go to Haoman 17 if I were you."

It was a Friday, the busiest night. Fighting to stay awake, I arrived at 1:30 in the morning, when Tel Aviv's nightlife begins to heat up. I found a crowd of hundreds pushing around three metal entrance gates, each protected by two huge men whose job it was to choose who could enter. Their title, in Russian and Hebrew: *selektor*. It was a madhouse. People passed identity cards forward so that their names would be called out. Others phoned friends inside to come get them. Heavily made-up girls elbowed each other, while I tried not to make eye contact with any of their muscled, tattooed, head-shaved boyfriends. Around the corner, music blared from cars with open trunks. Outside these cars, boys in jeans and T-shirts and girls in short dresses and high heels were passing around vodka bottles and dancing.

Gatenyo had told me that drinks are expensive inside the club, and so many kids get plastered outside first. By now I was yet again being pushed from all sides in a crush of hormone-crazed young people less than half my age. This was definitely not my scene. By 1:45, I hoped I would be rejected by the *selektor* so that I could go home to bed with a clean conscience. To my surprise and dismay, the bruiser in black with a sleek black ponytail pointed at me, crooked his finger, and rather brutally pushed people aside to allow me through. He probably thought that I, the old guy, had more money to spend.

I lined up at a metal detector, fought through the horde to pay forty dollars at the cash desk, and finally entered the club through a narrow door, where I had to squeeze past a surly fellow in black who tore my ticket. It was a cavernous, warehouse-type space with a sunken dance floor, bars, and stages. A thumping dull beat blasted my eardrums. I bought a beer and stationed myself at the corner of a railing, away from the wall of loudspeakers, a spot that allowed me a view of most of the largest room.

I don't know what I expected. From the sinister Queens Hotel in Zimbabwe to the New Florida above a gas station in Nairobi, I've been to a dump or two. In Kinshasa, I ate dinner at a seemingly respectable restaurant, only to find on my way out that the place had a Jacuzzi, and that a couple was frolicking shamelessly in the water. Gatenyo had primed me for Sodom and Gomorrah ("The girls are half naked, cocaine and ecstasy, knives, stabbings"), but I wound up finding just another drug-fueled, low-class nightclub.

Two young women, a blonde and a brunette, gyrated on a raised stage, wearing tiny black leather pants and matching bras. Disorienting strobe lights flashed across the heads of the massed dancers below. The music blared louder and faster, arms reaching to the ceiling, bodies swaying and sometimes falling. Mist clouds billowed from the sides and fanned over the crowd as a ship's foghorn blasted. I took in the noise from the people, the thumping beat, saw the flashing lights, the rising smoke, the manic smiles, the girls shimmying up and down their boyfriends like pole dancers, the men hurling themselves about and yelling, the beer spilling from plastic cups, and I thought, This is really not for me. I also thought, Someone here is getting rich. Eleven hundred people, said Gatenyo, forty dollars to get in, probably twenty dollars a head for drinks—they take in around sixty-six thousand bucks a night. How much can expenses be? Security, DJ, the dancers, the bar help; it's all cash, so not much tax: good business! That's what an old guy thinks about in a club full of flesh and hormones.

I did notice one thing of anthropological import. As talk was impossible, boy meets girl here entirely without language. The cell-phone camera appears to serve as the equivalent of a pickup line. Boy takes picture of dancing girl, eliciting one of two responses: Either she turns away and you're toast, or she laughs and wants to see the photo, which means touching heads, laughter, and you're in.

Around three o'clock, I left and walked over to Florentine Street, another party zone, albeit one with a different crowd. Here Hebrew was dominant, along with English and French. Cafés and bars were still packed and overflowing into the street, while in O'Hara's bar four boys danced self-consciously on the table as girls took photos and laughed. If Haoman 17 was supposed to be threatening, the scene here was innocent, with half the people on the streets eating ice cream. Almost like the good old days.

How quickly it changed, Gatenyo had said, looking out the window toward the sea. "Twenty years ago it was such a boring place. You went out, went to the beach, enjoyed the breeze. The best food was at home. That's all there was. And now? It's a great place." He had clapped his hands repeatedly in emphasis as he listed why: "Freedom. Gay life. The clubs. The bars. Great restaurants. Yes, it's a *balagan*, a mess. Young people can party till dawn. In the past, they went home at midnight. Now they go out at midnight. And the after-parties—they start at dawn and end in the afternoon. But there's positive and negative. We have to learn how to handle this."

His police work has taken him to major towns in Europe, and as rapidly as Tel Aviv is changing, he says, it's still a lot better than any European capital. "We don't have anything like their soccer violence, their attacks against policemen, killing, their level of drugs problems, prostitution, gambling. What we have is bad enough, though."

On another evening, I accompanied Gatenyo as he and other police officers guided twenty veterans of his paratroop unit and their wives around the seedier side of town, along with senior police officers from Holland. He was explaining the growing problem of drink and youth when three drunken girls in high heels and short dresses clattered and stumbled toward the group. As they passed, one of them literally fell into Gatenyo's arms and laughed up into his face. He said, "You see, you see? Imagine this was your daughter. We have to stop this while we still can." But he didn't say how.

SAVE YOUR SOUL

After making no impression on anybody at the club, and after wandering aimlessly around the bars of Florentine, I rested for a few days. The following Thursday I returned to Rothschild, where it was nice to be noticed at last and offered a drink—even if it was only by a pale man with a black hat and coat spreading the word of the Messiah. "Join us," he said, waving me to a chair. "What would you like to drink? Have some cake."

He was one of a half dozen bearded Hasidic Jews who had set up a long plastic table with chairs on the corner of Mazeh Street. They were toasting passersby, hoping to entice them to sit, listen, and, with luck, reconnect with their souls. They were clearly ready for a long night. A very pregnant woman in a wig and long dress offered candles to every female, regardless of how high the skirt or low the blouse. *"Shabbat shalom!"* she called out.[3] Most women smiled and dismissed her politely, while some took the candle and walked on. I accepted vodka in a little plastic cup and sat next to the bearded, black-hatted Ben Gur, a thirty-year-old former nightclub DJ, substance abuser, and bar owner. On his past, he wouldn't elaborate: "Let's not talk about it. That person wasn't me."

He certainly must have looked different than he does today. Ben is a member of Chabad, Hasidic Jews whose mission is to bring Jews closer to God, so as to hasten the Messiah's arrival. "A Hasid is he who surrenders himself for the benefit of another," Ben said, quoting his spiritual leader, Rebbe Menachem Schneerson. As he leaned forward, talking rapidly, two of his friends leaped from their chairs. Dressed straight from a Polish stetl, they linked arms and danced a jig, singing loudly, *"Moshiach, Moshiach, Moshiaaach! Aie, yaie, yaie ya ya yaieeeh!"* People strolling by paused to clap and laugh. Anywhere else in the world, this would seem bizarrely out of place, like the Hare Krishna chanting in Wall Street. In Tel Aviv, it seemed quite natural that Hasids would be accosting scantily clad boys and girls.

I asked Ben whether most people walking by were not beyond redemption. He shook his head and fingered his beard like an old man. "I was in a very bad place, and now I am in a very good place. Everyone can be reconnected to their soul, and that is why we are here."

Chabad has people like Ben in seventy-five countries, from Katmandu to the Amazon jungle, enabling Jewish travelers to celebrate religious holidays in a Chabad center. Ben waved to passersby, calling on them to join us. Most waved back with a smile and continued, while a few sat at the table and accepted drinks. "It's easier outside Israel," Ben continued. "Jews come by themselves to Beit Chabad. They feel they want to do something Jewish sometimes. Here in Israel, they don't feel like that. They already feel Jewish— just by living in Israel they think they are doing enough—so they don't connect to their religion." He filled my glass. "We have to remind them, help them, guide them back to their soul."

I raised my plastic cup. "Sounds good. But where does the vodka come in?"

"Aaaah," he said, smiling. He raised his eyebrows, and his beard twitched. "Offering drinks is spreading the word of the Meschiach. It is how we make a connection."

I glanced around at the throng of excited adolescents who flowed around our table like a river around a rock. "But why do you think everyone needs connecting to their soul? Maybe connecting with each other is better," I suggested, feeling a little light-headed with fatigue and vodka.

Ben, not to be sidetracked, shook his head. "Everything in nature wants to be connected to its source." He went on: "The plant wants earth; rain returns to its source; an animal wanders the land: these are all basic needs." With a deft hand he poured me yet another vodka. "And a Jewish person has a body and soul, too. He eats and drinks, but the source of his soul is God. As much as the body wants to eat and drink, the soul wants to be connected to God. But we don't always know how. I hope the meeting between the people and me will make the connection. That is actually the work of a rabbi: to remind everyone that the real essence is to be themselves."

I raised my glass in a toast and pushed my chair back to leave. "It's good vodka," I said. "It must be kosher?"

He nodded vigorously. "Of course. Have another one. And come back next week. We are always here, every Shabbat."

BAUHAUS BLUES IN THE WHITE CITY

I had failed to connect to my soul, and reconnecting with my youth in the fleshpots of Tel Aviv had left me somewhat deflated. Still, I was pleased to discover that the city held much else of interest for me. In 2003, UNESCO proclaimed the heart of Tel Aviv a World Heritage Site because of the many Bauhaus buildings that helped give the place its nickname, the White City. The world body declared: "The White City of Tel Aviv is a synthesis of outstanding significance of the various trends of the Modern Movement in architecture and town planning in the early part of the 20th century." As I discovered, however, the source of the White City's style is a bit more mundane.

"Nobody liked yellow, and of course blue and green were too Arab, so most buildings were painted white or off-white," said Nahoum Cohen, seventy years old, one of Israel's most prominent architects and town planners. He helped oversee the renovation of the Florentine neighborhood and Jaffa and has written numerous books on architecture and style, including *Bauhaus Tel Aviv*. I got in touch with him shortly after I had tasted Tel Aviv's nightlife, and he said that he would have loved to come with me. "Next time!" he said. On the phone he sounded lively, and as I surveyed the crowd at the corner of Dizengoff and Jabotinsky, where we had arranged to meet, I guessed who he was right away. Wearing shorts to his knees and an open white shirt, he was bronzed and unshaven and had a huge smile on his face. He waved, and we found a café nearby.

Many of the architects in the twenties were Russian Jews, while in the thirties they came from Germany, bringing with them the International Style and adapting it to local conditions. "They chose Bauhaus because with its simple straight lines and lack of any decoration, it was easy and cheap to build," Nahoum said, showing me a brochure he had brought along. "They added curves and balconies, but nothing else. In this desert place, there wasn't any wood or fancy materials, but there was lots of sand. So they built with concrete and glass, all local and inexpensive. So simple and so correct for the space." With the city's rapid growth in the fifties and sixties, many of the landmark houses they had built were destroyed to make way for towers and apartment buildings. Since the early sixties, Nahoum has been fighting to preserve the boxy Bauhaus structures, and now that fight has been adopted by UNESCO.

Although today Bauhaus structures evoke style and grandeur and are heavily protected landmarks, there was nothing grand about the vision of Walter Gropius. He chose the simplest name, Bauhaus, which means "house construction," because he had the simplest of goals. He didn't want all the fancy arches, friezes, and other adornments that marked grand European homes. Rather, he envisioned buildings made to fit the needs of the people inside. Goodness knows what Gropius would think if he knew what bureaucracy tenants endure today to make the slightest change to their protected homes. But there's one thing owners do love about their Bauhaus buildings: They're a potential gold mine.

Tel Aviv has about four thousand Bauhaus or Bauhaus-influenced buildings, although Nahoum says the number of true Bauhaus homes built in the twenties and thirties is closer to five hundred. I know well one of the Bauhaus-style buildings that was recently renovated. I can't give the address, because the owner spoke to me on condition that I wouldn't rat him out to the taxman. But the headline is this: He bought a building with nine small apartments for two million dollars, added two floors, and within a couple of years turned a profit, after purchase and renovation, of five million dollars.

Of course, the cost in terms of stress and annoyance was immense. The site manager, Uri, a large man who should lose weight urgently, shepherded the project through eighteen months of construction. He was always on the phone, arguing, browbeating, fighting. He was no longer on speaking terms with the owner. At one point during the project Uri was rushed to the hospital with acute stomach cramps diagnosed as stress. The reason for most of the aggravation: It was a Bauhaus building. Because many were built in a hurry, on poor foundations and using second-rate materials, renovating them takes longer and is usually more expensive than planned.

Yet that's nothing compared to the municipal instructions for altering protected buildings. "You can't touch this, you can't change that, everything is protected, for everything there is a rule, so we have to fight, fight, fight," Uri complained as we sat over lunch in a couscous restaurant. Later, Nahoum elaborated: "The trouble in Tel Aviv, as everywhere in Israel, is that nobody takes no for an answer. A negative response from the city planner is not the final word, but just another obstacle to overcome." Everybody argues. Why me? Why not him? Meanwhile, each Bauhaus building comes with its own unique needs and instructions. One can't have an elevator, another can't enclose its balconies, still another can enclose them, but only at the back. There's a rule for everything: plumbing, electrical, water, proportions, aesthetics, materials, public safety, garden appearance, the surrounding walls. "It's a complex thing," Nahoum concluded, "murder for everyone. So because they all argue, everything takes more time and costs more money."

On Uri's site, one tenant had ignored a supporting wall ("it didn't support much anyway") and built a window to the garden twice the size permitted. Upstairs, three apartment owners turned their external terraces into internal bathrooms, without permission. Upon the building's completion, a municipal inspector will determine whether to give the building a *tofes arbah*, the building license. Only then can the building connect to water and electricity.

"So if the inspector sees the bathrooms," I said to Uri, "that could screw the owner."

"Good!" said Uri, beaming. "I hope it does!"

Adding to the mix, the attention generated by the World Heritage designation has also helped attract foreign interest and investment. Now, alongside the preserved Bauhaus buildings, residential towers are going up on Rothschild, planned by architectural and design icons such as I. M. Pei, Richard Meier, and Philippe Starck. As a condition of their permits, the builders must renovate neighboring protected buildings and incorporate them into the design of the new tower. It's an attractive combination that bridges styles and time, and it has led to property prices comparable to those of Manhattan.

NOT A CARE IN THE WORLD

The transition from old to new that so marks Tel Aviv's architecture was underlined later that day, when I decided to grab a bite at a kiosk. There had once been dozens of these small brick huts along the boulevards, but today only a few remain, in gentrified form. The grubby, decades-old layers of movie posters and public announcements have been scraped away and replaced by polished brass and café signs. I walked to the corner of Rothschild and Allenby; there, in perfect harmony with the zeitgeist, the kiosk that had for generations sold cigarettes, lottery tickets, and fizzy drinks is now a sushi bar. I ordered California rolls and temaki and a small jar of hot sake.

This pleasant street corner had been the starting point for my two weeks of getting reacquainted with Tel Aviv, yet as I sat there eating sushi I looked forward only to this: never going to a bar or nightclub again in my life. Reliving one's youth rarely ends well, I suppose. Still, I had enjoyed some of what I found, especially Tel Aviv's unique youthful energy and complexity. Here, Orthodox Jewish neighborhoods exist side by side with the frenetic, Western lifestyle of the city's youth. When Hagar and I lit a candle at the site of the murders at the young gays' club on Nahmani Street, a religious couple entered the next building pushing a pram. He wore a *shtreimel*, a round hat of sable fur, and a grubby black suit with a white shirt; she wore a wig, and her dress touched the ground. I had asked Ben Gur, the Hasid who tried to save my soul, whether he had ever been to Haoman 17. He replied that at Hanukkah, he and his Hasidic friends go into nightclubs and bars to light Hanukkah candles and then to sing and bless the revelers. "Do you dance with them?" I asked.

"Of course, we always dance, wherever we are. It helps connect to the soul."

As for Arabs and Jews, they live alongside each other tolerably well; certainly they have come a long way since 1922, when Tel Aviv's Mayor Dizengoff received this warning from L. M. Jeune, an alarmed Jewish resident of Jaffa: "Mixed bathing is drawing the natives to the Bathing Resort, and to my knowledge, three Arabs have bathed there. They will spread the news that they are allowed to mix with the ladies, and there will surely be trouble."[4] Today, you'll often find as many Arabs as Jews on the beach near Jaffa, especially in the evenings. As Gatenyo told me, the number of crimes this provokes is so few as to be statistically irrelevant.

I had certainly enjoyed my leisurely strolls along the boulevards and side streets of central Tel Aviv, visiting their small museums and art galleries and stopping for coffee and cake in the neighborhood cafés. It is an intimate and pleasant place, and if you are so inclined, surely the easiest place in the world to start a conversation with strangers. But it is Tel Aviv's coastline that I loved the most: a mile and a half of unbroken sand crammed with surfers, sunbathers, swimmers, voyeurs, relaxing seniors, and screaming minors. Also a promenade full of chess players, runners, walkers, skateboarders, dancers, drummers, buskers, peddlers, and restaurants and cafés that spill onto the sand regardless of the rules. It could be a beach city anywhere on earth, which is its charm: Tel Aviv seems worlds away from the turmoil that surrounds it.

A LONG, HARD SLOG

On Day Twelve of my trek, when I left Tel Aviv heading south, I stopped to survey the city from the hill of Jaffa. It is a dramatic panorama, popular among wedding photographers: The azure waters of the Mediterranean break in a line of white froth on Tel Aviv's narrow yellow beach, which curves gently northward, while the city's red roofs and tall towers blend eastward into the coastal plain, toward the Samarian foothills of the West Bank. The Israeli artist Reuven Rubin painted from a similar vantage point in the twenties. One picture in his museum on Bialik Street off Allenby shows a handful of European-style red-roofed houses dotted among the ridges of sand dunes, while nearby are the dense orange groves of Arab Jaffa, where workers prune trees as a steam train puffs by. Today it's houses and offices as far as the eye can see.

I shifted the weight of my backpack and continued my journey, through Jaffa's old streets, through the alleys of Ajami, heading for the cliff top. It is a picturesque yet depressing walk. Ajami is the poorest of all Tel Aviv–Jaffa's neighborhoods, populated mostly by Arabs, descendants of the four thousand who didn't flee in 1948. Their houses are small, neglected, and often crumbling. Meanwhile, sprouting in the best locations are fabulous homes built by developers for the wealthy, most of whom are Jews. On walls everywhere, posters show a bulldozer crushing buildings while an Arab skeleton stands before it, arms raised, pleading for mercy. A caption quotes the Old Testament: "'harazachta v'gam yarashta'—you murdered and you inherit." Every poster had been defaced, presumably by supporters of the bulldozers. Overlooking the sea is an abandoned Muslim cemetery with dead bushes, smashed gravestones, and broken concrete graves. Grass grows on the sand and earth that spill through the cracks. It's a spooky place to walk about at dawn. I expected a skeleton's hand to break through the earth and grab my ankle.

There is much to explore in Jaffa, which looks down from the hill like Tel Aviv's guilty conscience. Yet I walked on, knowing I had a long slog ahead of me. The sand that floats up from Egypt's Nile Delta gives Israel its delightful golden beaches, the best in the eastern Mediterranean, but at the water's edge the sand is loosely packed and deep. It would be very hard going, on a very hot day. Moreover, of the roughly forty miles of Israel's coastline closed to the public, taken over by the military, port authorities, and factories, much of it is south of Tel Aviv, meaning I would have to walk all the way around them, adding miles to my journey.

In Bat Yam, immediately south of Jaffa, with only sand before me until Ashdod, twenty miles on, I stocked up on water, slathered myself in sunblock, and pulled my hat with its neck flap low over my head. For extra protection from the blistering sun, I opened my umbrella. Breathing heavily and sweating profusely as I plodded on in the hundred-degree heat, I must have looked like an English deserter from the French Foreign Legion. I wound up doing twenty-five miles that day, bypassing several intelligence posts and other military installations. Frankly, it was horrible. By the time I arrived in Ashdod eleven hours later and had found a place to stay, I was cursing this whole hare-brained project. I wasn't even cheered by the fact that I had unwittingly chosen a hotel where other people took rooms by the hour. As I checked in, a blonde in a tight-fitting gold top, black slacks, and high-heel shoes walked through the door and went straight to the stairs, looking at the floor as she walked. As for me, I was so tired that I didn't leave my room until the next morning. Then I set off at four o'clock, hoping to reach the next town, Ashkelon, in better shape.

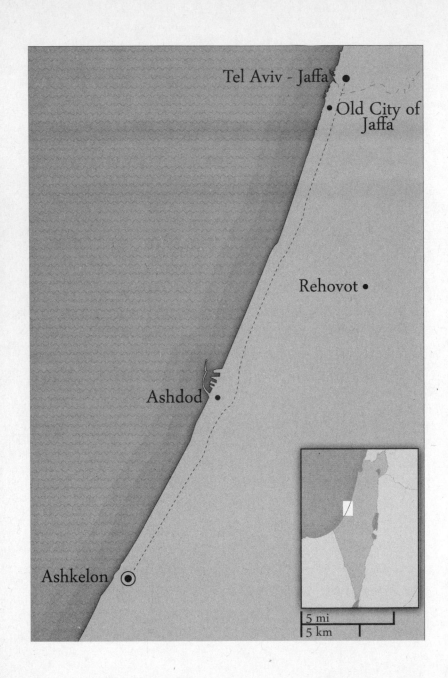

Tel Aviv - Jaffa •

• Old City of
Jaffa

Rehovot •

Ashdod •

Ashkelon ◉

5 mi
5 km

9

We're All in This Together

TEL AVIV TO ASHKELON

Ashkelon's charm lies in the people, not the place. The location is superb: Lying languidly along the water, the sea breeze cooling the sun-drenched streets, Ashkelon should be a tourist haven. But there is little to do. Although the seaport dates back to the Bronze Age, the marina is small, the promenade drab, and the town's cultural offerings meager. But the town grows on you, if you give it time. In the arts center, children compete noisily in a piano competition while parents take photos with cell phones. Outside, a group of elderly men and women practice tai chi on a green traffic island as traffic swirls by. In Roger's Café, it seems the whole town comes to gossip over cheese and spinach bourekas and strong coffee. The establishment bustles with immigrants from France, Ethiopia, Russia, Morocco, and Tunisia, but when rockets explode, it's like London in the Blitz: Everyone runs for shelter, joking, knowing they're all in it together.

Ashkelon is Israel's seventh-largest city, but the place has a five-thousand-year history of conquest, failing dynasties, and curious footnotes. It was here, the Bible relates, that Samson flew into a rage and killed thirty Philistines; here that the fair Delilah betrayed him by cutting his hair and sapping his strength. There are seven hundred dog skeletons in a mysterious ancient cemetery, which some believe may be left over from a cult practice that held dogs to be sacred. Saladin defeated the Crusaders here in 1187 until Richard the Lionheart led them back, only to lose again. For a journalist, the town has a passing interest as the first documented place to invoke censorship. After King Saul was killed, David commanded: "Tell it not in Gath, publish it not in the streets of Ashkelon; lest the daughters of the Philistines rejoice, lest the daughters of the uncircumcised triumph."[1]

One thing about Ashkelon I learned firsthand: It is best to drive there. It was hard enough walking to Ashdod the day before, but reaching Ashkelon's outskirts required trudging through another twelve miles of heavy sand. By high noon, I was groaning, sweating like a pig, exhausted, and miserable. Then the going got really tough. I had to maneuver around a mile-long condom (at least, that's what it looks like)—a giant, sand-filled canvas sheath, shoulder-high, wide as a barrel, that lies along the narrow beach, protecting the crumbling cliff from the pounding waves. Wherever I tried to walk—next to it on the beach, or along the top of it—waves kept smashing into me. Attempting to climb the cliff, I slid right down again with stones and rocks clattering around me. I was almost on my knees when I reached the first building in Ashkelon, which thankfully was the Holiday Inn, a white, round, jelly-shaped throwback of the kind that forty years ago must have made the city proud for a week or two.

I stayed in town one night, and with all due respect to the good people of the city, couldn't get out fast enough. Ashkelon is a harmless-enough place with a couple of quaint areas, but it mostly consists of sleepy streets and dreary malls. The beaches are fine, but the marina and seafront, much touted in the guidebooks, are soulless: concrete terraces, downmarket empty cafés with cold coffee and stale croissants, and people who shout instead of talk. In the evening I got lost near the hotel and was assailed by the macho street names: Paratroopers Street leads into Tank Street, which runs parallel to Pilots Street, near Givati and Golani Streets, named after Israeli infantry brigades. Imagine being an Arab here, I thought, and asking for directions. It would be doubly insulting because Ashkelon was built upon the ruins of two Arab towns, Al-Majdal and Al-Jura. Street names are not only a guide to a city but to its approved history, and here the Arab part had been erased.

To summon up energy for my trip's final leg, I treated myself to a morning massage in the hotel's health spa. The subdued light, jungle sounds, warm oils, and attentions of the masseuse went a good way to improving my mood. I was still on shaky legs when I left her little room, so I stopped for a final coffee at the marina to restore my strength. Then I set off. As Ashkelon's power plant and neighboring water desalination complex on the water's edge bar the public from the beach, I had to walk around them by going deeper into town and turning right along the main road. I was heading for the dunes but decided to walk through the fields for a change, a decision I would bitterly regret. It was another sunny day and from the peaks of the hills I could just make out the hazy, crowded slums of Gaza's Shati refugee camp and, a little farther on, Gaza City itself. I was on the home stretch, looking forward to touching the border wall and collapsing in a heap. As I plodded southward with my backpack and bottled water, I expected rarely, if ever, to visit Ashkelon again.

How wrong could I be? I had left in shorts and sandals and returned six months later in a bulletproof Cherokee jeep and flak jacket. I removed my writer's cap and strapped on my war reporter's Kevlar helmet. How quickly things change in Israel.

December 27, 2008, was a rare moment of almost complete Israeli unity. It was the day the Israeli armed forces hit back at Hamas, Gaza's reigning power, after eight years of intermittent shelling from the territory. Homemade Qassam rockets intimidated the people of Sderot and other communities that neighbored Gaza, but they were pinpricks that usually made more noise than damage. Then Hamas upped the stakes by firing fearsome Grad rockets smuggled from Iran, hitting more distant cities such as Ashkelon, until Israel could take it no more. Israel's air assault led to its ground invasion, which reduced anything in its path to rubble. It also led to fierce debate throughout Israel, and the world, about the cruelty and futility of it all.

As I covered the war through most of January 2009, Ashkelon became my home base; I rushed from town to town in southern Israel, chasing the bombs. Afterward, as I tried to make sense of it all, it dawned on me: Although I had thought my leisurely coastal walk would give me a truer sense of Israel than my frenzied work as a reporter, in the case of Ashkelon, it was the reverse. I found that the war had peeled back the layers and allowed me to discover the true nature of the place and its people. Not only did I meet many charming characters whose tangled and complex stories defy the accepted simple narrative of Jews against Arabs, but I confirmed several elements of Israel's inescapable reality: that everything and everyone is connected in the Arab-Israeli conflict; that one man's triumph is another man's sorrow; and above all, that no Jew or Arab should celebrate too loudly, because sure as hell, his turn could be next.

IT'S SAFEST BY THE CONCRETE

When we first heard that Israeli war planes were pounding Hamas targets in Gaza, I raced from Tel Aviv with my NBC cameraman and friend Amikam Cohen, a burly, blustering, larger-than-life character who had been my good-luck charm in conflicts for twenty-five years. As rocks bounced off our vehicle and shells exploded, he would always yell: "Don't worry, Martin, you're with me!" Now, as we approached Ashkelon warily from the north, police cars lined the road at intervals, waiting for bombs from Gaza. We turned off Highway 4 and were just pulling into the town center when the cars in front stopped dead, as if they had hit a wall.

Amikam's evasive action consisted of a stream of foul curses as he jammed on the brakes. We lurched forward, while other drivers leaped from their cars and flung themselves onto the street with their hands covering their heads, and pedestrians sprinted to the nearest building. In her rush, a grandmother pushing a stroller rammed it into the curb and the back wheels jolted upward. The head of a startled infant popped up, as if it were being tossed out of the stroller, and then quickly sank back out of sight. All this happened in a surrealist silence punctuated only by Amikam's cursing: Behind the inch-thick bulletproof glass, we couldn't even hear the siren warning of a rocket attack. We leaped out of the car but quickly figured we'd be better off inside the armored vehicle, so we leaped back in. An orange spilled from someone's shopping bag and rolled down the street, coming to a halt by the feet of two men sitting at an outside café. They were calmly ignoring the panic and sipping their coffee.

The maximum warning time given by the red-alert siren of a Grad rocket shooting from Gaza to Ashkelon is thirty seconds. We had hardly slammed the car door shut when there was a distant, muffled boom. The all clear quickly followed. Drivers dusted themselves, looked around sheepishly, returned to their cars, and drove off. Pedestrians returned to the streets, including the woman with the stroller, who leaned over it, cooed to the baby, and wheeled it away. A man at the table picked up the orange and offered it to his friend.

We parked the jeep and entered a café, hoping to learn where the bomb had fallen. Our mission couldn't have contrasted more starkly with my last, leisurely stroll through town for this book, but being here was better than reporting from the other side of the border, in Gaza, where I would have been cowering under Israel's assault, threatened by Hamas gunmen, working twenty-two hours a day, and sleeping in a hotel with little electricity, water, or food. Still, what had become routine for me as a war reporter was terrifying for Ashkelon's peaceful inhabitants, since they had only recently come within range of Hamas's improved rocketry. For six months, the town had been under sporadic missile attack, culminating now in a dozen attacks a day.

Just as we confirmed that the rocket had fallen harmlessly into a field, the siren rang again, a high-pitched whine that whistled around the streets from speakers across town. It rang from the television and the radio, which were both kept at top volume inside the small café. Through the wall-to-ceiling glass windows, I could see people pushing back their chairs and again rushing to safety, while the man behind the bar just laughed. He was a sun-bronzed, middle-aged fellow with white sunglasses perched on top of his cropped, dyed blond hair. He didn't move but lifted his cup of coffee to toast a big man seated in the corner by a concrete pillar. Later, I asked the man by the pillar why he hadn't moved. He said, "It's safest here, by the concrete."

I said, "But you're surrounded by glass windows. That doesn't make sense."

He answered, "What does?"

Good point, I thought. What better sums up Israel's sense of fragility—the paradox of a small country surrounded by enemies, that fears extinction, yet is seen as the neighborhood bully? And here's this big man, as the bomb falls, hugging the concrete pillar, surrounded by glass.

An elderly man sitting alone calmly informed me, as the stranger in town, while we waited for the rocket to hit: "If it's a quiet thud it means it fell in a field. If it's a sharp crack, it fell in the street. And if it's a whine and a whoosh, you're dead!" We all laughed and cocked our ears like terriers. I hadn't learned this from walking down the coast, and I wondered which was closer to the true nature of life in Israel—lazing on the beach with a book or running to the bomb shelter with a baby? And if it's a bit of both, then truly, this place must drive you crazy—like a serial bungee jumper guessing when the rope will break.

A few seconds passed until we heard a quiet thud. We relaxed; the rocket had fallen in a field. But then there was a sharp crack, followed by another louder, sharper crack. Two more rockets, and not far away. The men looked at each other.

After a few seconds the man behind the bar, whose name was Roger, said, "It fell by Yossi's house."

How could he know? I thought. He hadn't spoken to anyone.

"Where's that?" I asked. The phone rang and Roger answered it. Other men came in, shouting and nervous. It's close. One fell on Yossi's street. A woman saved her baby. No, she didn't. The baby died. There was no woman. There was no baby. Within a minute, four different versions of the story came flooding out, and when Amikam and I reached the house, we found that none of them had been true.

It was a street of pleasant little villas, and we had to elbow our way through the excited neighbors. Already emergency services had taken control, taping off the house, lifting the larger pieces of masonry and debris, clearing a way in and out, and evacuating victims of shock. There were no wounded, as everybody had followed orders and sought safety inside the bomb shelters. The rocket had smashed into the top floor, blasting a hole the size of a television in the wall, through which we could see a stuffed leopard on a bed, covered in dust and white plaster.

In the middle of the room, an emergency worker was comforting a young woman who was sobbing loudly. The social worker told her she needed to see a psychologist. "No, I don't," she gulped, "I'm fine."

"She's hysterical," a man interrupted, putting his arm around her shoulder. He was her brother, Itzik Ben-Dayan. He was lucky to be alive. He had heard the first rocket's distant thud and was just about to leave the shelter when "the house exploded." But he was calm. He stroked his sister's hair. "She panics, she always does."

"It's true," the seventeen-year-old girl, whose name was Mazi, told the social worker. "As soon as I hear the siren, I don't cry—I scream! I go crazy. Everything scares me, an ambulance, a dog, I don't sleep well at night. Ever since the missile hit the mall."

In May 2008 some genius in Ashkelon's city hall had turned off the missile alarm system, saying it kept sounding for no reason, upsetting everybody. So when Mazi was waiting at a bus stop by the Hutzot Mall, she had no warning. The first of Hamas's upgraded Grad rockets to hit Ashkelon just missed her head. "It landed right next to me," Mazi said, pointing to the corner of the room, as if that's where the rocket hit. "I saw it flying and falling, long and black; I saw the missile flying and landing, next to me; I saw all the wounded people; I was in the bus station, I am so afraid I don't wish it on a dog, the missile, smoke and fire, all black, less than four meters from me."

Four people were seriously wounded. Mazi was taken to the hospital, miraculously unhurt but in shock, unable to move her legs. Eight months later, she was still terrified. "I feel like I want to vomit, I'm giddy, fainting, suddenly I have low blood pressure, I take vitamins, B-twelve, I cry." Now she left the house only to go to work in a supermarket, and then rushed home to what she had assumed was safety. Luckily she had been at work when the missile hit her bedroom. It was her leopard we could see through the hole. "This place is cursed," Mazi said, "it is under an evil spell."

GAZA WAS LIKE TEL AVIV FOR US

War is the best time to feel the true nature of a people, and I have to say, war brings out the best in Israelis. It wasn't exactly London during the Blitz, but the sense of "We're all in this together" made Roger's Café in Ashkelon, on the corner of Herzl and Tsahal Streets, a riveting place. Israelis at war show an unaccustomed generosity toward one another, as well as rock-solid support for the fighters, healthy contempt for the politicians, and, too often, confusion about the war's goals. Roger Hatav, a local institution, was a gold mine of information and opinion. The whole world was speculating if and when Israel would send in the ground troops. One day, he brought my coffee and said, "Today's the invasion. Trust me." I asked him how he knew. "A soldier told me he got the order," he said.

Yeah, right, I thought. It's true that everybody in Ashkelon passes through Roger's Café, but there was no way Roger could know; if a soldier got the order, he wouldn't be allowed off base. Moreover, the army had taken away their telephones. They didn't want to make the same mistake as in their last war against Hezbollah, when soldiers in south Lebanon were ordering pizzas from Kiryat Shmona in Israel, giving away their positions to eavesdropping Iranian monitors. But sure enough, that day, as Roger said, Israel invaded. The little corner table by the door became my daily watering hole, my listening post, the ground to which I held my ear. As I discovered, to the people here the war was anything but futile; it was a defensive war, forced upon them.

We had left Mazi whimpering in the safe arms of her brother and the social worker and had driven back to Roger's Café for breakfast. After the three rockets had fallen, the pedestrian street outside had emptied. "Look after yourself," a female soldier was saying to a clearly drunken Russian who was sitting on a low wall. She handed him a piece of paper. "Read it; it says what to do if there's a bomb." She was from the Home Front command. Young male and female soldiers in baggy olive green uniforms with backpacks and M16 rifles slung over their shoulders were roaming the streets, looking for people to give their leaflets to, but there was nobody around. Shops were closed and shuttered; music blared from an abandoned DVD stall. The only pedestrians were pigeons waddling down the street. Mostly the soldiers were just flirting with one another.

The only place with a few people was Roger's Café, a name that hardly does it justice. It is more like a shrine. Every inch of wall space is occupied by a photo of Roger. Roger bare-chested, muscles flexed, as a handsome young man with full black hair; and bare-chested today, bigger and blonder. Roger with a large-bosomed Brazilian dancer on each arm, Roger with politicians, mayors, local soccer stars. Even the tabletops bore laminated photos of a young Roger with bare chest and white fedora. Outside was a life-size poster of Roger in blue-and-yellow Hawaiian shirt and pants. When Roger realized that we were reporters, he plied us with food and drink and refused to take a penny. When the young soldiers came in to rest, he sent them free food and drinks. For three weeks this went on. I think he gave away more food than he sold. When I asked why, Roger said,

"This is a war. This is not a time to make money." When I told him that in most places war was seen as a time to make lots of money, he answered, "Not in Israel—we are a family, but we only realize it when we are fighting someone else instead of each other."

Over the weeks, Roger sent over a steady flow of *hreime* ("It's spicy!"), a bizarre but tasty tuna-and-vegetable dish cooked by his mother, with whom he still lives. This was accompanied by bourekas stuffed with spinach, potatoes, and cheese; olives; cucumber and tomato salads; tuna sandwiches; boiled eggs; fruit juices and coffees by the pint, all carried on wobbly trays by Nanja Samsonoff, a blond Ukrainian who gave Amikam her telephone number. Whenever somebody came in, Roger waved him to my table so I could interrogate him. They were all men, and either from Tunisia, like Roger, who came at the age of six, or from Morocco or Libya. They all spoke Arabic, and they all agreed that they knew the Arabs better than the Arabs did themselves: "Gaza was like Tel Aviv for us," they said. Until the first Palestinian uprising in 1987, when the border became a real border, they shopped there, had Palestinian friends there, and went to each other's weddings and funerals. "Trust me," they all said, "if it was up to us, we'd have peace tomorrow!" But first, they said as one: "In war, as in war!"

These men should know Arabs. From the late forties, when Israel was founded, to the midsixties, anti-Jewish violence and Arab nationalism forced almost 900,000 Jews to flee their homes in Arab countries. Many were from the oldest unbroken Jewish lines in the world—Jewish families in Iraq, Syria, Yemen, and Egypt, tracing their roots back for two thousand years and more. Others escaped from Lebanon, Algeria, Morocco, Iran, and Afghanistan, emptying their proud Jewish communities. In Afghanistan today, there is only one Jew left. His name is Zebulon Simentov, and I met him just after I finished my coastal trek for this book. He cares for the synagogue on Flower Street in Kabul and is known locally as "The Jew." I brought him regards from friends in Israel, but all he really wanted was a bottle of Johnnie Walker ("black!") and a "contribution for the synagogue." About 600,000 of these Mizrachim (eastern Jews) settled in Israel. At first they were dismissed by the European Jews, who couldn't pronounce their names and wouldn't let them speak Arabic. Most of them were sent to poor, peripheral towns such as Ashkelon once was. After Gaza was conquered in 1967, the border was open; many of the eastern Jews felt more at home with the boisterous Gazan Arabs than with Tel Aviv's effete European Jews. So today, when the Mizrachi Jews in Roger's Café said if it was up to them they'd make peace tomorrow, I believed them. But as they told me, first they had a condition, based on their experience: Talk only from a position of strength.

Yaacov Zaguri, from Morocco, knew the answer to the Qassam rockets: "Hit them harder—then they'll think differently. Let America fight Al-Qaeda. Hamas is our enemy; we'll fight them our way. But we have to end it once and for all. If by talks, good . . ." Yaacov spoke clearly, out of consideration for my poor Hebrew, but there was something inapt and eerie for a man to enunciate so deliberately and precisely the words "or . . . we . . . will . . . smash . . . them."

Yaacov was the big man who liked to hug the concrete pillar when rockets fell. I asked him what he did at home. "We don't have a shelter," he said, "so we keep running down to the basement to hide. We knew all our neighbors, but not in our pajamas! Now we do. The worst is my son Itai. He's so scared, by the time I have my slippers on he's downstairs already, five steps at a time. It's hard to see your son trembling like a rabbit. He's twelve. I have a sixteen-year-old too, Gal. He just stays in bed."

"He must be cool," I said.

"No, just lazy. He takes after me. Three bombs fell nearby, one fell in our parking lot."

"Aren't you scared for Gal, then?" I asked.

"No—we trust in God."

"Yes," said Miro Hadjaj from Tunis, who had joined us while Yaacov was speaking. He was eating one of my bourekas and held two olives in one hand and a cucumber in the other, all poised by his mouth, waiting for space. He spat crumbs as he spoke. "It's amazing how many of their bombs fell in open areas or parking lots. People only got scratches. They've only killed one person here. And he's an Arab! Three Jews were downstairs when the Arab was killed, all construction workers. But nothing happened to the Jews. I think maybe God looks after us." Boureka flakes floated in Amikam's coffee, but he didn't notice.

Another man pulled up a chair. Whereas the others were around fifty or sixty years old, Chaim Hadad was only twenty-seven. He had also immigrated from Tunis. As he sat down, he shook hands with everybody and listened politely. They all had dark hair, swarthy skin, big hands, big smiles, and hearty gestures; from their looks they could all have been from one family, and in a sense, they were. Nodding at Chaim, Miro said, "He gives a lot. But he doesn't want to talk about it."

"Why not?" I asked.

Miro looked at me as if I were truly ignorant. "Because it reduces the value of the mitzvah."

Hadad's family owned supermarkets, which they opened up to every good cause. "I don't have much to give," Miro explained, "so I ask Chaim. He gives cases of drinks, boxes of bourekas, and I put them in my car and take them to the soldiers. He says, 'Miro, take what you want, because the people of Israel are together and that's what's important, we're together. Each does what he can.'"

"Why not talk about it?" I asked again.

"As soon as somebody lacks something and you have it, you give it," Miro said, finishing my *hreime*. "I must do what I can. That's a mitzvah. Give. Simple. At the end of life it all adds up. God judges what man has done. We believe that only God knows. We don't need to talk about it. Just do it. God judges us."

Yaacov added, "Chaim lost two million shekels from the war in two weeks, but he still donates all the time." I looked at Chaim. He smiled and remained silent, no doubt jacking up his heavenly points.

At another table, two men sat quietly, sipping coffee and looking at the news on TV. Roger took me by the hand and made me sit with them. One was an Arab and the other was the son-in-law of the mayor. Yossi Dayan spoke formally, as if speaking on behalf of the town, aware of his heavy responsibility addressing a foreign reporter: "There must be peace. We want it from our youth, but we can't give up on security. It is true there is a lot of hate on the other side; it depends on their leaders. They must have the same desire and need for peace that we have." He covered his friend's hand with his own. "Sa'id is a personal friend of mine," he continued, "he is an Arab, but our relations are like any Israelis together. I'm happy to have him as a friend. This is how it can be in the future. Is it so?" Sa'id nodded solemnly. Yossi went on, "Here's a Gazan guy sitting here but he leads an Israeli life like I do, an Israeli citizen, even though his wife is still in Gaza. As I said, Palestinians in Gaza want a normal life." Then he turned to Sa'id and said, "Right? You want a normal life?"

I almost laughed. What was Sa'id supposed to say—No, I don't want a normal life? And what is normal? And anyway, Sa'id was hardly representative. He must have been an Israeli agent in Gaza, or he would never have been granted Israeli citizenship without an Israeli wife. Yossi's arrogance annoyed me, so I challenged him in a way that I had not with Roger and his other friends.

"Actually," I pointed out, "you're living here on top of an Arab town, right? They did live a normal life, until you kicked them out." This part of Ashkelon was built upon the ruins of the old Arab town of Majdal. Three hundred yards down Army Street was all that remained—a minaret from a destroyed mosque that houses a museum, and a couple of Arab buildings converted into shops and bars. Israel's response is: If they hadn't started the war, they wouldn't have lost it. But Yossi ignored me and continued with his sermon to the press: "I believe most Arabs want peace. They are simple people; they want peace like us. Hamas brought chaos and catastrophe on the Palestinians . . ." He droned on but I had tuned out. Then through the café chatter I heard my name—"He's an American reporter"—and looked up to see a beaming Roger pulling yet another man by the arm toward me. Just as he was introducing Yossi Fartook, originally from Tunis, Nanja dropped a plate of bourekas that made a louder bang, and got more attention in this café, than a Grad rocket ever did.

HOPE STREET

These very Arab Jews showed that even if some of Israel's borders are neatly defined on the map, the borders between the people are anything but clear. Jews in the north once crossed freely to have tea with their Lebanese neighbors, while in the south, Israelis and Palestinians visited and traded with each other for two decades. While I talked with one building constructor in Ashkelon, he phoned his former Palestinian workers in Gaza to see how they were getting along under Israel's bombing. That led me to wonder about the fate of an acquaintance of mine in Gaza, the only Palestinian I had ever met who literally raised a white flag of surrender.

Iyad's family was originally from Majdal, and if ever a man's story defied the accepted narrative, it was his. Yossi Dayan, the mayor's son-in-law, would have loved to hear his story, but I didn't want to give him the pleasure. Iyad lived in Beit Hanoun in northern Gaza, five hundred yards from the border with Israel. His white flag was a large, grimy sheet hoisted on a tall branch above his stable, which housed his most prized possession, a bony white horse. His family must have once lived very close to where I was sitting—the Jewish neighborhood called Migdal, after Majdal, which had been home to ten thousand Arabs. It is an Aramaic name meaning "fortress"; four thousand years ago, a settlement here had been called Majdal Jad, after the Canaanite god of luck, but in more recent times, in 1948, the town had had the misfortune of being the forward headquarters of the Egyptian army under the command of General Gamal Abdel Nasser, soon to be Egypt's president. Majdal became a key target of the young Israeli army. When Jewish troops conquered the town and forced the Egyptian soldiers to flee, they also expelled most of Majdal's Arab civilians. The rest were deported in 1953. In the local museum, you can see black-and-white photos of the dejected Arabs sitting before the Israeli military headquarters. Most of them settled in Gaza. Now, to complete the circle, Palestinian refugees in Gaza were firing rockets at their old homes in Ashkelon, provoking Israel to attack their new homes in Gaza; and Iyad the farmer, this son of Majdal-Ashkelon, was in the middle.

Not that Iyad would have cared for the irony. When I first met him in the summer of 2006, Israeli tanks from the famed Givati brigade were poised to attack his town. They were lined up on the edge of Beit Hanoun's melon and tomato fields and firing the odd artillery shell, hoping to frighten Palestinian civilians into fleeing the area, thus clearing the path for an eventual attack. Iyad had a problem—several, actually. His biggest was that if the tanks came, his was one of the first houses they would crush. This was the area from where militants fired rockets at Sderot, less than a thousand yards away. Iyad lived on the last street of Beit Hanoun, and he described his dilemmas without ever changing his expression, a completely lifeless face, as if he were paralyzed. He was quite witty in his strange, deadpan way, so when I asked him the name of his street and he answered, "Hope Street," I burst out laughing. But it was true. Has a street ever been so ineptly named? I asked him why he was flying the white flag of surrender. Had he given up on the struggle for Palestinian rights? "Rights?" he spat, without moving a muscle. "All I want is for a shell not to kill me and my family." His mother, a wizened old lady, her head wrapped in a checkered shawl, chuckled. I asked her when she had last lived in peace and quiet, and she answered, as I knew she would: "Never." But then she added, "At least when the Israelis occupied us we could work the fields, we had some money. Not like now. Now we have nothing."

"So why don't you move away for a bit?" I asked Iyad. Every day, the Israelis were creeping their shells closer to the houses. Shrapnel had hit one girl in the mouth and a foreign journalist in the face. "Where to?" he shouted. "Where can I go? If I go to Gaza, I'll be killed!"

The farther you move from the centers of power, and the closer you get to the real people, the less their stories fit the political platitudes; it's a lesson I have learned repeatedly around the world, and it's why I love avoiding officialdom and talking randomly to Joe Shmo. Iyad's story isn't what I had expected to hear, and it certainly isn't what Palestinian leaders want their people to say. It turned out that Iyad's cousin, a nervous fellow, had moved into an apartment building in Gaza City and the landlord wanted him to leave. He refused to go. Finally, in desperation, the landlord paid the Daghmoush family, notorious thugs, to ask him to leave "their way." Half a dozen goons warned Iyad's cousin, and then turned up at his door, without knowing the nature of the man. Iyad's cousin greeted them with a hail of gunfire that killed two of them. He went to jail, but that wasn't enough for the Daghmoush family. An eye for an eye, a tooth for a tooth, and, as the biblical verse continues, a life for a life. In this case, two lives. In Gaza, jail is less a punishment for a crime, more a haven against revenge. The only fitting punishment is the same crime again. So Iyad couldn't leave Beit Hanoun because the Daghmoush family would kill him. But if he stayed, he risked getting killed by the Israelis. Shrugging, he said, "I'd rather take my chances with the Israelis than face certain death in Gaza City."

The next day, I returned with gifts of food and water for the family; they had run out and were afraid to leave the house because of the shelling. There had been explosions most of the day and night, and I asked if the tanks had actually moved yet. I thought they would be scared, but Iyad's mother answered, "I want the Israelis to come. At least it will be peaceful here and we will be safe. They'll stop the shelling and nobody can kill my son."

Now, two years on, the Israelis had come, at last, to stop the shelling of their own towns, and I wondered what had happened to Iyad. Had he surrendered again? Israeli armored vehicles preferred to crush homes by driving over them rather than risk mined roads; as a result, swaths of northern Gaza had been flattened. To protect their own homes, Israelis were destroying Palestinian homes. Iyad's family lost their home in Majdal; had they lost their home again in Beit Hanoun? And had Iyad, this family man who preferred Israeli soldiers to Palestinian gunmen, lost his life?

IT SAYS SO IN THE TORAH

Two weeks into the January war, after my daily breakfast at Roger's, we drove to an Israeli hilltop by the small town of Sderot, about fifteen miles from Ashkelon. It was mid-afternoon on a sunny day. The northern half of Gaza was spread out below me, and I was peering through binoculars, trying to see if Iyad's house was still intact. I wasn't able to make out his home because the line of houses bordering the fields a thousand yards away was too small and blurry. I could see an army position on a low hill with a few trees right in front of Beit Hanoun. The vegetable fields were muddy and ridged, demolished by the giant tracks of Israeli tanks, armored personnel vehicles, and huge armored bulldozers.

When I met Iyad in 2006, we had observed a similar scene from the Palestinian side. We were hiding in a destroyed building with the Palestinian owner of the melon fields, watching the tanks approach in a cloud of dust, dirt, and mushed-up melons. Next to us, another man was laughing.

"When they pass that tree," he said, pointing, "they'll start to ruin my land, too."

"That's funny?" I said.

"What else can I do but laugh?" he asked. "We have already lost everything. Look at my house."

He waved forlornly, pointing to the debris and damage from the shell that had plowed through the wall and smashed the furniture. I was standing on a burned tablecloth. "Now they are taking my fields, and I can't get to our water well. God is good!" He laughed again, close to tears. That was then, and now the people of Beit Hanoun were facing the same tanks again. All because gunmen from Hamas, Islamic Jihad, Al-Aksa, and other militias hid in their fields and streets and fired rockets at Israel. The militants' message was: As long as we suffer in Gaza, we'll make you suffer in Israel. But they were adding to the suffering of their own people, too.

Now, while we were still peering at Gaza, the siren wailed and we threw ourselves to the ground by our bulletproof jeep. Luckily the rockets flew over us, their thirty-pound warheads exploding a few hundred yards away in the center of Sderot. Eight thousand rockets had hit in the region in eight years, an average of three a day. But the area is poor and far from Israel's center, and nobody paid enough heed to do much about it. Only when larger towns such as Ashkelon and Ashdod came within range did the government pay serious attention: Hence Operation Cast Lead, which we were now observing.

As it turned out, one of the rockets that flew over us exploded in Sderot's bus station, miraculously hurting nobody; everyone was already in the bomb shelters. We raced after it and found, amid the debris, a tall, imposing young fireman called Moshe Geffen supervising the cleanup and calling out orders. Geffen's story mirrored Iyad's, only in reverse. While Iyad was a refugee in Gaza, expelled from Israel, Moshe was a refugee in Israel, expelled from Gaza. And while Iyad longed to return to his home in Israel, which he called Arab land, Moshe longed to return to his in Gaza, which he called Jewish land. They would have agreed on only two things—that they wanted peace, and that the other side was wrong. But like Iyad's, Moshe's story wasn't straightforward, either.

When I first got to know Moshe, my trusty television team—producer Paul Goldman and cameraman Dave Copeland—couldn't stop laughing. After we met Moshe in the bus station, we agreed we would follow him and his fire truck as they kept Sderot safe. That night, another missile fell, and the red fire truck raced off in hot pursuit, with us chasing in our jeep. But the fire crew couldn't find the rocket. They followed the highway until they reached an industrial site. Moshe jumped out and pounded into the night, looking for the impact site. He quickly returned, panting, one hand keeping his yellow helmet on his head, feet thumping the earth: "This isn't it." He jumped back into the truck, back to the highway, past signs to Ashdod in one direction, Beersheba in another. Police cars screamed by, in the opposite direction. The fire truck pulled into a side street, turned left, left again, right, and came to a halt in a cul de sac. The truck did a ten-point turn, then drove a bit, then stopped. We saw a flashlight go on in the cab as the crew pored over a map. Don't they have a GPS? I thought. Finally, they pulled off again, drove around for ten minutes, and eventually found a fire, 150 yards from the fire station where they'd begun.

Flames leaped, or rather, smoke wafted, from a green garbage container in the street. It wasn't the rocket, which fell in a field, but at least they'd found something to do. Pedestrians looked on in surprise as firemen swarmed the area. Moshe ran up and directed the jet into the garbage, and the fire was instantly extinguished. After a few seconds of hissing, and a few more minutes of water, I accused him of wasting precious reserves when the country was suffering a severe drought. He seemed rather hurt and said that smoke inhalation kills.

Moshe, born in Boston, had lived in a Jewish settlement in Gaza for eight years; his wife, Ayelet, from Passaic, New Jersey, had spent twenty years there. They had lived in a little house of sixty-five square meters with their two children. Moshe had five jobs—fireman, ambulance driver, medic, burial-society volunteer, and guard in the village protection unit. He loved his life in the sun—loved going to the beach anytime he wanted—and above all, he loved his community. The settlement featured mostly religious Jews, a good school, a low crime rate, and a sense of shared struggle. "Gaza is part of the land of Israel," Moshe said as we sat in the fire station, chatting on the bench in front of the TV. "The Torah says so, and what better source is there to prove it?"

We were watching the war on the news, while Moshe waited for the next rocket. "We weren't so extreme," he continued, "not like in Judea and Shomron. We were people of the beach, and they are people of the moun-tain. We're different, always have been. Sand shapes itself to the vessel it's in, rocks do not. To plant a tree they dig and hammer, each tree costs them blood. We just dig and water and five minutes later you planted a tree." Moshe glanced at the television, which showed Israeli burn victims in a nearby hospital. He watched with professional interest while he talked.

"Since the Second Temple, there were only two places with an un-broken Jewish presence, Pek'in and Gaza. And you know what? Our farm-ers are still getting calls from the Palestinians who used to be their workers. They ask, why can't we grow our lettuces? We were the first people in his-tory to grow food in those sand dunes in Gush Katif. It was a no-man's-land. So who does it belong to? Nobody lived there. We didn't steal it from any-one."

Herzl would have been proud of Moshe. This was the original Zionist logic, neatly packaged on the size of a postcard: a people without land for a land without people. And then we made the desert bloom. We grew let-tuces and they still can't. What dopes! Case closed. The trouble is, the other side doesn't place much importance in lettuce. The issue of the legal ownership of the land of Gush Katif is a minefield: Jews bought some land around Kfar Darom in the 1930s, and then Egypt annexed most of Gaza in 1946, only to lose it to Israel in 1967. While the Palestinians today claim all of it, so do religious Jews such as Moshe Geffen, for whom Gaza is an integral part of the Land of Israel, bequeathed to Abraham by God. "What better source is there?" Moshe asked again.

Yet life in Gaza wasn't meant to be for Moshe. As he admitted, it was a "bubble" that popped in the end. Moshe did enjoy one good moment during the traumatic expulsion of the eight thousand Jewish settlers from Gaza by the Israeli army in the summer of 2005: "Someone threw a plastic bottle at the chief of staff and it hit him in the head." Otherwise, he was so angry and upset that he couldn't trust himself not to kill someone, so he locked his own gun in his father's safe in Jerusalem, to avoid the temptation of using it. "People burned their own homes. I'm a fireman, but I didn't put out the flames. We went in to save lives, not to save the houses. We didn't want to leave them for the Arabs. An officer screamed at me to put out the fire. I didn't. I pushed him. I was about to punch him out, I was really upset, every day seeing another family lose their home, another house burning. My partner pulled me away and the officer walked off."

I had been there too, that hot summer week, watching Jewish settlers burning their own homes, sticking yellow stars on their children's coats, calling the Israeli soldiers Nazis, crying and screaming as young soldiers, some crying too, dragged them from their homes.

It was strange, listening to Moshe's passion, for the warnings of Israel's right wing had come to pass. They said there was no point leaving Gaza and hoping for peace, because it would just make it easier for the Palestinians to fire rockets at Israel. Now here was Moshe, the refugee from Gaza, waiting for the rockets to fall so that he could put out the fires. He remembered what had happened to his neighbors' homes, which they burned down on purpose.

"When the soldiers came to my house, my wife and I decided not to attack them physically. You see them come in, and your heart starts beating. You feel you're going to burst. We let them in, and they ordered us to leave. My five-year-old son said, 'You think the Arabs are not going to attack us? You think they only want Gush Katif?' A five-year-old boy! How much did he learn from me? He learned from me being shot at, many other things, you can't trust these people. He wanted an answer. He wanted to know why he had to leave his home. The soldiers didn't have an answer. We decided not to traumatize our kids. We would not object by force. Others can. *Gesundheit*. Not us. But the three steps onto the bus were the heaviest I have ever taken. Soldiers were crying as they carried my neighbor. He said, 'I won't fight, but I can't walk out of here, carry me,' so they did."

It had been agonizing that day—nobody could fail to be touched—but in all honesty, I hadn't felt that much sympathy for the settlers. Mostly I had marveled at how history repeats itself and how futile is this obsession with particular bits of earth, sand, and rock. I would think, as I saw the rage and the tears of the settlers, What's so bad about life on the other side of the hill? And now I felt I had to ask Moshe the obvious: "I wonder what the Arabs felt when they were thrown out of their homes in Israel in 1948? Do you, as a refugee, feel for them, too? You want to go back to your house, and they want to go back to their house. Do you have any sense of understanding for them?"

Moshe reacted as if stung. "But I wasn't bothering them, and that's what bugs me. Was I bothering them in Gush Katif? I'm asking you as the more left wing of the two of us—tell me, was I bothering them?"

I shrugged. "I have no idea. I guess you know from your life with them."

Moshe leaned forward, almost aggressively. "I'm asking you right now, Martin, let's shut off that recorder for a second. Was I bothering them in Gush Katif? In your eyes?"

"I'm sure not in your daily life, but probably you were like a daily irritation that they couldn't get rid of."

Moshe ignored that and answered with a bit of a non sequitur: "After the Oslo peace process, they had their own country, their own factories and life, agriculture, they had free water, Israel gives them electricity, water, okay, we gave them an army, weapons, and what do they do with it all? Shoot those rifles against us. Okay . . ."

"But do you understand that when they want to go back to their villages in Ashkelon . . ."

"Oh, those places. First of all, all those people aren't alive anymore. I am alive, thank God. Second of all, a lot of the places, the reason they were moved out, is they were troublemakers. And don't forget"—and here Moshe stressed each word separately, dragging them out, almost enjoying them, but also as if to emphasize that this justified everything that followed—"don't forget . . . they . . . lost . . . the . . . war! Again, sorry, my country is here. That's if we're talking politics." And then Moshe smiled, a beatific smile, and sat back with a satisfied sigh. "If we're talking religion, the land belongs to us, we came back in 1967, a *miracle*, an act of God." Then, with perfect timing, there was a siren, and we rushed to the bomb shelter.

ROGER'S CAFÉ

A few weeks after the war, Amikam and I went back to Roger's Café to thank him for all his help. Now, instead of just a handful of men staring at the television news and arguing about the war, each seat outside in the sun was taken by couples and families. Inside, it was so crowded and noisy we could barely hear each other. Instead of war news, the television showed a soccer game, Maccabi Haifa against Beitar Jerusalem; the radio worked through a medley of Rita, a local singer; and putrid cigar smoke wafted in through a door. Besides Nanja, there were three other waitresses, each of whom, with her blond and black hair, bright red lipstick, and tight jeans, looked as if she came from a different former Soviet republic.

To talk to Roger, I had to join him behind the bar while he dispensed coffee, change, and greetings to every passing customer. I didn't even have to ask a question. He just saw the recorder and started talking, while putting spoons on saucers, cutting slices of cake, and greeting everyone:

"The war was a waste of time. Just advertising for the politicians. Look, the Grads are still falling. We're still afraid, we still can't sleep. Avi, how are you? What's new? So what was it all about? They stopped too soon, that's the trouble. Should have gone on till they destroyed all of Hamas. Every time when there's a boom and I'm driving, I stop the car. I'm a wreck. And they've still got our boy Gilad Shalit, God bless his parents. Nanja, Shlomie likes brown sugar, give him brown sugar. It was all one big bluff. And you know, Hamas is nothing, but they got stronger. Don't turn it down! I like that song! Everyone supports them now and what did they do? Goal! Goal! They sat in the shelter, ate steak and drank champagne, while people died. They don't care. They turned the whole world against Israel. We're the suckers. And the tunnels? The tunnels! Give an Egyptian a thousand dollars, a pack of cigarettes, he'll do whatever you want. No way they'll stop arms smuggling. Motek, sweetie, I told you, warm the bourekas!"

A couple left the little table I had colonized during the war, beneath the giant photo of Roger grinning with the Hapoel Ashkelon soccer team, and for old times' sake Amikam and I sat there. Within moments, plates of salad and bourekas appeared, with coffee and orange juice. No *hreime*. A man I hadn't seen before came in and looked vainly for a table. Roger quickly came from behind the bar and led him to ours, gesturing from him to me, saying: "Israel Suissa—Martin, an American reporter." For the twentieth time, I said, "English, actually." Israel was born in Casablanca and had just returned from a vacation in Morocco, his first visit since 1963.

"My wife and I were walking in streets, narrow alleys. In Gaza, they would have burned us long ago; there they couldn't have been nicer. Thousands of Arabs. And what did they do? Help me. They argued among themselves about who could give me better directions. They knew I was Jewish. It was the old Jewish area. I gave them my address where I used to live. They walked with me to the house. I went in, took photos. I went to my mother's grave. My old school. It was moving. I already want to go back—now those are Arabs, a different kind . . ."

I listened fondly, and wondered if the Moroccans would be so different if they had lost their homes too. But Roger's Café is a lovely place with lovely people. I had walked through Ashkelon without having a clue that it existed, and now, thanks to the war, I had discovered that Ashkelon was much more than a sleepy beach town with five thousand years of history. The war became my window onto the real people whose experiences are so remote from those of the politicians and diplomats.

When war with Hamas broke out, I had been busy drafting early chapters of this book. At first, I had resented the intrusion of the real world into my writing, but after a few days of reporting the news from Ashkelon, I realized that this war was actually confirming the book's premise: that we in the media report from the coast only when the bombs are falling, and in so doing miss the real Israel. Moreover, as days and weeks went by, I met people whose stories illustrated a parallel, key theme: that because news reporting demands clear story lines and simple narratives, truth is easily distorted. Iyad, for example, with whom I finally caught up two months after the war ended, showed me around his fortunately intact home; his only regret was that the Israelis hadn't remained, and his sincere hope was that they had taught the gunmen a strong-enough lesson that they wouldn't return to fire more rockets at Israel. All he wanted was a quiet, secure life. His white flag was still flying.

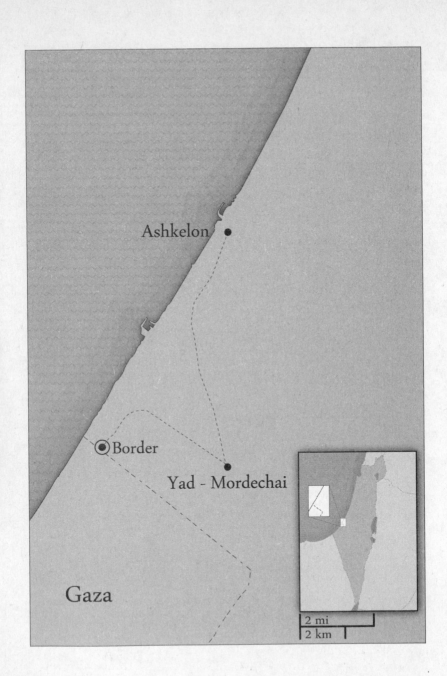

Ashkelon

Border

Yad - Mordechai

Gaza

2 mi
2 km

10

Journey's End

ASHKELON TO GAZA

On the white sandy beach about half a mile from Israel's border with Gaza, concrete slabs block the way, warning: no farther. A couple of miles offshore an Israeli navy patrol boat cuts through the waves, radar sweeping, guns ready. There are no Palestinian fishing boats; Israel banned them from leaving Gaza's little port, fearing they'll smuggle weapons or terrorists. It is a pretty beach with low sand dunes and inviting green hillocks of grass and bush, but it's as deserted as the sea; the only sounds are the crashing waves and muffled booms of explosions from distant Gaza City. Behind a wide channel carved by the tide stands a gray concrete watchtower with dark narrow slits. Soldiers watch through high-powered binoculars, judging whether the man with the backpack is a threat or just another innocent tourist heading for trouble.

After sweating through Ashkelon's baking streets and highways, I was relieved to reach the cooler fields and forest of the plain. I strolled through the Yad Mordechai woods, enjoying the shade of the eucalyptus and sycamore trees, observing birds sitting on the branches and trilling to one another, and anticipating the end of my trek, which I had begun almost two weeks earlier. I felt warm and fulfilled. I had set off later in the morning than usual, after my massage and coffee, and had been walking for three hours. Yet with the sun off my face, I was feeling better and better with each step I took. The Gaza border and the end of my journey were only about six miles on, assuming I could find the coast.

Unfortunately, I couldn't. I became confused in a maze of fields, trees, and hedges. I followed a dirt track this way, cut through a grove of pistachio that way, followed another dirt track along a fenced-off water-pumping station, came to an impenetrable wall of spiky cactus plants with luscious ripe yellow-pink sabra fruits, followed another dirt track until it reached a fork, took the one that seemed to go southeast toward the beach, then chose another dirt track among thick bush that unfortunately funneled me into a U-shaped enclosure of low white boxes. Here I heard a strong buzzing sound, like a thousand bees, and I realized two things: that I was really quite lost; and that this sound was indeed a thousand bees.

Kibbutz Yad Mordechai is famous for its honey, and I had stumbled into the very mother lode. Bees swarmed and buzzed and settled on my clothes, neck, bare legs, and arms. I backed away, careful to make no sudden movement. A cloud of insects buzzed about my head, their high-pitched whine as loud as a chainsaw. I closed my eyes. I knew I just needed to stay calm, keep moving gently, and they would fade away. A bee hovered at my nostril, tickling me, and I blew sharply out of my nose. I turned and walked away slowly, my eyes fluttering, open just wide enough to see where I was going, until the bees thinned out and finally they were gone.

I hadn't been stung, but I was shaken. Earlier, I had been keeping the smoke from the Ashkelon power plant to my right, to guide myself south, but I hadn't seen it for an hour. The trees were too thick. The land was flat, the sun directly overhead, and I had no idea if I was heading toward the coast. Fantasies took hold. So close to the Gaza border, I imagined getting screamed at by an Israeli soldier for wandering into a closed military area, or shelled while in a practice fire zone, or even murdered by a Palestinian terrorist who had just climbed the border wall. I wasn't scared, just aware after years of reporting on wars around the world that people die in the silliest of ways, often by wandering into the wrong place at the wrong time. I looked warily into the bushes and picked up a rock. I took out my trusty Swiss army knife with its broken blade; the tweezers would make a handy weapon.

Then it occurred to me to do what any reasonable man does when lost and in danger: Call the missus. Hagar phoned Yad Mordechai's switchboard, was transferred to the security officer, and gave him my cell-phone number. He quickly called, and as I described the landmarks around me, he guided me by phone to the highway, a mile to the east, and then to the kibbutz. From here it was a three-mile walk through fields and past the Zikim army base to the coast, and then another couple south to the border. Close enough, but my goal of ending the trek today was out of the question. It was midafternoon now, and I didn't want to be anywhere near the border in the dark. Neither did it feel secure to sleep alone under the stars. I'd have to spend the night somewhere safe and finish my journey the next morning. The nearest hotel was back in Ashkelon, but luckily I had a friend on the kibbutz.

OY BUBELE!

Twenty-two years ago, Shuli Schneider had been our family's first live-in nanny. A typical blunt kibbutznik, she had not hesitated to put me in my place. During her first week on the job, we held a dinner party, and as the guests took their places, I asked Shuli to bring a jug of cold water. Her response, before all the guests, was "I'm the nanny, not the slave." Chastened, I fetched the water, Shuli joined us at the table, and we became firm friends. She had left our family two decades earlier, but when I knocked on her door, sweaty, dirty, and unannounced, it seemed as if I'd seen her just yesterday. She handed me a clean towel, showed me the shower, fixed up a bed on the sofa, and assigned her sweet and chatty five-year-old son, Ben, to show me around the kibbutz.

Yad Mordechai, like Kibbutz Lohamei Hagheta'ot in the north, has a special place in Israel's story. It, too, has a Holocaust museum that commemorates the fighters of the Warsaw Ghetto, in particular the resistance leader Mordechai Anielewicz, after whom the kibbutz is named. A huge statue on a hill shows twenty-two-year-old Mordechai, open-shirted and muscled, grasping a hand grenade, before he was killed by the Nazis. It is a heroic legacy that inspired the kibbutz founders in 1948. About a hundred of them, reinforced by a handful of Palmach fighters, waged a bloody battle against a thousand Egyptian soldiers. The kibbutzniks held back the Egyptians for five days, granting valuable breathing time to the main line of Israeli defenders closer to Tel Aviv. Since then, this defiant and selfless resistance had become the stuff of Israeli military folklore. On the hills where the battle took place and almost a quarter of the defenders died, sheet-iron soldiers in silhouette portray the fighters crawling, firing, and running.

When Ben and I returned from our tour, Shuli had a question for me: Would I like to meet somebody who was present at the battle, a wonderful lady? Sure, I said, I'd love to. This turned out to be a stroke of great fortune, for Hollywood casting could not have found me a more fitting character with whom to conclude my journey. Rifkah Reicher, ninety-five years old, lives independently in the kibbutz's nursing home. She is tiny, deeply wrinkled, and frail, with short white hair and big round spectacles framing wide brown eyes. After arriving from Poland as a twenty-two-year-old in 1936, she helped found the kibbutz, defended it in war, and raised her family here. Today she serves as the kibbutz's official wise woman, a role she handles with the utmost charm and sweetness. When her mind wanders for a moment, she strikes her cheek with her hand and reminds herself, "Oy, I must give short answers."

During the buildup to Israel's War of Independence, Rifkah's job was to help sustain radio communications with the outside world. Climbing atop the water tower with a flashlight, she sent messages in Morse code to the headquarters on a neighboring kibbutz. During the battle, she scurried between trenches with food, water, and ammunition and helped carry the wounded on stretchers. "You couldn't be aboveground, there were so many bullets and explosions," she recalled in her little kibbutz room. "I was peppered by earth and sand, but we had no choice. Was I frightened? Luckily the Egyptians were useless soldiers, that's how we survived, although we buried our friends." Her voice broke a little and her eyes teared. I looked away. Twenty-six Jews died and the Egyptians suffered some 350 dead and wounded before the Jewish fighters fled and the Egyptians overran the kibbutz.

That was the last time Rifkah abandoned the kibbutz in war. "It's true," she said, leafing through photographs. "I'm tied to this place. It's personal, everyone can understand that, right?" But it isn't the same kibbutz. Reflecting on the privatization movement, she laughed brightly and exclaimed, "We were so left wing that in our dining room we had posters of Stalin!" Yet Rifkah didn't mind the changes so much. "I knew that was what the young people wanted. They wanted to share big things like health and education, but with separate family lives. So I voted for the change. Anything to keep the community in one piece. That's our strength, the community, like a family, in whatever form."

When I shut down the recorder and thanked her, Rifkah looked up at me. "Good luck to you, I hope you succeed with your book."

"I'll bring you a copy," I replied, smiling.

She threw her head back in laughter. "*Oy, bubele*, I won't get a chance to read it. Any day now I will die."

"Of course not," I said, "I should be as sharp as you. You will live that long, you must, you will be in the book."

"No," she said, "Eliyahu is waiting for me." She pointed to the photo of her husband, who died twelve years earlier, a tall, smiling man with a shock of gray hair. I brought it to her, and she stroked the glass. "Eliyahu was such a good man, a strong man. He built the first five houses in Yad Mordechai, he helped build the dining room, and he planted the trees at the entrance to the kibbutz." She paused and swallowed. "Now he is preparing our bed together again. I am ready."

I had tears in my eyes as she pushed herself from her chair and showed me to the door. I grabbed her matchstick arm to support her when her legs nearly gave way.

GAZA FROM THE HILL

Toward sundown, Chaim Azar, the kibbutz security chief who had guided me out of the woods, offered to drive me to a nearby hill to see the Gaza border. I was delighted to accept what quickly became a guided tour of rocket attacks. "Ten fell in the kibbutz, about five hundred outside, in eight years," Azar said while hunched over the wheel of his Mazda jeep. The vehicle jolted and leaped along the rutted path, and he began pointing out the landing site of each individual missile strike, excitedly reliving the moments of impact. "There, one, two, three, four, five, and over there, and there, six, seven, eight, nine, *ooooaaaahhh*, smoke, all around, *wowowwheewhaa!*"

A deeply lined, bronzed man with an impish smile, Chaim has never lived outside a kibbutz in his sixty-two years, and he says he is all the happier for it. We raced along dry wadis, past fields and greenhouses, while he pointed out the crops: potatoes, cucumber, tomato, eggplant, avocados. There were chicken coops and cowsheds, as well as thick green orchards of pomelos and grapefruit. "A rocket fell here, and there," he said, "and over there! *Wowowowow!*" He pointed out where two Palestinians had climbed the border fence and were killed by Israeli troops. "We don't want to shoot them, but each time they shoot us, we will hit back twice as hard."

The path ended below a steep rise of sand and scraggly bush. Leaving the jeep, we climbed up, slipping, my sandals filling uncomfortably with sand. I smiled to myself, excited, knowing what I would see once we'd reached the top. And as we took the final steps, there, sure enough, at our feet, about three hundred yards distant, was my goal, the Gaza border.

I've been to Gaza maybe a hundred times, in peace and at war. When I first crossed over in 1974, there was no formal boundary. Today, by contrast, the international crossing point has cavernous arrival and departure halls, the most sophisticated electronic monitoring devices, a concrete wall twenty-seven feet high, and a hidden army of soldiers, border police, and surveillance cameras. But nothing quite felt like seeing it through Chaim's binoculars from the top of the sand dune. It was my journey's end, although not quite. Looking was one thing. I still had to walk along the beach to achieve my goal: walking all the way from the Ladder of Tyre to the Gaza border.

Chaim pointed out the wall around the nearest Israeli community to the border, Nativ Ha'asara, a surprisingly upmarket village with smart villas and lush gardens, financed in part by tax breaks granted by the central government to the border communities. The wall was not the border barrier, but rather an interior, secondary wall on Israeli land. Eighteen feet high, it was painted green at the bottom, blue midway up, and sky blue at the top, helping it blend in and appear less menacing; its function was to stop Palestinian snipers who might breach the real border wall and shoot at residents. After this inner wall came a few hundred yards of empty dunes and bush, followed by the twenty-seven-feet-high border wall itself.

On the Palestinian side of the border, I saw a no-man's-land of barren dunes. Faced with constant infiltration attempts, Israeli troops had crushed crops and trees, bulldozed homes, and cleared out the residents to better monitor approaches to the border. Scanning the no-man's-land are cameras that send live pictures to intelligence centers manned 24/7 by young soldiers. As the wall cuts west, where I stood, it becomes a high-tech fence that continues all the way to the beach and even a few hundred yards into the Mediterranean. That was the border I hoped to reach the next morning, to complete my trek along the coast of Israel.

Beyond the border in the distance, I could make out the surprisingly built-up Gaza suburbs of Beit Lahiya and Iyad's Beit Hanoun, from where Palestinians fired most of their Qassam rockets. The tower blocks and residential areas gradually spread until they bled into the sordid refugee camps of Shati and Jabaliya. Farther on lay Gaza City itself, and then the rest of the Gaza Strip, which clings to the coast in a narrow band of homes and farmland. The sun was close to setting, and a pleasant orange glow settled over the landscape as flocks of birds flew by. It was quiet here, and I could only imagine how startling it must have been to experience this calm shattered by rockets, bombs, and planes. Shielding my eyes with my hand, I could see Israel's intelligence zeppelin, a giant white balloon framed against a blue sky, bristling with surveillance cameras and tethered to the ground by immense coils of rope and steel. The craft floated just inside Israel's border, its cameras trained on every suspicious activity in the Gaza Strip. It is only airborne when there is tension, and its presence in the sky boded ill.

SEA OF MEMORY

The next morning, I took no chances and set off early along a dirt-and-asphalt track that Chaim had described. I walked three miles through the fields and orchards and within an hour or so reached yellow dunes. Zikim Beach had once been a popular spot, but years of rocket attacks in the area meant I had the place to myself. The waves rolled gently in, settling white froth on the sandy beach before sucking out again. With my goal so close, I decided to savor the moment and play in the waves. Flinging off my backpack, I stripped down to my underpants and dove in. I'd have taken those off, too, but I knew that my every move was probably being monitored by twenty-five young soldiers staring at surveillance screens.

I swam for a bit and then lay on the sandy incline, the cool water sloshing over my feet as the waves came in. Already the day was growing hot. I looked up at the sky and followed the few puffy gray clouds moving slowly across it. I smiled to myself. This is it: journey's end. In a few minutes I would get up, walk to the Gaza border, and go home. I felt great. For years I had wanted to walk the coast and take a calmer, deeper look at this turbulent place I had reported on for so long: I even had the title of the book I would write. I wanted one of my sons to accompany me, and I would call the book *The Father, the Son, and the Holy Coast.* But my boys had other ideas, and I was left alone with my journey, and now, my thoughts.

Although I had wanted to avoid the conflict as much as possible during my journey, this had proven impossible, for the burden of the past was too heavy. No country lives its past as Israel does; not only the Jews, but the Arabs, too. William Faulkner wrote, "The past is never dead. It's not even past," but Israel's preeminent modern poet, Yehuda Amichai, was able to relate that universal truth uniquely to Israel, and even to Yad Mordechai, with sadness and resignation.

> *Yad Mordechai. Those who fell here*
> *still look out the windows like sick children*
> *who are not allowed outside to play.*
> *And on the hillside, the battle is reenacted*
> *for the benefit of hikers and tourists. Soldiers of thin sheet iron*
> *rise and fall and rise again. Sheet iron dead and a sheet iron life*
> *and the voices all—sheet iron. And the resurrection of the dead,*
> *sheet iron that clangs and clangs.*
>
> *And I said to myself: Everyone is attached to his own lament*
> *as to a parachute. Slowly he descends and slowly hovers*
> *until he touches the hard place.*

Everyone here knows that hard place: Life here is a succession of laments, and they begin early. Shuli had asked her son, Ben, to tell me what it was like when rockets fell on the kibbutz. She had smiled at me and nodded proudly. But Ben had looked away and said, "I can't remember," and when Shuli prodded him, he looked away again, unresponsive. For a moment, this chatty little boy with unruly blond hair and blue eyes seemed adrift, as if he'd come to his own hard place, caught, as Amichai wrote else-where, between his own "sea of memory and sea of forgetting."

Sometimes memory is the solid ground we stand on, sometimes the morass we sink into. Jews and Arabs, whose memories here extend thousands of years, are stuck in the morass. In walking the coast of Israel, even while passing through some of the most bitterly disputed land on the planet, I had not wanted to accuse or to examine who was right or wrong or to come up with solutions; I had simply wanted to observe. Ambivalent as I am about the country Jews have forged, I do respect the people who created it, and as I progressed on my journey, I became ever more determined to convey some of my admiration for their fascinating contradictions.

Where else would a car driver knock you down, curse you, and then drive you to the hospital, comparing notes on mutual friends? Where else would a shopkeeper hesitate to sell you twelve kilos of apples and pears for a juice diet, saying you must be crazy? Where else would ten friends sit together for coffee on Friday, all talk at the same time, and afterward have not the foggiest idea what anybody else said? And where else would a group of strangers break the ice, not by discussing last night's TV program or the latest news, but by posing the question, So, how did your family survive the Holocaust?

SURVIVING IS JUST THE BEGINNING

At one point during my trek, a brave lady who survived a terrorist attack said to me, "Surviving is not enough. Surviving is just the beginning." I understood what she meant in Café Europa, when I saw the boys and girls serving coffee and cakes to laughing Holocaust survivors, who in turn danced the waltz in an imitation Viennese café to the violin of an imitation Gypsy. The joy of these survivors was real enough, like an extended family reunion—what Smadar Haran in Nahariya, whose child was beaten to death by a terrorist, had called the Jewish revenge.

The elderly kibbutz founders, those once-young and -vital men and women, pioneers in shorts and silly floppy hats, immigrants from Europe and America, who had picked the soil of the Holy Land from beneath their fingernails, buried friends, and sent their children to fight for what they had built, now puttered around in electric carts, shouting, "Speak louder!" For the most part they were satisfied with their lives, because even if Israel didn't turn out the way they had dreamed, it was still a safer place for Jews. Nobody here would call Sonya Arieli a Yid. The founders had done their best, and the Jewish people had more than survived here—it had flourished.

Yet I could not ignore a certain obtuseness in their celebrations of the Jewish state. When Rifkah and Chaim told me of the trouble they had in Yad Mordechai in the late forties and early fifties with Palestinian fellahin who raided their farms and stole crops and fruit from the trees, I wondered how I would have reacted if I had been an Arab then. Imagine being a refugee only a few miles from your stolen home, watching strangers tilling your fields and harvesting the fruit from the trees your father planted. Who wouldn't be bitter? If an Arab creeps up at night and picks fruit from his old trees, is that stealing? Who here is the thief? Yet close to the Lebanon border, among the refugees from Al-Zib, I hadn't found a single Arab who had an unkind word to say about Eli Avivi, the Israeli who lived in the ruins of their family homes and had turned them into a bed-and-breakfast.

The conflict, I think, is Amichai's hard place, emotional terrain to which everybody's lament, their sad story, their history and memories and dreams, compels them to return. Only peace, I think, may change this. Until then, Arabs and Jews will depend on these hard memories as a falling man does a parachute; they remain something tangible on which to grasp. There is no forgetting here, and little forgiveness; the wounds are too fresh. And the circle of pain grows wider each year as more boys and girls prepare for war. Even little Ben, who couldn't or wouldn't remember the rockets, will no doubt one day come home with an M16 strapped across his manly chest.

On the other hand, I also found many who were already trying to build a better future. Ran, who helped transform the kibbutzim and now wanted to improve the world, starting in the forest; Abdu, the Acre tour guide, who loved to show Jews and Arabs how much they have in common; Yuval, who prepared high school kids for the army, but most of all taught them to care; Nahoum, the architect, devoted to Tel Aviv's beauty; and many more who humbled me by their optimism in the face of Israel's challenges. Even Sonya, the innkeeper who had an unkind word about everyone, nevertheless helped them all.

Israel is a hard country to live in. Mothers pray for peace before their babies join the army, and then eighteen years later they cry as they wave good-bye to the bus taking their kids to basic training. Many men remain reserve soldiers well into their forties, by which time they will have fought in at least two wars and buried friends. Wages are low and prices are high. Income tax approaches 50 percent. Luxury taxes double the price of a car, and the price of gas is among the highest in the world. One in three children lives below the poverty line—Jews as well as Arabs. It is a tiny country in a very hostile region, and it is increasingly isolated in the world. Yet the achievements of its seven million people in the fields of medicine, agriculture, high tech, weapons development, scientific innovation, and the arts rival the world's largest countries. And the beaches, the weather . . .

In short, basking in the sun, with waves washing over me and sand sucking pleasurably across my body, I knew that tough as it is, I really do love this place.

CAN YOU COME AND GET ME?

My skin tightened as the sea salt dried in the heat. Time to move. I showered in fresh water at the single functioning tap outside the shuttered old beach café. I put my shorts and shirt back on, and headed south again along the beach, but it wasn't clear how far I could walk. I could see the haze of Gaza City before me; to my left, concrete walls, wire fences, and razor wire rose from the shrubs of the sand dunes, protecting an Israeli intelligence post and communications tower. A line of concrete blocks linked by barbed wire lay across the beach, without quite reaching the sea, leaving room for me to pass; and about half a mile farther on, I could make out another, larger, fence that stretched deep into the water. I heard a sudden loud but muffled *ba-boom*, like a cough from the chest, and then way inside Gaza black smoke rose over the houses and merged with the clouds. The day before, a few rockets had been fired from Gaza, and this must be Israel's retaliation. Then, more booms and smoke. Maybe they were hitting the smuggling tunnels that link Gaza to Egypt? That's why the zeppelin was up. I hadn't chosen the safest day to end my trek.

I walked by the concrete blocks. Two words in Hebrew were scrawled in red ink, but the writing was faded, and I couldn't read it. Admittedly, I didn't try too hard. I wanted to reach the actual border, then get the heck out. I could see clearly the bullhorns on the concrete watchtower, one facing north and one south, but I heard nothing. About fifty yards past the barrier, a female voice boomed from the army post. She sounded rather agitated. I couldn't understand the muffled words through the bullhorn, but it seemed I was being told to halt. So I did. I gestured, raising my arm and pointing toward Gaza and twisting my hand in a question, miming a request to continue. More unintelligible words from the watchtower. I turned back. I knew better than to continue against orders, even if I couldn't understand them, and anyway, I felt that actually touching this barrier or that

barrier hardly made a difference to my trek. I had made it, and I was floating; I felt like dancing in the waves. Instead, having retraced my steps to the
permitted side of the first concrete barrier, I took my camera from my
backpack and photographed myself first by the concrete and barbed wire,
and then with Gaza in the distance. Next I shot more photos of the army
watchtower and the tall red-and-white communications tower next to it.

I sat on the edge of one of the blocks and took a long pull from my water
bottle, sighing in satisfaction. I held the digital camera in the shade and
looked at the photos I had just taken. The best were of the army watchtower with its slit windows and loudspeakers and all the antennae and
communications dishes sticking from the top. I took off my sandals, stretched
my legs, crossed my arms, and gazed at the sea, deeply content. Then I
closed my eyes as if to sleep. I was in good company, if only in spirit. The
soldiers of Alexander the Great, Richard the Lionheart, Napoleon, and
many more had passed this way. Samson and Goliath, too, and the Mamluks from Egypt, as well as the Canaanites, the Babylonians, the Persians,
the Greeks, the Romans, and still others. They probably camped right
here, midway between Ashkelon and Gaza, both ancient cities. But when
I opened my eyes again it was the olive green fatigues of the Israeli army
that held my attention. Two soldiers atop a dune a hundred yards away
were sauntering toward me, M16 assault rifles slung across their chests,
pistols on their belts. One was a lieutenant, the other a sergeant. "Hello,"
I said in English. "Good morning."

The lieutenant, whose name was Elad, answered in English, "The police are on the way." I must have looked surprised because he continued,
"You didn't stop when you were told."

"Yes, I did," I said. "As soon as I heard something, I stopped." I explained that I hadn't known where the border was, that I couldn't understand the faint muffled sounds from the bullhorn, that I had no intention
of breaking any rules, and that I couldn't read the Hebrew on the concrete

barrier. He was a reasonable young man. "Yes," he said, "it should really be in English, too. And Arabic." We asked each other where we were from; miraculously we did not have a mutual friend, but pretty soon we were chatting anyway. "Did you take any photos of the army base?" he then asked. I admitted I did, and he ordered me to delete them. Now, for a reporter, this is like a red rag to a bull. If I'd been on a news assignment, I would have refused and demanded to see a written paper showing that this was a closed military area. I would have insisted on waiting for the police to arrive, and then I would have protested my rights and invoked freedom of the press all the way to jail, and then deleted the photos. Not this time. My only thought was how apt it was that I was ending my journey as I had begun it, in trouble with the border guards.

After I deleted the pictures, I was allowed to leave. I parted from the two soldiers, armed with a piece of paper from the lieutenant; I was to give it to the police if they found me on the beach. Elad had written his name, phone number, and these words in Hebrew: "Leave him, checked and secure."

Elated, I took the first steps home. I walked about half a mile north, toward the path I would follow back to Yad Mordechai, and thence to the main road to catch a bus to Tel Aviv. The water was blue and enticing and I was hot, so I decided to take one final dip in the sea. The waves were bigger now and rolling powerfully onto the sharp incline of the beach. I stripped off, dove into the swell, and swam out about fifty yards. It was still shallow, and I could stand easily with water to my waist. A wave broke just ahead of me. I caught the next one and body surfed to within ten yards of the sand. I did it again and again until a set of big ones appeared. I stood, my body twisted, half facing the sea, my arms stretched ahead ready to dive forward, and as the wave reached and began to pass me I hurled myself, catching the curl of the wave perfectly. I surged ahead, arms forward, legs straight back, body taut, head straight as if in a dive. I was swept along with the wave, which seemed to grow in strength as it approached the beach. Faster and faster I went, until *wham!* I hit the ground. I continued underwater along the sand, scraping my face until a small rock or stone smashed into my nose. The water sucked out again, leaving me exultant, crumpled, and bleeding profusely.

A couple of hours later, I called Hagar from the clinic at Yad Mordechai with good news and bad news; fitting, because in Israel there's always a sting in the tail. "The good news is I finished the walk," I informed my long-suffering wife. "The bad news is it looks like I broke my nose. Can you come and get me?"

Notes

Introduction

1. Benny Morris, *Correcting a Mistake: Jews and Arabs in Palestine/Israel, 1936–1956*, in Hebrew (Tel Aviv: Am Oved, 2000).

1. In the Beginning

1. Genesis 17:2.
2. Mark Twain, *The Innocents Abroad, or The New Pilgrims' Progress* (1869).
3. Dan Senor and Saul Singer, *Start-up Nation: The Story of Israel's Economic Miracle* (New York: Twelve, 2009).

2. The Bride of Galilee

1. I later found out that Avivi's collection was legitimate. A law was introduced in 1974 making all antiquities the property of the state. But before that, objects found along the coast could be kept by the owner.
2. Dr Sharif Kana'ne, Bir Zeit University.
3. On July 15, 1951, on the steps of the al-Aqsa mosque in Jerusalem, a Palestinian killed Jordan's King Abdullah with three bullets fired into the head and chest. The assailant was afraid the monarch would negotiate peace with Israel.

3. Revenge of the Jews

1. Time tempers passions. For an account of acts of Jewish revenge, see Tom Segev, *The Seventh Million: The Israelis and the Holocaust* (New York: Hill and Wang, 1993).
2. Peter Lagerquist, "Vacation from History: Ethnic Cleansing as the Club Med Experience," *Journal of Palestine Studies* 36:1 (2006), p. 43.

3. Primo Levi, *If This Is a Man* (English publication in 1958).
4. Conversation with the former Supreme Court judge Dalia Dorner.
5. The traditional Jewish seven-day mourning period.
6. Hannah Arendt, "Eichmann in Jerusalem," *The New Yorker*, February 16, 1963.
7. Conversation with Michal Havazellet.

4. Four Faces of the Truth

1. James Reston, Jr., *Warriors of God: Richard the Lionheart and Saladin in the Third Crusade* (New York: Doubleday, 2001).
2. Fra Bonvicino da Riva, "Fifty Courtesies for the Table."
3. In 1917, Lord Balfour declared on behalf of the British government support for a Jewish homeland in Palestine. It laid the political groundwork for the State of Israel.
4. *An Account of the French Expedition in Egypt; Written by Bonaparte and Berthier; with Sir William Sidney Smith's Letters.* With an English translation (London: Edward Baines, 1800).

5. The Cream Arabs of Haifa

1. *An Account of the French Expedition in Egypt*, op. cit.
2. Ibid.
3. Liver, lungs, stomach, and intestines were washed and packed in natron to dry them out.
4. His numbers are hotly disputed by official sources, but no established figure is available.
5. Central Bureau of Statistics, Abstract of Israel, 2008.
6. Ben Caspit, "The State of Israel—National Demographic Policy," *Maariv*, 2008.
7. Knesset speech, November 12, 2008.

7. The Call to Arms

1. Exemptions allow some Israeli youth to avoid service legally.
2. Joshua 12:23.
3. Kurt Ravee, the longtime antiquities director of Israel's coast, estimates there must be about five thousand shipwrecks in the area. "It's been a harbor for five thousand years and a ship must have sunk about once a year. As the sea receded and sand built up, it stands to reason that underneath the fields and hills here there must be many shipwrecks."
4. B. W. Johnson, *Young Folks in Bible Lands* (1892).
5. Flavius Josephus, *The Jewish War*.
6. Ibid.
7. The higher proportion of Arabs and Orthodox Jews accounts for other alarming

statistics. A 2009 Ministry of Education report said that in 2008, only 44 percent of seventeen-year-olds received high school graduation certificates, down from 49 percent in 2004. Jewish numbers were stable but Arab numbers dropped from 40 to 32 percent. Unemployment figures are similar. With Arabs unable to participate equally and fully in education and employment, and Orthodox Jews choosing not to, the trend is significant. "This trend, which will become more pronounced in coming years, is a great danger to the future of the country, whose security and economic prosperity depends on human resources." *Haaretz* editorial, July 12, 2009.

8. Not his real name.

9. All the special units have a very rigorous training plan, as a result of which about half the recruits are eventually rejected.

8. The Off-White City

1. The answer to the eternal argument about who was here first, Jews or Palestinians, is clear concerning this particular stretch of land—neither. Manshiyeh, like Tel Aviv itself, was barren sand dunes until it was settled by immigrants from Egypt in the mid-nineteenth century: "home to freed slaves, Africans, Gypsies, Persians, Indians and Baluchis" (Adam LeBor, *City of Oranges: An Intimate History of Arabs and Jews in Jaffa* [New York: W. W. Norton, 2007], p. 68).

2. Not her real name.

3. The Hasid Sabbath observance begins on Thursday night.

4. LeBor, *City of Oranges*, p. 69.

9. We're All in This Together

1. II Samuel 1:20.

Index

Abdul Hamid, Sultan, 98

Abdullah, King of Jordan, assassination of, 43

Abraham, 11, 13

Absentees (Arab refugees), 39

Abu Musa, 133

Achziv (Al-Zib), 26, 28–53, 166
  called The Bride of Galilee, 29, 48
  holiday village at, 28–29

Achzivland, "independent" state of, 32

Acre, 39, 47, 66, 122, 219
  decline of commercial importance, 117
  history of, 99–105
  Napoleon's siege of, 103–5
  Old City, 91, 93–105
  Yom Kippur riots (2008), 109–13

Afghanistan, 256–57

airport security, 27

Ajami neighborhood, Jaffa, 241

Al-Aqsa Martyrs' Brigades, 177

Algeria, 256

al-Jazzar, Ahmed Pasha, 102–3

Al-Jura, 248

Allon, Yigal, 69

Al-Majdal (neighborhood of Ashkelon), 248, 259–61

Alon (not his real name), getting out of military service, 194–98

Alumot kibbutz, 156

Amichai, Yehuda, 283–84

Anielewicz, Mordechai, 277

Arabic language, 98–99

Arab-Israeli conflict, 44–45, 283–86

Arab Jews. See Jews in the Arab world

Arabs
  can't separate fact from fiction, 44–45
  justifications of terrorism, 63–64, 220
  need to feel superior, 107–8
  stereotypes about, 44–45, 179

Arabs of Israel
  angry and ready to explode, 135–36
  birthrate among, 17, 130, 184
  called collaborators by younger
    generation, 127
  called "Cream" Arabs, assimilating
    to Israeli ways, 128
  on the coast, 182
  conversions to Judaism, 42–43, 52
  cultural diversity of, 16
  discrimination against, 134–35
  dispossessed but still living in
    Israel, 34–35, 127
  elites, coexistence with Jews,
    117–18
  glass ceiling for, 131, 134
  identifying as Palestinian, 126–27
  not allowed in military, 184
  policing of, by Israeli defense forces,
    190–92
  population size, 19
  poverty of, 241
  secular, 118, 125–26, 129–31
  those loyal to Israel, 38–53
  those who did not flee in 1948, 26
  threatened with expulsion, 136–41
  See also Christian Arabs
Arab villages, destroyed in 1948, 38,
    248, 259–61
Arendt, Hannah, 80
Arieli, Sonya, 177–80, 184
Ashdod, 242
Ashdot Ya'akov kibbutz, 178
Ashkelon, 245–71
  history of, 247–48
  joylessness of, 248
    rocket attacks on, 249–55, 257–58,
      264–65
Ashkenazim, 15–16, 19
Atlit, 145, 151, 153, 181
  British detainee camp at, 144, 153
  secret naval base, 154, 176
Auschwitz, 58–59, 62, 70, 80, 83–84
  revisited by survivors, 80, 85–86
Avivi, Eli, 28–38, 40, 45–46, 50
  private museum of, author steals
    a glass bottle from, 35–37
Azar, Chaim, 280

Baha'i faith, 123
Balfour Declaration, 103
Banana Beach, Tel Aviv, 218
Barak, Ehud, 177, 184
Barbara (not her real name) (author's
    informant in Tel Aviv), 223–24
Barghouti, Marwan, 50
Barrito, Khalouf, 214–15
bathing, mixed, 240
bats, 227
Bat Shlomo, 143
Battadan, Margalit, 165–68
Bat Yam, 242
Bauhaus, 235–39
beach going, 240, 282
Bedouin Arabs, 16
bees, 276
Begin, Menachem, 219, 221
Beit Hanoun, 260–64, 281
Beit Lahiya, 281
Beit Oren kibbutz, 143, 145–48,
    154–65, 168, 170–71
  financial restructuring of, 163–65

reinvention and rebirth of, 147,
155–65
Ben-Dayan, Itzik, 253
Ben-Gurion, David, 3, 71, 171
Ben-Gurion Airport, 27
ben Zwi, Ari, 169
Bible, the, 15
birthrates, Israeli and Arab, 17,
130–31, 184
Bonvicino da Riva, Fra, 101–2
borders of Israel
crossing them, 25–27
with Gaza, 273, 280–81, 287–89
with Lebanon, 25–27
Bosnia, 160
British in Palestine, 144, 153,
219–20
brothels, medieval, 101

Caesarea, 173, 181
ancient, 183–84
modern town of, 182–83
Café Europa, Tel Aviv, 82–83, 86
Canaanites, 28–29
Carmel Nature Reserve, 143
cell-phones, used to navigate, 276
cemeteries, 241
Chabad, 234
checkpoints, 191–92
children, communal living of, 178
Christian Arabs, 16, 99
Club Med, 28
coast of Israel
Arab towns on, 182
author's hike along, the basis of this
book, 4, 7–8, 241–42

glorious stretch of between Atlit
and Netanya, 181
history of, 5–6
coexistence of Arabs and Jews
breakdown of, in Acre, 108–13
in Haifa, 117–18, 125–41
in Jaffa, 222–23, 240
in old Acre, 94
Cohen, Amikam, 250, 256, 269–70
Cohen, Nahoum, 236, 238
Coleridge, Samuel, *Rime of the Ancient
Mariner*, 95
combat, scenes of, 202
communal living, 178
conscription, 177, 206
Copeland, Dave, 265
Cornelius (Roman officer), 173,
183
"Cream" Arabs, 128
crossing points, 280–81
Crusaders, 96–97, 100, 118, 153,
247

Daghmoush family, 262
Dagon, Orna, 157, 159–60, 163, 169
Daher el-Omar, 102
Daka, Nawar, 222–23
Dan, Danielle, 206
David, 247
Dayan, Moshe, 146
Dayan, Yossi, 259–60
death camps, 69
Declaration of Independence (1948),
71
defense forces, Israeli, 176–206
Diaspora, 184

Dor, 181
Dor Habonim nature reserve, 181
draft dodgers, 177, 184
drinking, 230
Druze Arabs, 16
    stereotypes about, 179

Eastern Jews. *See* Jews in the Arab
    world
Egypt
    annexation of Gaza (1946–, 267
    Jewish refugees from, 256
    in 1948 War, 261, 277–79
Eichmann, Adolf, trial of, 75–80
Eilan, Yuval, 185–87, 201
Ein Hod, 143
elections, 137–41
Elijah, 150
Elijah's Cave, 150
elite military units
    high status of members of, 186, 189
    training for entry into, 176, 185
Ethiopian Jews, 19, 160
etiquette, medieval, 101–2
European Jews, discord with Eastern
    Jews, 257

Farhi, Chaim, 102–6
Fartook, Yossi, 260
Faulkner, William, 283
Felix (Tel Aviv old-timer), 214
Fields, W. C., 121
fighter pilots, 176
Fijians, stereotypes about, 179
fishing boats, banned, for Palestinians,
    273

Flavius Josephus, 183
Fletcher, Martin (author)
    boating accident, 1–4
    dangers encountered as a foreign
        correspondent, 151–53
    English upbringing of, 62–63
    nose broken during final dip in the
        sea, 290
    parents of, little help given to as
        Holocaust survivors living in
        England, 62–63, 71–72, 87
    stopped at the Gaza border, 288–89
    walk down Israel's coast, 4, 7–8,
        20–21, 241–42
French in Palestine, 149

Gal, Reuven, 184–85
Galante, David (descendant of Chaim
    Farhi), 105–8
Gatenyo, Itzhak, 229–33, 240
gays, 224–25, 227–29
    attacks on, 228–29
Gaza, 249, 260–71, 273, 280–90
    closed border with, 280–81
    Israeli army house demolitions in,
        263–64
    Israeli settlers in, expelled by Israeli
        troops, 264–69
    open border with (after 1967),
        256–57
    part of historic Israel, 266–67
Gaza City, 249, 281
Geffen, Moshe, 264–69
Georgians, stereotypes about, 179
German atrocities, 73, 76–80, 83–84
Gesher Haziv kibbutz, 165–68

glass, discovery of, by ancient
    Phoenicians, 120
Golani army base, 66
Goldman, Paul, 265
Goldwasser, Nachman, 166–67
Gonen kibbutz, 158
Grad rockets, 249, 253
Gropius, Walter, 237
Gur, Ben, 234–35, 239–40
Guri, Chaim, 67
Gush Dan conurbation, 213
Gush Katif, 266–68
Gypsies, stereotypes about, 179

Habadniks, 41–42
Hadad, Chaim, 258–59
Hadjaj, Miro, 258
Hagar (author's wife), 4, 33–34, 57,
    67, 96, 178–84, 205, 217, 276,
    290
Haifa, 23, 115–18, 122–41, 145
Hamas, 46, 177
    Israeli war against, 257–71
    rocket attacks from Gaza (2008),
        249–55, 257–58, 264–65
Haoman 17 nightclub, Tel Aviv,
    229–32
Haran, Smadar, 58–64, 66
Hariri, Yishai, 166–67
Hashomer Hatzair, 74
Hasidim, 41–42, 233–35
Hassan Bek Mosque, Tel Aviv,
    220–23
Hatav, Roger, 254–56, 259–60, 270
hate, not harboring, 86
Hausner, Gideon, 75

Havazellet, Michal, 81
Hebrew language, 98–99
Herod, King, 183
Hersey, John, 146
Herzliya, 1
Herzliya Pituach, 212
Hezbollah, 66, 111
    rocket attacks (2006), 64, 148
    war with (2006), 201–2, 206,
        254–55
Highway 4, 55, 93
hiking, getting tired and fearing
    heatstroke, 150–53
hiking gear, author's, 28
hippies, 1960s, 28
Hlehel, Ala and Abir, 123–31
Holocaust, refusal to talk about it in
    Israel, a taboo subject, 63–66,
    69–82
Holocaust memorials and museums,
    55, 65, 277
Holocaust survivors, 58–59, 62–63
    immigrating to Palestine and
        interned by British, 144
    little support for, in Israel or the
        West, 71–81
    present life of, 81–88, 284–85
    rebuilding lives in Israel, 68–69
Holocaust victims, reasons for
    nonresistance, 75–80
Holy Land. See Palestine
Horowitz, Miki, 82
hummus, how to eat, 97
Hummus Sa'id (eatery in Acre), 97
Husayn, Ataya, 36
hymen, "closing" of, 129

Iceberg, ice cream bar, Tel Aviv, 225

Imi (in Beit Oren), 159–60

immigrants
from Arab lands, 71
difficulty of fitting in, 19–20
and population growth, 17–20

International Style (Bauhaus), 235–39

Intifada, first (1993), 109

Intifada, second (2000), 50

Iran, 256

Iraq, 256

Irgun, 219–20

Islam, 108
Jewish conversion to, 50

Israel
cultural diversity of, 14–20
economic, scientific, and financial
success of, 20, 286
faces Europe, not the Middle
East, 20
geographical diversity of, 14
a hard country to live in, 286
historical richness of, 13–14
love of country in, 186
media coverage of, focused on
violence, 7–8
pleasant aspects of, 6–8
population, size and composition,
13–14, 19, 213–14
right to exist, 8, 103–4, 136
a safer place for Jews, 285
security operations, 46–47
uniqueness of, 284
"What a country!" remark, 4

Israel Defense Forces, 177

Israeli Arabs. See Arabs of Israel

Israeli government, hatred for, 32

Israeli-Palestinian conflict, 44–45
future of, 177
is peace possible? 49–51
See also Arab-Israeli conflict

Israelis. See Jews of Israel

Iyad (a Palestinian living in Gaza),
260–63, 271

IZL Museum, Tel Aviv, 219

Jabaliya refugees camp, 281

Jaffa, 240
Arabs of, 222–23
competition with Tel Aviv, 212

Jaffa, battle of (1948), 219, 220–21,
222–23

Jamal, Tawfik, 110, 112–13

Jerusalem, 136–37

Jesus, 183

Jewish Agency, 160

Jewish identity, 234–35

Jews
ancient, in Palestine, 183–84, 266
conversions to Islam, 50
Roman massacres of, 183–84
who decides who is one, 15

Jews in the Arab world (Mizrachim)
connections of friendship with
Arabs, 260
exodus of, and immigration to
Israel, 256–57
low status of, 106–7

Jews of Israel
birthrate among, 130–31
land purchases before
Independence, 266–67

medieval, 101
  secular, 15, 125–26, 129
Jisr al-Zarqa, 182–83
Jordan, 133
Judaism
  Arab conversion to, 42–43, 52
  See also Orthodox Jews

Kahane, Meir, 137
Kaiser, Yaacov, 59
Karmiel, 120
Katyusha rocket attacks, 64
Katzrin kibbutz, 158
Kfar Daroum, 267
kibbutzim
  failure and bankruptcy of, 93,
    146–48, 161–62
  history and mythic stature of,
    145–46, 168
  memories of childhood in, 178
  need to adapt to modern Israel, 146
  reinvention and rebirth of
    (privatization), 147–48, 158–59,
    165–71, 279
  socialist, utopian ideals, 74, 146–47,
    158, 169–70, 279
Kiryat Haim, 122–23
Kishon River, 120–21
Klezmer music, 16
Krayot, 122
Kuntar, Samir, 66
Kziv creek, 51–53

Ladder of Tyre, 13, 25
Lebanon, 23, 46–47, 107, 256
  border with, 25–27

Palestinian refugees in, 43,
    46–47
Lebanon War (2006), 205
"Letter to the Jewish Nation" (by
    Napoleon), 103–4
Levanon, Ziv, 2
Levi, Primo, 70
Lieberman, Avigdor, 110, 135, 137–41
Lohamei Haghetao't, 55, 65–71, 76

Ma'agan Michael kibbutz, 145
Maglan (commandos unit), 176, 200
marriages and weddings
  of Ashenazim with Sephardim, 16
  modern Arab, 124
  traditional Arab, 48–49
Masai talking stick, 191
mass executions, 76–80
Matta, Abdu Salvatore (tour guide),
    98–106, 108–12
Maxim eatery, Haifa, 150
media. *See* news reporting
Melamed, Ariana, 76
memories, harbored by Arabs and
    Israelis, 284–86
Mengele, Joseph, 83
Merom Golan kibbutz, 225
military service
  early release from, 194–98
  evasion of, 184–85
  lack of enthusiasm for, 177, 180,
    184–93, 204–6
  willingness to serve, 198–206
Minsk, Ofir, 187–89
mitzvah (donation), 258–59
mixed bathing, 240

Mizrachim. *See* Jews in the Arab
world
Mizrahi music, 16
Moore, Jenny, 112
Morocco, 256, 270–71
Morris, Benny, 6
mosques, 220–21
Mount Carmel, 143–44, 148–50
Muhammad Ali, 148
Muslims, 16

Na'aman River, 120–21
Nachmias, Yoske, 219–21
Nahariya, 57–71
Nahmani Street, Tel Aviv, gunman
attack on gays (2009), 228–29
Nakba (the catastrophe), 38
Napoleon, invasion of and retreat
from Palestine, 103–5, 118–20,
149–50, 181
Nasser, Gamal Abdel, 261
Nativ Ha'asara, 281
navy commandos, 121
Netanya, 181
Neve Yam, 178
news reporting, interest in bad news,
not good, 93–94, 271
New York City, 96
nightlife, 223–33, 239–40
nudism, 32, 33–34

October (Yom Kippur) War (1973),
211
Olmert, Ehud, 134
"one of us" (*achad mi shelaanu*), 27
Operation Solomon, 19

Orthodox Jews, 14–15, 16
birthrate among, 17, 184
not required to serve in military,
184
stereotypes about, 179
Ottomans, 99

Palestine
ancient, 183–84, 266
Jewish homeland in, 103
Mark Twain's view of, 13–14
medieval, 101–2
Palestinian refugees
dishonored, 43
in Lebanon, 43, 46–47
Palestinians
Arabs identifying as, 126–27
goals of, 16–17
number of, 38
policing of, by Israeli defense forces,
190–92
terrorist, 133
Palmach (Jewish militia), 29, 52, 69
Partition of Palestine (1947), 64
past, living in the, 283–84
Paul, Saint, 173, 183
Pek'in, 266
"a people without a land for a land
with a people" (Zionist slogan),
35, 266
Peres, Shimon, 146, 165, 229
Philistines, 247
Phoenicians, 120
Pinsk, 76
Pisgat Ze'ev, 136–37
plastic pollution, 95

Plato, 44
pollution, 95, 120–22
Pontius Pilate, 173, 183
population, 13–14, 17–20, 213–14
Present Absentees (Arab refugees), 39
Promised Land, Abraham's view of, 13
prostitutes (hookers), 3–4, 123
protekzia, 20, 32

Raban, Havka Folman, 67–71, 76, 87
Rabin, Yitzhak, 59, 146
refugee camps, 281
refugees, Arab
    forced to flee by Israeli soldiers, 49
    internal, remaining in Israel, 39–53
    number of, originally, and their
        descendants, 38
Reicher, Rifkah, 278–79
religions of Israel, 14–16
reservists, 203–4
revenge, overcoming the desire for, by
    rebuilding, 60–62
rocket attacks, 64, 148, 245, 249–55,
    257–58, 264–65, 287
    siren warnings of, 250–51
Roger's Café, Ashkelon, 254–57,
    269–71
Romans, ancient, oppression of Jews,
    183–84
Ronen, Ran, 155–57, 159–65, 167–68,
    169–71
Rosh Hanikra, 23, 25, 30, 53
Rothman, Moshe, 82–88
Rothschild, Baron Edmond de, 144
Rothschild Boulevard, Tel Aviv, 225,
    233

Rothschild family, 182–83
Rubin, Reuven, 241
Russian immigrants (from former
    Soviet Union), 95, 137–40, 230
    occupations of, upon arrival in
        Israel, 17–19
    stereotypes about, 179
Ruttenberg, Dodik, 157–59, 161–65,
    169–71

Sa'adi, Hussam (Yohanan, Hanan),
    39–47, 49–50, 51–53
Sa'adi family of Al-Zib, 31, 39–53
Sadeh, Yitzhak, 69
Saffron, Hannah, 138–40
Sa'id (a Palestinian, perhaps Israeli
    agent), 259
Saladin, 247
Salomon, Tamir, 205
Sami, Captain, 39–47
Samson and Delilah, 247
Samsonoff, Nanja, 256
Sarafand, Lebanon, 46
Saul, King, 247
Sayeret Matkal reconnaisance unit,
    176
Schneerson, Menachem, 234
Schneider, Shuli, 277–78, 283–84
Sde Dov, 218
Sderot, 263–65
Second Temple in Jerusalem, 183
secret military units, 176
security operations, 46–47
Sela, Yigal, 30
Sephardim, 15–16, 19
Shaki, Daniel, 198–200

Shalit, Gilad, 270
Shati refugees camp, 281
Shavei Zion, 66
Shayetet 13 (navy SEALs), 176,
    187–89
Shefayim kibbutz, 168
Sheikh Munis, 214
Shimon, Dov, 44
Shimon, Matan, 200–204
shipwrecks, 3, 181
Shtraim, Yulia, 138
Sidni Ali, 175
Simentov, Zebulon, 256–57
Six Day War (1967), 107–8, 127
socialist ideals, 74, 146–47, 158,
    169–70, 279
Sokolowsky, Manny, 66
Stalin, 279
Stella Maris monastery, Mount
    Carmel, 148–50
strangers
    harsh queries from, 25–26
    intimate conversations with,
        215–17
suicide bombers, 41, 63, 150, 228–29
Suissa, Israel, 270–71
summer, heat of, 145
survival
    Jewish, and building new lives,
        61–62, 284–85
    from terrorist attacks, 58–61
Syria, 133, 256

Tamir, Yuval, 121
Tel Aviv, 209–42
    Bauhaus architecture of, 235–39

beach life of, 240
European nature of, 209
founding of, 213
nightlife of, 223–33, 239–40
pleasure capital, 211
the White City, 236
Tel Baruch, 3, 215
Tel Hai, battle of, 201
terrorism
    Arab attacks, 133, 228–29
    justification for, 63–64, 220
    survivors of, 58–61
Titus, Emperor, 183
Toameh, Khaled Abu, 131–37
Toameh, Massad, 132–33
Treblinka, 69
Trumpeldor, Yosef, 200–201
Twain, Mark, 13, 15

Um Mohammed, 47–49
UNESCO, 235–37
United Kibbutz Movement, 162,
    165
Uri (construction manager),
    237–38

Vaad Habayit bar, Tel Aviv, 226
Vilnay, Zev, 11

Wall, the, 137
war, inevitability of, 180, 193
War of Independence (1948), 29, 64,
    70, 84, 127, 146, 219–21, 261,
    277–79
Warsaw Ghetto, resistance of, 68,
    69–70, 277

West Bank
  policing of, by Israeli defense forces,
    190–92
  walling off of, 137
wheelbarrow, scuffle over a, 18
Winkler, Yehudit, 72–73

Yad Mordechai, battle of (1948),
    277–79, 283–84
Yad Mordechai kibbutz, 276–80,
    289–90
Yad Mordechai woods, 275
Yad Vashem Museum, 67
Yassin, Ahmed, 46

Yavin, Chaim, 94
Yemen, 256
Yom Kippur, 109
Yom Kippur riots (Acre), 109–13
Yom Kippur War (1973), 211
Yosselevska, Rivka, 76–80

Zaguri, Jaacov, 257–58
Zikhron Ya'akov, 144
Zikim
  army base, 276–77
  beach, 282
Zionism, 35
  heroes of, 200–201

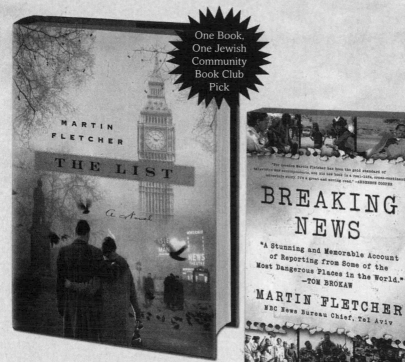